Contents

Educational Futures

Educational Futures: Dominant and contesting visions provides an overview and analysis of current tensions, debates and key issues within OECD nations, particularly Australia, the USA, Canada and the UK, with regard to where education is and should be going. Using a broad historical analysis, this book investigates ideas and visions about the future that are increasingly evoked to support arguments about the imminent demise of the dominant 'modern' educational model.

The text focuses on neither prediction nor prescription; rather the goal is an analysis of the ways in which the notion of the future circulates in contemporary discourse. Five specific discourses are explored:

1   globalization
2   new information and communications technologies
3   feminist
4   indigenous
5   spiritual.

The book demonstrates the connections between particular approaches to time, visions of the future, and educational visions and practices. The author asserts that every approach to educational change is inherently based on an underlying image of the future.

This fascinating exploration of futures education will be of interest to academics and students of Futures Education, members of futures organizations and academics interested in educational change throughout the world.

Ivana Milojević is a Postdoctoral Research Fellow at the University of Queensland, School of Education.

Futures in Education
Edited by Richard A. Slaughter

New thinking for a new millennium
Edited by Richard A. Slaughter

Educating beyond violent futures
Francis P. Hutchinson

Reframing the early childhood curriculum
Jane M. Page

Lessons for the future
David Hicks

Futures beyond dystopia
Creating social foresight
Richard A. Slaughter

Educational futures
Dominant and contesting visions
Ivana Milojević

Educational Futures
Dominant and contesting visions

Ivana Milojević

 **Routledge**
Taylor & Francis Group

LONDON AND NEW YORK

First published 2005
by Routledge
2 Park Square, Milton Park, Abingdon, Oxon OX14 4RN

Simultaneously published in the USA and Canada
by Routledge
270 Madison Ave, New York, NY 10016

Transferred to Digital Printing 2006

Reprinted 2006

Routledge is an imprint of the Taylor & Francis Group, an informa business

© 2005 Ivana Milojević

Typeset in Palatino by
Integra Software Services Pvt. Ltd, Pondicherry, India
Printed and bound in Great Britain by
MPG Digital Solutions, Bodmin, Cornwall

British Library Cataloguing in Publication Data
A catalogue record for this book is available from the British Library

Library of Congress Cataloging in Publication Data
A catalog record for this book has been requested

ISBN 10: 0–415–33374–1
ISBN 13: 978–0–415–33374–0

To Saim Dušan and Mariyam Lena
And to Ivana, when she was a child – for persisting

Figures

Tables

Acknowledgements

During the last ten years of my life the greatest personal and professional support came from Sohail. I thank him for everything.

I owe my gratitude to my friends and colleagues from the School of Education, University of Queensland – especially to Simone Smala, Ravinder Sidhu, Annette Woods and Julia Tilling – for their professional input and personal support. Special thanks goes to Julie Matthews for endless discussions during our commute to and from Brisbane and also for her friendship. Professionally, I am also indebted to the various forms of support I received from my many colleagues at the School of Education; from, among others, Peter Galbraith, Ray Land, Martin Mills, Bob Lingard and Pam Christie. The leadership role of the Head of School, Professor Allan Luke, has been incredible, and his departure to Singapore was a great loss. My supervisor, Professor Carmen Luke, provided administrative support, references when needed and thorough editing of my PhD thesis. I thank them both for all their assistance, including helping with my postdoctoral research application and their invitation to work on the School Responses to Racism project as a researcher and project manager. Their generosity in giving me the lead authorship for the monograph that came out of this project is, I believe, extraordinary.

My non-academic friends also provided emotional support and have contributed to me having a more balanced life. I single out my dear friend Kim Zafir, who believes that this is her one chance to have her name mentioned in a book.

Colleagues from the World Futures Studies Federation have helped by engaging with, and publishing, my work or by otherwise supporting my professional growth in the field. I would especially like to thank Richard A. Slaughter, David Hicks, Marcus Bussey, the late Jennifer Jayanti Fitzgerald, Dada Jyotirupananda, Paul Wildman,

Tom Poole, Ziauddin Sardar, Vuokko Jarva, Wendell Bell, Kuo-Hua Chen, Art Shostak, David Wright, Dušan Ristić, Pentti Malaska and Felix Marti. I thank Eleonora Masini, Elise Boulding, Riane Eisler and Hazel Henderson for their inspiration.

Susan Leggett is my editing and formatting fairy – I thank her for her persona and for her thoroughness.

Use of images in the book has been graciously permitted as follows:

Figure 2: The futures triangle is reprinted, with the author's permission, from Sohail Inayatullah's *Questioning the Future: Future Studies, Action Learning and Organizational Transformation* (2002).

Figure 3: Villemard's *A l'Ecole* (At School), *Visions de l'an 2000* (Visions of the year 2000) (1910). Chromolithograph, Bnf, Département des Estampes et de la Photographie.

Figure 4: Mural painting, *Cosmic Evolution*, by Robert McCall. Web home page image http://www.futurefoundation.org/. Used by permission of Foundation for the Future, Bellevue, WA, USA.

Figure 6: Cynthia G. Wagner, 'Facing the Electronic Future in Classrooms: Classroom design integrates computers into the learning environment', in *The Futurist*, January–February 2001, 68. Previously, this photo appeared accompanying the article 'The classroom of the 21st century', by Kofi Akumanyi, London Press Service, International Press Unit, FCO, www.londonpress.info. Photo by Winston Hamilton and reprinted by permission of UK Foreign and Commonwealth Office.

Figure 7: *Millennium Tree* © Josephine Wall. www.josephinewall. co.uk. Used under license from Art Impressions, Canoga Pk., CA.

Figure 8: *The Wilson Quarterly*, 1995, Vol. XIX, No. 3. It referred to the article by Alan Ehrenhalt, 'Learning from the Fifties' in that issue. Copyright www.photolibrary.com.

Special thanks goes to my Yugoslav friends, relatives and colleagues:

Prilikom objavljivanja ove knjige želela bih da se duboko zahvalim svojim roditeljima Zoranu i Jeleni za njihovo ulaganje u moje obrazovanje; svojim nezvaničnim i zvaničnim mentorkama za vreme studija sociologije i kasnije: Jeleni Milojević, Slobodanki-Seki Markov, Jeleni-Jelici Tabak, Milici Bujas i Andjelki Milić; svojim dugogodišnjim prijateljima Darku Kosovcu – Kokiju, Dragani Parlać-Dadi, Biljani (Došenović) Periz i Mariji Murinji-Madži; sestri od strica Sanji Milojević; kao i tetki Zagi Kovačević i Baki – (pokojnoj)

Miri Weinberger Vlahović kod kojih sam jedno vreme tokom studija stanovala.

Takodje se zahvaljujem svojim kolegama sa Filozofskog Fakulteta u Beogradu i Novom Sadu, pogotovo koleginicama (pokojnoj) Žarani Papić i Svenki Savić, kolegi Boži Miloševiću i profesoru Draganu Kokoviću. Ljubinku Pušiću dugujem zahvalnost što me je informisao o radu World Futures Studies Federation i pomogao da stupim u kontakt sa tom organizacijom.

Svima – prethodno imenovanim rodjacima, prijateljima, i kolegama – hvala što su mi, svako na svoj način, pružili podršku za vreme dugogodišnjeg školovanja i za vreme rada na Filozofskom fakultetu u Novom Sadu. Sva prethodna iskustva tokom mog školovanja i rada osnova su uspešno odbranjene doktorske disertacije, na osnovu koje je ova knjiga napisana.

Ivana Milojević, 2005

Introduction

Is anyone satisfied with the current dominant model of schooling and education? And is there such a thing as the dominant model of education? Or is there just a vast variety of diversified philosophies and approaches? What does the future hold for the current ways education is commonly understood and practised?

By undertaking a broad historical analysis, this book investigates ideas and visions about the future that are increasingly evoked to support arguments about the imminent demise of the dominant 'modern' educational model. There is, of course, a diversity of educational theories and practices, but there is a valid argument that the dominant model of education is still the one where schools:

> 'take' children at age 5 or 6, put them into class groups composed of children of the same age, place each class in the charge of one teacher and allocate students and teacher to a self-contained classroom where pupils are led through a curriculum based on the notion that human knowledge is divided into 'subjects'. Schools are still ranked according to upwards progression (kindergarten, pre-school, primary, secondary, tertiary) and 'expert' teachers still transfer knowledge to 'learners' who are seen to be 'relatively ignorant'. And finally, most schools tend to look the same the world over: they are set in a large geographical area called 'the school grounds' or a campus implying 'a self-contained institution'.
>
> (Beare 2001: 1)

Or, as described and critiqued by Slaughter, current school systems are:

> quintessentially 'industrial era' organizations. In their stereotypical form they are rigid hierarchies, mandated and controlled by

Central and State governments, with top-down structure. One of their key features, therefore, is inflexibility. Typically there is a minister at the top; teachers and students are at the bottom – not unlike a nineteenth century army. The 'meat in the sandwich' is a layer of bureaucracy that must, at all times, obey prevailing political priorities. Teachers and students remind one of marginalized, disempowered 'foot soldiers'. Indeed, it is vital to appreciate that prevailing 'system imperatives' are not necessarily about human beings, society or, indeed, the future. They are largely abstract in nature and may be summarized as: power, control, economy and efficiency.

(Slaughter 2004: 195)

In her pictorial representation of the history of education, Rousmaniere (1998) argues that we now commonly and universally accept and recognize the image of 'the school' and 'the teacher'. School photographs from America, England, Mexico and Africa all tell a similar 'story'. Of course, we could add Eastern Europe here as well, as seen in Figure 1. For – at the very least – over 100 years the image of education was of children ordered, stiff, grouped together, with a teacher looking stern and authoritative (Rousmaniere 1998).

The futures discourse – ideas and images about possible, probable and preferred futures – is increasingly used to support arguments

Figure 1 School photo, Novi Sad, former Yugoslavia, 1975. Copyright the author.

about the impending decline of such a – modern, industrial – form of education. The critique of modern education ranges across the political spectrum (from 'the Right' to 'the Left'); across countries (both 'western' and 'non-western'); across genders (within men's, queer and feminist movements); and across worldviews (e.g. post-modernism, critical theory, neo-Marxism, critical traditionalism). These critiques all imply that 'modern' education has by now become 'outdated'.

For example, religious scholars critique modern education for helping create selfish, driven individuals and anxious, materialistic societies. In this case, modern education is mostly accused of separating the 'inseparable' – from this perspective, education makes little sense if it is removed from a religious and 'values'-laden context. At the other end of the political spectrum (e.g. humanist, multicultural, feminist, neo-Marxist approaches), modern education is critiqued because it reproduces existing, social/economic/gender hierarchies. Authors informed by these theories and perspectives argue that education should instead promote human rights, equality and diversity. In contrast, proponents of elitist education maintain that there is nothing wrong with hierarchies. Students should be given the best opportunity to 'achieve and excel' within existing societies. Yet others, for example authors that can be located within spiritual, holistic and eco-centric approaches, argue that modern education is based on an outdated worldview/paradigm/narrative. They argue for the 'mainstreaming' of the 'Gaian narrative' – seen to be more in tune with 'the emerging future'. Postmodernists, on the other hand, do not want to replace the current model with any other meta-narrative, but rather with diversity, ongoing processes and negotiations.

One of the main features of modern education – the reproduction of the nation state 'citizen' – has been increasingly challenged by various globalization processes. Proponents of globalization would 'push' education even further towards this 'New Pedagogy' where it becomes 'advantageous to learn well, to learn quickly and learn continuously' (Ellyard 1998: 61). Others, however, see globalization as a new threat to their 'traditional' (national, ethnic, cultural, religious) identities and believe education should remain mostly about national and cultural preservation. Parallel to this, an ongoing process of 'de-colonization' – from both 'modern' and 'globalized' education – is taking place. Crucial to this process is the recovery of various non-western traditions, including indigenous ones, that were forcibly replaced by European colonizers. Lastly, new technologies seem to be placing education based on print literacy increasingly 'out of step' with the 'new times'. Proponents of a cyber-education vision see classrooms transforming into new 'networked' classrooms existing within new information/network societies. Here too, education is to satisfy both the needs of future societies and those of the present generations of children who are to inhabit them.

The main question, then, is not whether modern education is going to change. Change, as defined by the modern and the postmodern, is 'the only constant'. The main questions have thus become: (1) What *should* education be like? (2) Should education be about 'preparation' for certain given futures as predicted by many (both 'official' and 'unofficial') scholars, or should it be about the creation of desired, preferred visions for the future? (3) If it is about preparation for given futures, what exactly are these futures going to look like? and alternatively (4) If it is about the creation of preferred visions, what kind of visions *are* desirable?

But, despite the deep and continuous social changes our global society/societies have been undergoing, and despite the obvious connection between a particular desired future and the corresponding desired educational change, the futures dimension remains marginalized within educational discourses. Furthermore, the future is too often conceived in terms of: (1) tacit inferences; (2) token invocations; or (3) taken-for-granted assumptions (Gough 1990). Exploration of the future still remains a neglected issue in education (Beare and Slaughter 1993; Gough 1990; Hicks 2002; Hicks and Holden 1995; Hutchinson 1996; Page 2000; Slaughter 1996b, 2004). Finally, the future is almost always defined in terms of technological progress, or, alternatively and more recently, by its exact opposite – as ecological regress leading to civilizational collapse.

Educational Futures: Dominant and contesting visions actively engages with the previously mentioned futures discourses about educational futures by providing an overview and detailed analysis of arguments about where education, particularly state-based education systems, is and should be going. It thus summarizes current tensions, debates and the main issues developed within OECD nations in general, and Australia, the USA, Canada and (to a lesser extent) the UK in particular. In addition, by way of discussing already existing visions of the future of education it also moves away from criticism towards 'substantive vision' (Giroux 1989) and the construction of alternatives (Brodribb 1992; Grosz 1990; Gunew 1990; Hughes 1994). While this book is, to a large extent, presented in the tradition of *critical* futures studies and *critical* social theory and as such is engaged within the *'negative* or *reactive* project...of challenging what currently exists...criticizing prevailing social, political and theoretical relations' (Grosz 1990: 59), it also discusses alternative strategies. This is because:

> To say something is *not* true, valuable, or useful *without posing alternatives* is, paradoxically, to affirm that it *is* true, and so on. Thus coupled with this negative project, or rather, indistinguishable from it, must be a positive, constructive project: creating alternatives.
>
> (Grosz 1990: 59)

Of course, normative discourses are always inclusive of the desired, the hoped for, as well as the feared. However, the exploration of the desired (*utopian* and *eutopian*[1]) and the feared (*dystopian*[2]) is also often missing from current debates. Moreover, the argument has repeatedly been made by theorists influenced by postmodernism that utopian/dystopian themes should 'best be avoided', mostly because they constitute 'binarist approaches' and as such tend to overlook 'complexities and contradictions' (Kapitzke 1999: 3). This argument itself overlooks recent theoretical developments that influenced the movement from a singular notion of 'utopia' to dystopia, eutopia and *heterotopias*.[3] Heterotopia, in particular, acknowledges that what is seen as 'utopia' by one social/cultural group can be considered as 'dystopia' by different social and cultural groups and/or within different social and historical contexts. It also acknowledges that at any given time there are competing utopian and dystopian visions that are constantly being negotiated, locally and globally. As well, the critique of utopias overlooks the development of *eupsychia*. This term is used to denote a prescriptive and improved imagined state of not only *collective* (as in utopia, dystopia, eutopia and heterotopia) but also *individual* being (self/soul).

A central argument in *Educational Futures: Dominant and contesting visions* is that an active and ongoing engagement with utopian thinking remains crucial. This is because while all futures visions, whether dominant or marginal ones, are inclusive of utopian, eutopian and dystopian elements, it is only the dominant futures imaging that succeeds in convincing about the inevitability of its own desired vision. That is, when there is no dialogue between various utopian, eutopian, dystopian and other futures imaging, dominant social groups and ideologies continue to define what is seen as utopian (implying impossible and naïve) and what is to be seen as 'the truth about the future'. By labelling visions that challenge their dominant utopian view, powerful social groups and mainstream discourses succeed in expressing their own desires, their own desirable futures. Mannheim (1936) made this argument long ago: 'The representatives of a given order will label as utopian all conceptions of existence which *from their point of view* can in principle never be realized' (ibid.: 176–177).

So, the first task in discussing mainstream/dominant/hegemonic, counter and alternative discourses in relation to desired/prescribed educational and social change is to unmask alleged *'realistic' futures* that are usually championed by dominant social groups and/or those benefiting from 'more of the same' futures. That is, these futures should *also* be seen as *emerging from particular utopian discourses*, rather than from some universal and neutral space.[4] For example, capitalism and economic globalization in many ways continue a particular tradition within the west. This tradition focuses on expansion, an unlimited supply of material goods, and the successful control of natural and biological processes. Another dominant image of the future, that of a technologically advanced information society, is also located within a particular western tradition, that of 'discovery, exploration, colonization and exploitation' (Bell 2000: 697). For example, cyberspace is routinely referred to as a 'new world' or a 'new frontier', even a 'new continent', whose conquest and settlement is often compared to the conquest and settlement of the 'New World'. This destabilization of the 'realistic' futures is the main focus of my inquiry in Part II: *Destabilizing dominant narratives*.

The second key task, which runs parallel to unveiling utopian elements within hegemonic futures discourses, is to *discuss alternatives* – as equal to hegemonic ones and not as inferior or naïve. That is, both should be seen as equally valid discourses about the future, as simultaneously real, imaginary, utopian, desired and feared. However, at the beginning of the twenty-first century, hegemonic discourse labels as 'utopian' only those images and visions that counteract the capitalist, technological, patriarchal and western civilizational project for the future. This project is perceived to be 'realistic' as it entails the continuation of the present realities, no matter how harmful they may be to a local and global society or to particular social groups. Articulation of alternative eutopian visions is therefore important in opening up the future and breaking down common assumptions of what is 'imminently' going to happen. Development of alternatives to the present, coming from the perspective of disadvantaged groups/worldviews, is one of the important strategies in both rethinking the present and developing informed decisions for the future. This is because power may not necessarily be a 'possession' of economic and cultural elites. This view actually 'cements' power relations, the critique becoming another disempowering system. Rather, as argued by Foucault, power is not only everywhere, it is also creative, positive, existing only when it is put into action (Foucault 1982: 219). While Foucault 'does not deny that there are individuals and organization that rule over other people' (McPhail 1997), he also argues that resistance is always possible because the process of normalization is never complete (ibid.). That is, '...knowledge is never fully co-opted and...there will always be subjugated forms of (power/) knowledge that can be used to resist prevailing and hegemonic forms of (power/) knowledge' (ibid.).

Articulation and analysis of dissenting, alternative futures visions thus become one avenue for paradigm shift/epistemic change. The expression of desired visions for the future is one place where the possibilities for social transformation are a means by which we can 'put power into action'. As Sardar, Nandy and Inayatullah – futures researchers informed by postcolonial theory – argue, 'dissent has to go beyond mere protest', and must formulate alternatives 'from the perspective of the excluded, exploited, disempowered, and the marginalised' (Sardar 1999: 142–143). Those who dissent, argues Nandy, become neither players nor counter players but are engaged in 'a different game altogether, a game of building an alternative world' (Nandy, in Sardar 1999: 146). This articulation and analysis of alternative, dissenting futures is the main focus of my inquiry in Part III: *Searching for social and educational alternatives*.

Third, while we might assume that utopias are not relevant to us, in fact, we *daily live* the many *utopian and dystopian visions* of the past. Utopian thinking, or design of prescriptive and improved imagined states of collective and/or individual being, has been to some extent responsible for many successful and unsuccessful social experiments. As argued by Hertzler (1965: 266): 'Not all of any of the utopias has been realized, but as much of them have been, as is the case in any improvement scheme'. Similarly, Polak (1973) has argued that yesterday's utopia often becomes today's social philosophy:

> Many utopian themes, arising in fantasy, find their way to reality. Scientific management, full employment, and social security were all once figments of a utopia-writer's imagination. So were parliamentary democracy, universal suffrage, planning, and the trade union movement. The tremendous concern for child-rearing

and universal education, for eugenics, and for garden cities all emanated from the utopia. The utopia stood for the emancipation of women long before the existence of the feminist movement. All the current concepts concerning labor, from the length of the work week to profit-sharing, are found in the utopia. Thanks to the utopists, the twentieth century did not catch man totally unprepared.

(Polak 1973: 137–138)

Fourth, being aware of the full range of discourses is especially important in the light of the current *prevalence of the dystopian* genre and its (negative) impact on young people (Hicks 1998, 2002; Hutchinson 1996). As well, the articulation of positive futures visions is also crucial in the light of the *colonization of the future* by technological/scientific, uni-civilizational and androcentric worldviews. As shown by critical educational futurists, such as Slaughter (1993, 1996a,b, 1999, 2004), Hicks (1994, 1998, 2002), Hicks and Holden (1995), Hutchinson (1996) and Boulding (1990), the future is most often envisioned in terms of its technological orientation, unbridled linear progress and its exclusion of the Other – women, traditional cultures and nature. This can partly be attributed to the exclusion of women and non-western cultures in the development of various futures (both 'utopian' and 'realistic') projects. It was assumed, and still is, that non-western societies could not develop images of advanced future societies because they themselves were 'pre-industrial' and 'pre-modern'. The colonization of knowledge by the dominant (western) perspective has thus led to a view of the future that is most often defined by three pillars: (1) the capacity of technology to solve all problems; (2) linear progress as the underlying mythology; and (3) the accumulation and expansion of material goods as the main goal of civilization. This has resulted in looking at the future as singular, '... dominant by myopic projection' (Sardar 1999: 1):

The future is little more than the transformation of society by new Western technologies. We are bombarded by this message constantly from a host of different directions. The advertisements on television and radio, in newspapers and magazines, for new models of computers, cars, mobile phones, digital and satellite consumer goods – all ask us to reflect on how new technologies will transform not just our social and cultural environments but the very idea of what it is to be human.

(Sardar 1999: 1)

Similarly, since the 'place' of women was defined by patriarchy to be in the private sphere, women's contributions to the future were primarily limited to the personal domain. As a result, argues Daly (1978: 1), 'even outer space and the future have been colonized' by patriarchy.

Finally, we must remember that *education* has always been the *utopian measure par excellence* (Hertzler 1965). Ozmon further elaborates this by stating that:

> [Since utopians believed]... that the great social problems of a society cannot be solved without changing the entire structure of the society within which these problems reside... they saw a twofold necessity for education, first, for the purpose of educating man to the need for great and important changes, and secondly, they saw education as a vehicle for enabling man to adjust to these changes.
>
> (Ozmon 1969: ix)

In one of the rare books (*Utopias and Education*, 1969) that explicitly focus on the connection between utopias and education, Howard Ozmon has argued that utopian thought played an important part in influencing educational thought in the west. He points at ways in which utopian thought has influenced education in the past, and also asserts that utopians have, by and large, placed a high priority upon education (Ozmon 1969). In addition, 'most utopian writers not only have a high regard for education but are educationists themselves' (ibid.: x).

It is important to stress, however, that this utopian sentiment has, in western thought, always been 'in competition' with those alternative approaches towards social change that put an emphasis on *reform* rather than on *radical transformation*. These two streams are well summarized by Wright (1999, par. 4):

> On the one hand, radicals of diverse stripes have argued that social arrangements inherited from the past are not immutable facts of nature, but transformable human creations. Social institutions can be designed in ways that eliminate forms of oppression that thwart human aspirations for fulfilling and meaningful lives. The central task of emancipatory politics is to create such institutions. On the other hand, conservatives have generally argued that grand designs for social reconstruction are nearly always disasters. While contemporary social institutions

may be far from perfect, they are generally serviceable. At least, it is argued, they provide the minimal conditions for social order and stable interactions. These institutions have evolved through a process of slow, incremental modification as people adapt social rules and practices to changing circumstances. The process is driven by trial and error much more than by conscious design, and by and large those institutions which have endured have done so because they have enduring virtues. This does not preclude institutional change, even deliberate institutional change, but it means that such change should be piecemeal, not wholesale ruptures with existing arrangements.

To complicate matters further, these two approaches to social change have also always existed within a context in which *education has primarily been an instrument of social control*. As Foucault's work so clearly demonstrates, the structure and organization of schooling firmly locates bodies and minds in place. By the teaching of particular knowledge and skills that are based on educational regimes of truth (incorporates 'futures knowledge base'), a particular subject is always developed on the basis of these normalizing regimes. The governed subject becomes the self-regulated subject, therefore successfully fulfilling 'the practical needs of schools, businesses, and society as a whole for discipline and order' (Cromer 1997: 118). As a result, 'systems that had been developed by reformers to restructure society were adopted by society to maintain the social order' (ibid.). As well, changes take far longer to implement in formal education than in, for example, business or private households because: '...schools are citizen-controlled and nonprofit. As systems, they are multipurpose, many-layered, labor-intensive, relationship-dependent, and profoundly conservative' (Cuban 2001: 153). This tension is summarized in Figure 2 (adapted from Inayatullah 2002: 186).

Educational institutions, practices and discourses are therefore torn between demands to, on one hand, create and respond to social change and, on the other, maintain the status quo. Still, all these demands are informed by particular futures discourses. While this is more obvious in the case of demands that more explicitly engage with social change, even demands and desires for *maintaining* the status quo (or returning to a 'perfect' past) depend on projection of the current (past) system as a desirable vision for tomorrow.

Educational Futures: Dominant and contesting visions actively engages with these various desirable visions for the future. It also makes explicit some of the implicit assumptions within current debates on

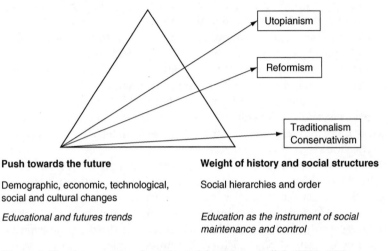

Pull of the future

The vision or image of the future – Personal and collective

Educational and futures visions – Desired futures

Utopianism

Reformism

Traditionalism
Conservativism

Push towards the future

Demographic, economic, technological, social and cultural changes

Educational and futures trends

Weight of history and social structures

Social hierarchies and order

Education as the instrument of social maintenance and control

Figure 2 The futures triangle. Adapted from Inayatullah (2002: 186).

educational change, in order to clarify current choices. One of the aims of this book is to show the connection between a particular desired future and the corresponding desired educational change. The text focuses on neither prediction nor prescription; rather, the goal is an analysis of *the ways in which the notion of the future circulates in contemporary discourse.* The subject of this book, therefore, is not to investigate what education in the future is *going to be like.* Nor is it to determine what education *should* look like in the future. Instead, the thrust of the book is to investigate multiple discourses about the future in general – the social future – and the educational future in particular. So, instead of predicting and/or prescribing, *Educational Futures* offers deconstruction of 'the future', that is, it provides an analysis of the ways in which current predictions, images and ideas about the future influence decision and policy making today. The focus is on the future seen as 'an active principle in the present' (Slaughter 1998: 39) rather than 'misconstrued as an "empty space" '(ibid.).

To summarize, *Educational Futures* provides: (1) an overview and analysis of arguments about where education is/should be going, thus actively engaging with both the futures and normative (utopian) discourses; (2) a relocation of the future as *contested space*, a (meta) narrative that can be deconstructed and problematized; and (3) an investigation into 'the truth' claims about the future and ways in which such 'truth' claims of what the future will be like or should be like (predictions and preferred futures) privilege certain class, civilizational and epistemological interests.

This book is informed by multiple theoretical frameworks. These include postmodernism/poststructuralism, feminism, postcolonial theory and critical futures studies. Thus, this book does not merely deconstruct the future, but presents alternatives. It does so by comparing contesting discourses in terms of their ability to help create peaceful, multicultural, gender-balanced and economically, ecologically and socially sustainable future societies.

The book is in four parts. Part I: *Historical futures discourses in education* (Chapters 1–3) provides a historical and theoretical overview. First, the analysis used in the book is itself put in a historical and theoretical context. Second, the current dominant education model and the current dominant view of the future and approach to time are contextualized and historicized. And third, an alternative reading of educational history is offered, one that incorporates different civilizational approaches to time. That is, instead of theorizing all historical educational practices solely from within the western approach to time, non-western historical educational practices are theorized from within their own frameworks. Connections between various approaches to time – for example, linear or cyclical – visions of the future and educational practices are shown. An alternative historical reading is given in order to provide the background and epistemic context for current views of educational futures.

In Part II: *Destabilizing dominant narratives* (Chapters 4–7), dominant futures and utopian visions are thoroughly analysed and discussed. Two main visions identified as hegemonic futures and utopian discourses are the Globalized and WebNet vision of the future with the corresponding globalized (not global) and cyber model of education. Although these visions are often seen to be realistic discourse of the 'imminent future', discourse analysis shows that they are also constituted by desire and imagination, about what is hoped for. In addition, the analyses show that these desires and hopes are still firmly based on western and patriarchal worldviews. The main argument here is that dominant futures visions succeed in capturing public imagination because they 'make the most sense' – are easily intelligible – from within our current social structures and dominant worldview.

Part III: *Searching for social and educational alternatives* (Chapters 8–10) outlines numerous alternatives proposed to the current dominant educational model as well as to hegemonic futures visions. Three alternatives are presented and analysed in detail because these visions most deeply challenge assumptions and preferred visions coming from the dominant, hegemonic 'regimes of educational truths'. These dissenting alternative futures are feminist alternatives, the recovery of indigenous traditions and the spiritual education model. They fundamentally challenge patriarchal and western assumptions about what constitutes knowledge, history, future and 'ideal' education. The analysis of these alternatives is thus important because it broadens the 'educational canon'. By bringing civilizational and gendered frameworks of desired futures into the futures of education debate, the analysis shows that the way in which 'reality' (historical, present and future) is perceived changes depending on the underlying worldview and civilizational, cultural and gender priority. Thus, works of numerous non-western and feminist educational thinkers are investigated and summarized in the context of their respective desired futures.

Part IV: *Towards educational eutopias and heterotopias* (Chapters 11–12) compares hegemonic, counter and alternative educational futures discourses. In this Part, I focus on showing how different understandings and views of time and the future are implicit in the creation of different goals and aims for education. The hegemonic and alternative visions are compared so as to clarify the choices – as well as to identify the main hopes and fears – of each desired future. As well, I assert that utopias, even when officially abandoned, continue to return in our discourses. They remain the implicit lenses that frame our futures. Thus, the main argument made is that the transformation of society and education is not possible without the transformation of how we see and imagine our futures.

Part I

Historical futures discourses in education

> Every imagined future has its past, just as every historical moment has its own vision of the future.
>
> – Thacker (2001)

Figure 3 Villemard's *A l'Ecole* [At School], Chromolithograph, *Visions de l'an 2000*, 1910. BNF, Département des Estampes et de la Photographie.[1]

1 Future, time and education: contexts and connections

The futures context

Knowledge about *the future* or even *futures* is, like any other knowledge, 'rooted in a life, a society, and a language that [has] a history' (Foucault 1973: 372). As we cannot know something which has not yet happened, knowledge about the future comprises ideas and assumptions about the future, images and visions of the future as well as the investigation of causalities that bring the logical consequences of certain events and trajectories. Given that the future is not predetermined, every study of the future is 'strictly speaking, the study of ideas about the future' (Cornish, cited in Wagar 1996: 366). It is an inquiry, or 'the study of possibilities that are plausible in terms of present-day knowledge and theory' (ibid.).

The previous and the following discussion on social and educational change arise from the particular tradition of investigating the future or from 'modern futures studies'. This multidisciplinary and systematic field of inquiry of probable, possible and preferable futures that emerged in the twentieth-century western world is based on the following key philosophical assumptions:

- The future is not predetermined and cannot be 'known' or 'predicted'.
- The future is determined partly by history, social structures and reality, and partly by chance, innovation and human choice.
- There is a range of alternative futures which can be 'forecast'.
- Future outcomes can be influenced by human choices.
- Early intervention enables planning and design, while in 'crises response' people can only try to adapt and/or react.
- Ideas and images of the future shape our actions and decisions in the present.

- Our visions of preferred futures are shaped by our values.
- Humanity does not make choices as a whole, nor are we motivated by the same values, aspirations and projects (Amara 1981; Bell 1997; Cornish 1999; De Jouvenel 1996; Fletcher 1979; Masini 1993a; Slaughter 1996a).

More specifically, the theoretical approach in this book follows the 'critical/poststructural' and 'cultural/interpretative' (Inayatullah 1990) tradition within modern futures studies. It also provides an analysis of 'normative' (Moll 1996) approaches. The critical/poststructural approach expands the discourse of the future across cultures, and 'by historicizing and deconstructing the future, creates new epistemological spaces that enable the formation of alternative futures' (Inayatullah 1990: 115). To contest the given future and create alternative futures, critical futures thinking is crucial as it helps us recognize that *every approach to educational change is inherently based on an underlying image of the future* (and of time). The normative approach incorporates utopian and imaginative thinking, visioning and the consideration of social and cultural dynamics (Moll 1996: 18).

In addition, theoretical influences include three distinctive and overlapping approaches within social sciences – postmodernism, feminism and postcolonial theory. The inquiry focuses primarily on the western and patriarchal imprint on the dominant futures visions, on alternatives that have developed outside and on the margins of the western paradigms as well as within women's/ feminist movements. Deconstruction, genealogy, critical discourse (methods which have become increasingly familiar) and causal layered analysis (CLA) are used in order to investigate how particular ideas and images about the futures of education have become dominant – the accepted norm – and thus now frame what is possible.

Causal layered analysis, developed by Inayatullah (1998a), enables analyses of how data within various discourses are contextualized, interpreted and located in 'various historical structures of power/knowledge – class, gender, *varna* [caste] and episteme (the critical)' (ibid.: 816). CLA complements methods that focus on the horizontal spatiality of futures discourses, such as scenarios, backcasting and emerging issues analysis. It focuses on the vertical dimension of futures studies (ibid.: 815) and takes a layered approach to the future (Slaughter 2002). This layered approach to the future, as developed by Inayatullah, consists of four levels. These four levels are:

1 Litany – the description or visible characteristics of the issue. The trends and problems that are often exaggerated and used for political purposes are part of the public debate.
2 Social cause – qualitative interpretation of data and economic, technological, cultural, political and historical systemic factors are explored.
3 Discourse/worldview – focuses on finding deeper social, linguistic, temporal, cultural structures and the discourse/worldview that supports them.
4 Myth/metaphor – consists of deep stories, collective archetypes, the not-so-apparent-and-obvious dimensions of the problem under inquiry (Inayatullah 1998a).

As a critical futures studies method, CLA asks what layers of understanding are missing from conventional trend analysis (linear futures). It seeks to explore the politics of knowledge and meaning nested in conventional statements of the future. It intends to go beyond the litany of statements (e.g. 'the Internet will revolutionize education') by asking which social, economic and political causes and factors can create revolutionary change in pedagogy. Moreover, it asks who has access to power, in this example, to the Internet. At a further level, issues of worldviews and discourses (e.g. feminist, non-western) are explored. In the case of the Internet and education, it considers the ways in which the Internet is a representation of instrumental rationality. How does it privilege sense-based education and avoid knowledge that comes from spiritual modes of learning? At an even deeper level, constitutive myths and metaphors are explored. For example: Is education mainly about the speed of access to information, or is education predominantly about inner transformation, as with spiritual education? Is the purpose of education mainly to control, achieve and compete, or is its purpose mainly for the improvement of the self (as in eupsychia) or society (as in utopia)?

These approaches acknowledge that various individuals, communities and civilizations all have their own 'futures knowledge base' – that is, the way they see and understand time – as well as their own assumptions and visions about the future. These are neither universal nor ahistorical as they vary through space and time. However, in our current world there are also many commonalities and similarities. For example, there is hardly any geographical or psychic space left that is not being imprinted with both western modernist views of progress and development, and western educational models. Still, various local sites all have their own 'regimes of truth' about social and educational futures; that is, they are not free from exercising their own hegemonic future visions. However, this book focuses on the manifestation of hegemonic visions of the future that imprint on the global – and English-dominated – space, and alternatives that contest this hegemony. Hegemony is here used in terms of Gramsci's notion designed to explain how a dominant class (or social group) maintains control by, as Lewis (1990) describes it:

> projecting its own particular way of seeing social reality so successfully that its view is accepted as common sense and as part of the natural order by those who in fact are subordinated to it [Jaggar 1983: 151]...In this respect, hegemony is accomplished through an ongoing struggle over meaning not only against, but for the maintenance of, power.
>
> (Lewis 1990: 474)

So, the following section asks which view of time and of the future is currently hegemonic – taken for granted, accepted as common sense and as part of 'the natural order'? More importantly, how and why has this happened?

Civilizational approaches to time

Conception of time and the future exists in every known society (Bell 1994). The practice of divination, rites of passage (transitions to future social roles), agricultural planning, seasonal migrations, development of calendars all testify that 'conceptions of time and future exist – and have existed – in human consciousness everywhere' (ibid.: 3). The future is 'an integral aspect of the human condition', because 'by assuming a future, man makes his present endurable and his past meaningful' (McHale 1969: 3).

Although the conception of time and the future exist universally, they are understood in different ways in different societies. Masini (1996: 76) argues that there are three main representations of time. The first representation is:

> A variation of cyclical motion, as in the enclosed circle of life and death in living organisms, or of night and day in cosmic time. This representation is well reflected in the Hindu and Buddhist 'cosmic eras' (*kalpa*) which are delimited by mythological events in time periods through which all beings continue ad infinitum.

The cycle is represented by a snake. In this conception we see the future as part of an unending continuum. The future is part of life and death. Naturally this influences one's perspective of the future: there is little reason to despair or to strive to achieve.

(Masini 1996: 76)

The second representation is based on the Graeco-Roman and the Judaeo-Christian conception of time:

Founded on the idea that all people are the same in relation to God. Time is perceived to be a trajectory towards something more, towards accomplishment. In this representation time is symbolized by an arrow; the future is better than the present and the past and may be in contradiction to the historical present, as in utopia. The possibility of the future being worse than the past or present is out of the question. This is the conceptual base of 'progress' ... the time of scientific and technological development, where every success has to be bigger and better than anything in the past or present ... (but) this concept of time and the future is being challenged by environmental barriers and barriers emerging from its own frame of reference.

(Masini 1996: 76)

The third representation has been developed, according to Masini, by Vico and others and has been extended by Laslo (ibid.: 77). According to this representation, 'Time is a spiral, an evolutionary process of world civilization giving a structure to spatial and temporal events ranging from the natural to the social, that develops over time' (ibid.).

These three basic metaphors for time – circle, arrow and spiral – influence the type of futures thinking – and the very understanding of the future – across cultures. Sohail Inayatullah writes:

Different visions of time lead to alternative types of society. Classical Hindu thought, for example, is focused on million-year cycles. Within this model, society degenerates from a golden era to an iron age. During the worst of the materialistic iron age, a spiritual leader or *avatar*, rises and revitalizes society. In contrast, classical Chinese time is focused on the degeneration of the Tao and its regeneration through the sage-king seen as the wise societal parent.

(Inayatullah 1996: 200–201)

What is missing from Masini's discussion on the three main representations of time is an understanding of time as 'non-flowing', as part of an 'eternal now' or as 'Dreaming'.[1]

Having western and some eastern societies in mind, Masini further argues that while some cultures have focused on development and progress of the society, others have focused on the development of the self – an 'accomplishment of the ideal person' (Masini 1996: 77). Views of time and the future have practical implications for individual and social lives. For example, different views of time and the future seem to have contributed to some societies (e.g. those based on the Judeo-Christian tradition) developing in accordance with the expansion principle, and some (e.g. many indigenous societies) in accordance with the conservation principle. Thinking about time and the future is an integral part of cultural and civilizational worldviews, which in many ways determine particular directions, decisions and choices that are made.

This enunciation of four approaches to time does not mean that the linear concept of time is exclusively western, the cyclical inclusively eastern and eternal time exclusively indigenous. Temporal structures should not be essentialized. Adam (1995: 29), in particular, warns about social construction of 'other' time, based on a division between 'them' and 'us'. The recognition that the experience of time is integral to human existence, but that the way we perceive and conceptualize that experience varies with cultures and historical periods, underpins all studies of 'other' time (ibid.). These anthropological, historical or sociological studies recognize that 'the meanings and values attributed to time are fundamentally context-dependent' (ibid.). But they also 'dichotomize societies into traditional and modern ones in which the time perception of the former is constructed through its opposition to the dominant image of "our Western time"' (ibid.). 'Other time' thus becomes the 'frozen present of anthropological discourse' (ibid.: 30). The main problems with this are that 'alien' time is 'commonly explicated in terms of what it is not, and that the existing dualistic models of "own" and "other time" are fundamentally flawed' (ibid.: 30). But any analysis of 'other time', concludes Adam (ibid.: 31), is also a 'simultaneous commentary on "our time"'. Thus, what is important to mention here is that each of the three civilizations that I next analyse understands, or has understood at some point, that all three 'times' are inherently interwoven together. The concept of time can only be derived from the concept of change, composed observationally and relationally (Lippincott 1999; Prasad 1992). Experiences of linear and cyclical movements, as well as feelings of eternity, are all universal human experiences. Most importantly, this division does not imply in any way that 'cyclical' and 'eternal time' are to be found only in previous historical periods. As I will argue in Parts III and IV, many alternatives, many current educational visions *are based on these alternative* 'traditions' rather than on linear ones. In that sense, *both cyclical and eternal time can still be found*, or, alternatively, *can still be* 'reinvented' or 'reconstructed' to suit present issues and dilemmas. *Time is* thus, or can be, *a resource* – not an independent variable – to be used to create other futures. Some of the alternatives do exactly that: use different approaches to time to argue for a new (even a meta) narrative about the future. This is extremely important, because if the dominant views of time and the future remain uncontested, the discourse remains controlled and managed by dominant social and cultural frameworks of meaning. The transformation of educational structure, process and content becomes almost impossible. What critical futures thinking enables is the recognition that there is an underlying image of the future in every educational change approach.

It is also important to stress here that although various experiences of time are indeed based upon universal human experiences, the way in which time *is experienced* is also 'profoundly influenced by theories or beliefs about the nature of the world' (Morphy 1999: 265). It is both this experience of time and a particular ontology that have always influenced education in a particular way. Though rarely explicit, 'teaching time' has always been part of a 'hidden' curriculum. Both current educational practices and all educational visions for the future significantly incorporate this hidden curriculum.

Hidden curricula: The dominant view of the future and approach to time

Over the last 500 years – with the help of the expansion principle intrinsic to capitalism and colonialism, and the way 'progress', 'development' and 'time' were seen and defined – the 'victory' of western models of civilization has occurred. This hegemony of western civilization has also meant the implementation and imposition of western concepts of time (time being linear) and of the future globally (e.g. the idea of 'millennium'), and, as we will see in the following section, western models of education. Futures thinking thus became linear, concerned with progress and with ways for controlling the future. 'Science', including 'social sciences', developed within this context.

The roots of the current linear understanding of time lie within both Christianity and modern science. In the Christian view, God has created the world and at some point. He is going to bring it to an end (Taylor 2001). The scientific view of the universe follows a strictly linear pattern. Time is divided into past, present and future and into hours, minutes and seconds. The Universe was created in a Big Bang and either it will end in a Big Crunch or, after it expands indefinitely, it will slowly fade away. In the end, reports Lemonick of *Time* magazine (2001: 52), the universe – 'once ablaze with the light of uncountable stars' – will become an unimaginably vast, cold, dark, empty and profoundly lonely place. Since no biological matter can escape, the only consciousness that can possibly survive could perhaps be in the form of a 'disembodied digital intelligence' (ibid.). It is this view of time that is behind some futures alternatives, such as that of globalized cyber education. I discuss this in more detail in Part II: *Destabilizing dominant narratives*, which deals with dominant futures and utopian visions.

The linear movement of time is implicit in current notions of progress and its reverse image, regress. When the linear future is understood as regress, a certain historical period from the past is idealized as a more, or the most, desirable way of living. One example is 'back to the basics' demands that idealize the mid-twentieth century in countries such as the USA or Australia. Behind these demands there is a perception of that time as a period that was stable and secure, a period when the nation was strong and the Other less threatening. Another current example can be found within some parts of the New Age movement that often glorify agricultural or indigenous societies where food, water and air were clean and the spirit able to roam free, prior to industrialism degrading the physical, social and spiritual environments.

When the linear future is understood as progress, the earlier social stages are seen as less developed and simple or rudimentary and primitive. Most importantly, such discourse has had real-life implications in regard to the suppression of indigenous languages, ways of knowing and educational practices. There have been serious practical repercussion for those that were 'theorized' as, for example, uneducated and, therefore, in a need of (western, modernist) 'education'. The discourse itself was instrumental in creating colonial policies that intended to impose western educational models on subjected peoples. But these policies were designed according to the perceived development phase of different colonized peoples. While colonized peoples were generally seen as inferior, compared to advanced western civilization, there were important differences. For example, during the debate between Anglicists and Orientalists in colonized India on whether the language used in administration and in schools should be English or native, Anglicist Thomas Macaulay exclaimed, '...a single shelf of a good European library is worth the whole native literature of India and Arabia!' (Macaulay, quoted in Spring 1998: 16). In a single sentence, Macaulay manages to write off a whole tradition – which is especially disturbing given that 'no other living tradition can claim scriptures as numerous or as ancient as Hinduism' (Klostermaier, quoted in Reagan 1996: 95) – and close off an entire alternative future. The actions by Macaulay and others and the discourse they created helped firmly to establish English as the administrative language of India (Spring 1998: 16). But this debate was only possible because 'Europeans recognized the import- ance of the languages and cultures of what they called the ancient civilizations of the East' (ibid.: 17). Other peoples were not so lucky:

> In contrast to the cultures of Asia and Northern Africa, Europeans in Africa south of the Sahara and in the Americas simply dismissed indigenous languages, religions, and cultures as primitive...[so] the British colonialists did not attempt to pre- serve languages labelled as primitive...To a greater extent than Orientalism, Primitivism allowed Europeans to believe in their cultural superiority to the others of the world population. Under the rubric of Primitivism, colonialism, as an expression of white love, was considered a cultural rescue mission.
>
> (Spring 1998: 17–18)

Thus, in colonized Africa, there was no debate over educational poli- cies comparable with that which occurred between the Anglicists and the Orientalists in India. Rather, 'the British simply introduced an English educational model' (ibid.: 18). Likewise, in North America – and we could here add Australia as well, which Spring does not discuss – 'they [the British] ignored local educational practices and languages' which they encountered upon arrival (ibid.).

Western philosophical orientations such as evolutionism and euchronic utopianism also reflect this progressivist discourse. While evolutionism is more recent, utopianism followed a change in western approaches to time:

> Before the late eighteenth century, history had been interpreted as being cyclic and thus repetitious. The late Enlightenment

produced several thinkers who made the Age of Reason's implicit notion of the idea of progress explicit and placed it in a novel time-forward scheme that challenged the notion of cycles. The shift in utopian approaches from a future ideal place to a future ideal time – euchronia – marked a major departure from the traditions begun by Thomas More and prepared the way for the revolutionary era ahead.

(Hollis 1998: 78)

Both evolutionism and utopianism imply that 'social institutions can be rationally transformed in ways that enhance human wellbeing and happiness', but they disagree about how and how fast change is to be achieved (Wright 1999). As discussed earlier, evolutionists focus on piecemeal change and slow, incremental modifications (ibid.), while utopians, on the other hand, focus on 'wholesale ruptures', grand designs for social reconstruction, conscious design, rational calculation and political will (ibid.).

It comes as no surprise then that, until very recently, educators from both the Left and Right ends of the political spectrum still relied on 'modernist notions of progress to justify their theoretical, empirical, and political strategies' (Popkewitz 1998: xiii). This has been done without reflective examination and with 'almost missionary zeal' in order to obtain the 'salvation' of the masses through education (ibid.: xiv). In most cases, these strategies remained locked within the dominant, modernist model of education.

The dominant model of education

The current mainstream educational model, also referred to as 'modern education', grew out of the debate and out of the tension between the previously mentioned main approaches to social change – utopianism, evolutionism and progressivism. It replaced the previous dominant educational model, which can best be described as a *religious model* of education, having finally won the centuries-old battle. The 'educated' person of the twentieth century finally became 'an effect of teachable knowledge, not an effect of divine dispensation or natural evolution' (Fendler 1999: 40). This new, scientific, secular and rationalist discourse was based on an alternative vision of the future and an alternative reading of the past. The paradigm of evolution eventually replaced the paradigm of Creation, reason replaced faith, empirical evidence replaced the Truth of God, scientific inquiry replaced the given text that is to be memorized and so on. The particular vision of the future, as progressive movement from the past to the present rather than as regress from the Golden Age, which better served the needs of a more secular, scientific, industrial civilization, also 'won'.

Within this (scientific/industrial) worldview, life is divided into four life stages – child, student, worker and retiree. The main focus of education is to prepare a child and a student for a productive economic life within a chosen vocation (thereby creating or mould-ing the complete human being). In schools, time is broken into smaller and bigger units such as classes, working days, weekends, terms, semesters and school years. Education is divided into early, primary, secondary and higher. Short courses that focus on improvement of vocational skills are also introduced. Lifelong education is the exception rather than the rule. Punctuality is highly valued and so is effectiveness and efficiency. Tests are established to measure individual, school and national educa-tional effectiveness and achievements. As the scientific and secular worldview dominates, a particular emphasis is put on intellectual intelligence and reason.

Reason rather than faith, and awareness about objectives rather than internal phenomena, started to form the core nucleus of modern education. The meaning of life was to be found within the vocational sphere and intellectual development. Other real-life issues – for example, family-related ones, sickness, death, emotional upsets and so on – were to be kept either outside of the public discourse or confined within specialized institutions (e.g. the church). Education became predominantly about the preparation of a productive labour force as well as about the creation of a complete human being as previously defined. Neither includes the emotional nor the spiritual self. Emotions are seen as inferior to reason, while spirituality became identified with what is often claimed to be a particularly bleak period of western history, known as the Middle Ages. This was a 'by-product' of the Renaissance period which attempted to liberate people from the oppressive social conditions of the day, including the brutality of church inquisitions, religious suppression of other ways of knowing and seeing the world, or religious justifi-cation for the feudal organization of political, social and economic relations. Other characteristics of the current 'modern' education model include the democratization of education, an increase in literacy levels, compulsory education for all primary-school-aged children and focus on achievement, intellectual development and the importance of standards, certificates and diplomas. Education came to be about the creation of a productive nation and about preparing children to become responsible members of that nation.

This model particularly reinforces linguistic and logical mathematical forms of intelligence. According to Gardner (1983, 1993), who argues that humans possess not one but eight distinct forms of intelligence, what is neglected are the spatial, bodily kinesthetic, musical, interpersonal, intrapersonal and naturalist intelligences ways of learning and knowing. As a result, such an education system predominantly caters for children who are good with words and logic, while children who show ability in dance, art, music, social relations, intuition, drama, nature and other areas of self-expression tend not to receive as much recognition (Armstrong 1996).

There are different opinions as to why this particular model spread throughout the world. According to Connell (1980: 16), western-type schools expanded rapidly throughout the world in such a way that in 'non-western countries, few indigenous schools survived to the middle of the [twentieth] century'. Those that did, such as in Islamic countries and in India, found their influence 'somewhat restricted and specialised, and they were outdistanced by their western rivals' (ibid.). Connell explains this expansion of western educational models in the following way:

> The western school, with its carefully organised grades and classroom procedures, its hierarchy of teachers and administrators, and its readily recognisable standards, certificates, and sequences of studies, established a pattern suitable for a program of mass education. It was a pattern that was easily grasped and readily exportable. Migrants from Europe and America and colonial administrators helped to set it up throughout the world and it was also actively sought and introduced by non-colonised countries such as Japan, China, Thailand, and Turkey. It was seen as an essential instrument of national development. It took root because it met a current need. Through the western school, education had been systematically institutionalised and packaged; and in that form it could be readily distributed to the mass audiences that were *seeking it* [italics added] throughout the world.
>
> (Connell 1980: 16)

Others (e.g. Said 1993; Spring 1998) argue that this model was *imposed* on other peoples because their cultures were seen as subordinate, inferior and less advanced. Education was a consequence and means of maintaining colonization. For example, education was seen as crucial in liberating 'backward' peoples: justifying enslavement of native Americans. Morcillo, in the sixteenth century, wrote this: 'They should be civilized by good customs and education and led to a more human way of life' (Morcillo, quoted in Spring 1998: 10).

Investigation of educational histories – written records – seems to support the second view. In addition, investigation of existing texts on educational history/histories also shows a connection between the particular approach to time, visions for the future and educational visions and practices. Written within the framework of a worldview that assumes linear time and defines the future in terms of distance from the rudimentary past, these educational histories are further good examples of the connection between futures and educational discourses.

2 Using time and the future to colonize and educate the other

Eurocentric and patriarchal bias in twentieth-century educational history

In this analysis of 'generalist' educational histories, one can easily find that the main approach used is the systematization and cataloguing of educational practices, ideas and 'great' educational philosophers and reformers according to strict chronological order. The writing is focused more on the presentation of facts than on interpretations and the meanings given to these facts. Of course, while allegedly broad, general and universal (as shown by their titles), these histories are mostly concerned with the educational history of the west. Non-western educational history is only sporadically reviewed in 'the context of ancient civilizations' (*Encyclopaedia Britannica* 2001), or, alternatively, in the context of 'comparative education'. While some non-western educational histories, such as the history of medieval Muslim education, are given attention, this is most often because of their 'impact upon western education' (ibid.). But while exiled from generalist educational histories, non-western education histories do represent a corpus of their own, as accounts of *Ancient Indian Education* (Altekar 1957; Mookerji 1960) or histories of Japanese (Kaigo 1968), Chinese (Kuo 1972) or Muslim (Shalaby 1979) education attest. This corpus is, of course, much more limited, occasional and highly specialized. And, perhaps most importantly, very few non-western educational histories are available in English. The general knowledge production in the west privileges those that are located within it, which is not a problem limited to the west; Mandarin-speaking theorists living in China, for example, might equally be 'privileged' by companies that publish books in Mandarin. The problem, however, generally lies in the one-directional movement from west towards non-west. As argued by, for example, Altbach, there is 'the gulf' between:

> the power and influence of the major central nations of the Western industrialized world which produce knowledge and the vast hinterland of consuming nations of the Third World, many of which are hardly part of the [international] system at all...

> (Altbach 1987: xii)

While Altbach's analysis is here focused on the Third World, the general principle of uni-directional movement is true for the west and non-west. Within such a movement, it is western authors that almost always remain both generalized and localized experts. They are experts on 'general' education and, as well, authorities on, for example, 'Chinese' education. The writings of Chinese authors, on the other side, either remain unavailable in the current 'global' language or, alternatively, are translated many decades later. This perhaps helps explain why the above-mentioned non-western educational histories are all 'dated'. And it explains why it is still Mookerji's (though seminal) text (1960) that is used to study traditional Indian education, almost 50 years after it was originally written. Finally, when non-western authors write on universal issues, their work is bracketed as the Chinese or Indian perspective. Western authors are rarely labelled by their tradition.

In addition to the general invisibility of non-western perspectives in all these broad educational histories, there is also a silence surrounding the issue of women's engagement with educational practices and discourses. Except for Maria Montessori, women are always objects of educational histories never subjects. In available educational histories the issue of gender is discussed as a separate and specialized entry, usually under the rubric of 'the education of women'. This theme focuses mostly on how women used to be, are and should be educated rather than on how they did/do *educate*. In sum, 'human' experience is predominantly based on men's experience of education, while women's experiences and engagement with education are either invisible or marginalized.

Thus, western history and discourses are generalized and universalized, while non-western discourses are located within specialized categories. When it comes to women, there is no equivalent to either generalized and universalized educational histories or non-western educational histories. That is, women's educational histories are defined as either histories of exclusion or as a special entry within broader, general histories. However, feminists and women futurists have provided alternative readings of broad social histories (e.g. Boulding 1992; Eisler 1987; Miles 1993). Feminist scholars in the area of education have particularly focused on how 'men controlled education...[how] they prevented women from learning, and then condemned women because they were ignorant' (Spender 1982: 9). I discuss this alternative reading of history from a feminist perspective in Part III: *Searching for social and educational alternatives*.

No Greeks, no education

As discussed earlier, Eurocentrism is evident in generalized educational histories in definitions of the universal and the particular, and in relation to the issues of authorship. But what might be most relevant for the argument I make in this book is that *chronological content* (the stages of history) is determined by *particular epistemic understandings of time* (linear, progress-based), which are firmly based in western intellectual history. That is, time is understood as movement from the past towards the *future*, which is again *defined in a very specific way, as progress or development*. This, in turn, maintains and further creates a persistent theme in western mainstream discourses: the future is the one created in the west (by an intellectual male elite) and the only choice for 'others' is to progress towards this particular future. Non-western histories are either silenced or superficially included within this particular discourse. For example, the most common organization or structuring of educational ideas and practices from the past follows a general western chronology in the way progress and development are conceptualized. Other historical cultures and educational systems are forced to fit into a western 'artificial divisions of history as early, middle, and present' (Nakosteen 1965: 4). In practical terms, this means that education is firstly divided between primitive and civilized people. Then, early civilizations of Mesopotamia, Egypt, India and China are explored in general terms until the appearance of the Hellenistic Civilization. After that, more attention is paid to the Greeks, whose contribution is discussed in detail. This is because Greeks are seen as 'the beginners of nearly everything, Christianity excepted, of which the modern world makes its boast' (Castle 1961: 11). As Castle further eloquently puts it:

Certainly the Greeks were the first real educators of our western world. No history of education can neglect them; for they were the first western people to think seriously and profoundly about educating the young, the first to ask what education is, what it is for, and how children and men *should be* [italics added] educated.

(Castle 1961: 11)

In this particular paragraph, Castle asserts that the Greeks are the first 'real' educators of our western world. In all of the educational histories I review here, this position is contested only by Nakosteen (1965). Nakosteen's main disruption of the hegemonic canon is in his extension of the conventional time frame, challenging the history of origins. That is, in a place usually reserved for 'the Greeks' – as the sole beginners of 'western' civilization – Nakosteen discusses the Indian educational system, arguing that Indian educational influences upon the Middle Eastern nations and upon Greeks were substantial (ibid.: 19–20). More recently, Martin Bernal has, 'since the early 1980s, been arguing that the civilization of classical Greece has deep and important roots in Afroasiatic cultures' (Reagan 1996: 5). More problematic than erasing earlier influences on western civilization is that not only are the Greeks seen as *the first* real educators but as the originators of *civilization* itself. Western civilization is equated with *the civilization* – a civilization that developed through stages and reached its peak in the current stage of modernity. Modernity is then defined according to western understandings of history, that is, as the present, which is also often seen as the highest and the most rational historical moment in the development of (western) civilization. According to this narrative, modernity arose out of philosophical debates in the west and because of particular western inventions: scientific, economic, theoretical and cultural. As such, modernity follows a strict chronological order and makes a radical departure from the pre-modern past. While non-western civilizations are recognized for their early contributions, the advent of modern (western) civilization annuls their further development by default. In educational histories, the cultural developments of so-called 'early' educational systems (such as Chinese, Hindu, Persian, Hebrew and Egyptian) are therefore treated 'as though their cultural developments terminated with the beginning of the Christian era' (Nakosteen 1965: 4). This approach becomes especially confusing, argues Nakosteen, when the advanced stages of educational systems such as those of India, Persia, Egypt or Judea are surveyed as 'though they constituted the primitive beginnings of Western educational traditions' (ibid.).

To discuss or not to discuss: 'Savages' and their education

As indigenous education is perceived to belong to the earliest stages of human history, which are by definition simple and undeveloped, the mainstream discourse assigned a particularly limited and inferior place to traditional indigenous education. At the beginning of the twentieth century, mainstream Eurocentric discourse on indigenous education was an account of 'non-progressive education (among) savages or nature peoples' (Graves 1909). This particular discourse within Eurocentric educational histories reflected a particular view of time and the future that was culturally and temporally specific. That is, education practices within traditional indigenous societies were judged not in connection with the indigenous approaches and understanding of time, but exclusively from the framework of the western one. This resulted in an understanding and labelling of indigenous education as undeveloped, inferior and simple. In its early phases, some hundred years ago, the narrative on traditional indigenous cultures and education read:

> 'One set of savages is like another', said Samuel Johnson, and this dictum of the eighteenth-century sage has stood the test of modern investigation. The government, customs, and mentality of all savages have proved to be strikingly similar in their simplicity and crudity. When the human race is yet in its intellectual infancy, which it seems to be in the case of all primitive peoples both of the present day and the past, society is found to be on a comparatively simple basis, and there is little differentiation of thought or occupation... [The savage's] social organization is undeveloped, he is absolutely incapable of abstract thought, his religion is superstitious and crude, his occupations are largely limited to securing the products of nature that are at hand, and the education he receives is imitative and fixed...Because the life and thought of savages are so crude and undeveloped, histories generally give little or no account of the educational process among the most primitive peoples.
>
> (Graves 1909: 8–19)

Although generally undeserving of much space within educational histories, savage education, Graves (ibid.: 13) argues, is still 'worthy of some consideration' because:

> the very simplicity and uniformity of the organization, method, and content of savage education, by constituting an instructive

contrast to later complexities, and affording a means of interpreting them, form a natural starting-point for studying the history of education.

(Graves 1909: 13)

Writing at about the same time, Laurie (republished 1970) contests this view. For Laurie, since the savage is lacking in ethics, there is nothing he can offer the world:

In a historical survey we can afford to ignore the vast variety of tribes which are still in a savage state, and which, either by innate incapacity for development, or by the force of irresistible external circumstances, have risen little above the beasts that perish. The human possibilities of such tribes may be, in germ, as high as those of many more favoured races; but this is doubtful. They labour to acquire skill in getting food by the exercise either of bodily vigour or successful cunning, and they cherish the virtue of bravery in warding off the attacks of others like themselves. As they have, however, no political or ethical ideal, they can have no education in the sense in which we use the term in this book. *They can teach us nothing* [italics added].

(Laurie 1970: 2–3)

A similar approach is taken by Painter (1908). While, 'fortunately for mankind', education in some form or other is as old as our race, 'progress in education' follows 'general human progress' and so:

Following the course of human progress, the history of education naturally divides itself as follows: I. The Oriental countries, including China, India, Persia, Palestine, and Egypt. II. The ancient classical nations, Greece and Rome. III. The Christian education of Europe and America, which is divided into – (1) the period before the rise of Protestantism and (2) the period after that great movement.

(Painter 1908: 9–10)

While among all peoples 'barbarous as well as civilized' each generation has received some special training for their subsequent career, this was often done in 'a very defective and one-sided way' (ibid.: 3). Naturally, when the state of civilization was in general 'low', education has correspondingly been 'narrow and imperfect' (ibid.). 'The beautiful world of science and art' remains 'undreamed of' (ibid.).

His classification therefore takes no account of 'uncivilized peoples', because '…education with them consists almost exclusively in training the body for war and the chase. Their education is thus too primitive in its character to bring it within the scope of our present undertaking' (ibid.: 10).

And the same (hi)story of education continues

Such an approach to educational history, seen in the work of early twentieth-century writers such as Graves, Laurie and Painter, remains a consistent theme throughout the century. Mulhern's (1959: iii) *A History of Education: A Social Interpretation* is indicative of the mainstream classification of societies and cultures that prevails in the twentieth-century western (and colonial) discourses. Mulhern first defines progress as 'the adaptation of man to his changing environment' (ibid.: 10), and then distinguishes between three 'clearly differentiated types of society – primitive, Oriental, and Western'. (ibid.). He argues that the main difference between primitive and oriental cultures is in the greater flexibility of oriental cultures, their greater mastery over the physical environment and their higher level of overall progress:

> Primitive peoples, living in a natural environment whose operations they did not understand, and in an imaginary environment which they themselves created, and fearful of these real and imaginary enemies, opposed all material and spiritual changes… But, into primitive life and society change came, usually, it seems, after a long period of fixity…Thus, driven *upward* [italics added] probably in the main by a changing environment, men found, eventually, a new mode of social life, new certainties and new security in the larger social unities of Oriental nations… Whenever or however the change to the Oriental social level first occurred, the dawn of history finds that man has definitely passed *far beyond* [italics added] his primitive social beginnings.
> (Mulhern 1959: 3–16)

Naturally, educational practices were also different among primitive and oriental peoples. The main difference is seen to be whether education was conscious in its aim or not:

> As in primitive, so again in Oriental times the folkways were passed on from generation to generation by education in one

form or another, but on this latter level the process, in its formal aspects at least, was unlike that of the primitives, a clearly conscious one, directed generally by a privileged priestly class, which was the strong right arm of a political despot who was regarded and worshiped as a god.

(Mulhern 1959: 15)

Still, both primitive and oriental cultures are seen as inferior to the western civilization that emerged later. For writers like Mulhern, the main achievement of western civilization is that it had discovered the values of individual liberty, individual intelligence and individual initiative on which the foundations of modern democracies have been established (ibid.). Reflecting another dominant theme in the west, Mulhern argues that both primitive and oriental societies are deficient in this respect. While among primitive peoples there is only an occasional individual – usually an extraordinary warrior – who enjoyed a measure of personal liberty, in oriental societies liberty became the privilege of a small fraction of the population. The small fraction was usually a political and religious aristocracy – but even among them, 'the minds even of the priests of the ancient Orient were uncritical and submissive' (ibid.: 20). Education is seen as crucial to continuing modernity and 'modern democracies', which will continue only so long as they:

continue to provide an education which will develop in their citizens a critical, forward looking, vigilant attitude. 'Eternal vigilance is the price of liberty', and in thoughtful, intelligent planning for the future lies the promise *of a better world tomorrow.* [italics added].

(Mulhern 1959: 20)

As I have previously argued, it was the particular western understanding of time, progress and development that influenced colonial educational discourses and policies. As can be seen in many of the passages quoted above, the futures discourse was used in a particular way, usually to chronologically 'theorize' non-western cultures as uneducated, and non-western educational practices as somehow deficient. What is implied, therefore, is that non-western cultures are in a serious need of real (western, modernist) 'education'. Some parts of these discourses remain extant in our so-called postcolonial world. A hundred years after Graves and Laurie so eloquently expressed the mainstream western views on indigenous cultures at that time, western chronology and the reading of history still dominate. For example, in an otherwise satisfactory as well as thorough account of educational history by *Encyclopaedia Britannica* currently available online, a distinction between education within primitive and civilized cultures is still made. Brian Simon's *The State and Educational Change: Essays in the History of Education and Pedagogy*, published in 1994, also includes only western educational history. In fact, although using a generalized title, Simon's book is almost entirely concerned with English and British educational history. This is not an accident, but a product of the worldview that equates western with universal. The worldview creates the system of knowledge, which then defines what is to be included and not included in scholarship. The non-west is not included as it has nothing to offer.

Another recent example of Eurocentrism is Rorty's (1998) *Philosophers on Education: Historical Perspectives*. This account continues the traditional Eurocentric approach by beginning with Socrates' and Plato's ideas on education and finishing with an article on 'Civic education in the liberal state'. Out of 33 chapters, only two deal with education that exists on the margins of the western paradigms (Shi'ite's education in Qom and traditional Yeshiva's education in Israel). In addition to the culturally inappropriate spelling of *Qu'ran* (as Koran) in her introductory essay, Rorty locates Islamic and Jewish educational practices at the very end. Their inclusion is contingent on their specialization and location as the Other. In another article, Rorty clearly describes education of Shi'ite Mullahs and traditional Yeshiva's education of interpreters of the Torah and the Talmud as arising from '*other* [italics added] philosophic traditions' (ibid.). But the choice of articles that describe educational discourses based on these 'other philosophic traditions' is rather odd. While the majority of articles in *Philosophers on Education* assign a space for individual western philosophers, the articles that deal with Islamic and Jewish education describe specific educational practices that occur in one place (Qom) or within a system (Yeshiva's education). There is no explanation for these particular choices and one can easily remain puzzled about where and what exactly Qom and Yeshiva are – as these categories are neither contextualized nor explained. Rorty's account is, however, in line with previous works on a similar subject by other authors, albeit she includes two articles that describe education of the Other.

Meyer's (1975) selection in his *Grandmasters of Educational Thought* also begins with Socrates and Plato (and finishes with Dewey). Surprisingly, Meyer's account also ignores Maria Montessori, the only woman for whom the space in historical reviews on educational ideas and theories is usually reserved.

Another example of western bias is Bertrand's recent overview of *Contemporary Theories and Practices in Education* (1995). For example, Bertrand acknowledges that one particular approach in education – 'spiritualistic theories', and spiritualistic visions of the world – stems from both western (Platonism and Neo-Platonism) and non-western (Hinduism, Taoism, Zen) philosophies. But, within this tradition, he chooses to discuss the work of Abraham Maslow, Willis Harman, George Leonard and Constantin Fotinas; Bertrand acknowledges that these authors were variously influenced by particular non-western philosophies but does not actually discuss any of the non-western authors within this tradition.

Acknowledging the non-west

There are, however, two more recent and important attempts to include non-western educational traditions when discussing educational history. One is Timothy Reagan's *Non-Western Educational Traditions: Alternative Approaches to Educational Thought and Practice*, published in 1996. The other is *Globalization and Educational Rights: An Intercivilizational Analysis* by Joel Spring, published in 2001. These two books break away from the tradition of 'comparative education', in that they take broader units of analysis. While most comparative education overviews do so in the context of particular nation states, both Reagan and Spring discuss various non-western traditions within *civilization* frameworks. In addition, they both (to a greater or lesser degree) incorporate insights from feminist theory. Most importantly, both texts imply that non-western traditions are 'still alive' and relevant to educational futures. That is, instead of relocating non-western traditions in the 'reservoir of backward' (pre-historic, pre-modern, 'early', 'simple', etc.) practices, they locate them as part of a global human heritage.

To sum up the preceding discussion, twentieth-century educational histories define educational practices in line with the general organization of history as a linear progression from primitive, savage states towards the more civilized and modern. This particular project excludes both non-western peoples and women from having any import in the past and any say on the future. Postmodern, feminist and postcolonial theorists have challenged this exclusion. The result of their critique has not been, however, the writing of more balanced grand narratives, but an abandonment of macrohistorical writing altogether. Educational histories are now usually highly localized. They exist within a particular, usually short, time frame and narrow geographical space. At the same time, educational histories that still attempt to incorporate broader historical periods are currently very rare. When written, they are still produced within paradigms hardly touched by feminist and postcolonial deconstruction. However, the rewriting of general educational histories is crucial if we are to both recover futures lost by exclusion and create new, balanced, peaceful, sustainable futures. Recovering the past does not mean lamenting those parts of tradition that were also damaging to non-dominant social groups. Rather it means using the past as a resource to create new futures. Until these general educational histories are rewritten, transforming the current curriculum will be nearly impossible, since the exclusionary western template will remain defining. The litany – the day-to-day curriculum practices of education – will continue unchanged.

One question that remains, assuming a paradigm shift does occur, is what to do with these histories. If not rewritten, at least they have to be 'removed', argues Moorcroft (1997: 74). In the light of 'the wealth of excellent material now available' – on partnership, peace, multi-cultural and environmental education – that libraries can acquire, perhaps some of the older materials should 'have no place in public and school libraries' (ibid.). Academic libraries, on the other hand, need to keep a record of the past, because by 'weeding out such materials, we would be wiping the slate clean in a way that would be historically deceptive' (ibid.). However, Moorcroft (ibid.) also suggests that alternative strategies may be used to deal constructively with this 'offensive material'. For example, these texts could be reclassified under 'colonial writing', or warning stickers could be placed on some material, depending on what local indigenous (and other ethnic) communities would find appropriate (ibid.). One problem with this approach, however, is that almost the entire library stock could then be located in the 'western, colonial, patriarchal' section and librarians would never tire of placing warning stickers! Rewriting of broad educational histories to better reflect our present theoretical and social movement would then, perhaps, be something that could be more easily done.

Teaching time and imposing a future

In any case, part of this colonizing process was also 'teaching time'. As Tuhiwai Smith (1999: 53) describes, western observers were 'struck by the way time was used (or rather, not used or organized)' by indigenous peoples in Africa, the Americas and the Pacific. Representations of 'native life' described this life as 'devoid of work habits' and native people as 'being lazy, indolent, with low attention spans' and so forth (ibid.: 55). Explanations of why this is so ranged from the 'hot climate' argument to those that made a direct connection between race and indolence, that is 'darker skin people [were]... considered more "naturally" indolent' (ibid.: 54). After the arrival of missionaries and the development of more systematic colonization, the connection between time, work and education became even more important:

> The belief that 'natives' did not value work or have a sense of time provided ideological justification for exclusionary practices which reached across such areas as education, land development and employment. The evangelical missionaries who arrived in the Pacific had a view of salvation in which were embedded white lower middle-class English or puritanical New England work practices and values. It was hard work to get to heaven and 'savages' were expected to work extra hard to qualify to get into the queue.
>
> (Tuhiwai Smith 1999: 54)

Of course, it was forgotten that before industrialization, in the west too, time was measured by human activities or environmental changes and not so much 'by the clock'. It was forgotten that clock time was also at one time 'invented' and that this was done in order to respond to the needs and desires of particular societies/cultures/ civilizations. As argued by Boorstin:

> The first grand discovery was time, the landscape of experience. Only by marking off months, weeks, and years, days and hours, minutes and seconds, would mankind be liberated from the cyclical monotony of nature. The flow of shadows, sand, and water, and time itself, translated into the clock's staccato, became a useful measure of man's movements across the planet...Communities of time would bring the first communities of knowledge, ways to share discovery, a common frontier on the unknown.
>
> (in Levine 1997: 54)

Clock time was invented to satisfy the needs of industrialization, not the environment, argue Levine (ibid.), Nowotny (1994) and

Adam (1998). The clock, and not the steam engine, is 'the key machine of the industrial age' argues Lewis Mumford (in Levine 1997: 63). In turn, the discovery of industrial time had an enormous impact on both human societies and the natural environment (Adam 1998; Levine 1997; Nowotny 1994). Adam (1998) argues that when time became a commodity, both the environment and the future became simultaneously devalued. This remains the main principle in the neo-classical economic approach and reflects the general attitude of modernism:

> The future...is discounted which means giving the future less value than the present...This means, by today's value and at a discount rate of 10 per cent per annum over a period of ten years, the future $1,000 is calculated to be worth a mere $386 today...the future is devalued by a sleight of the economic hand...[which] makes many an incomprehensible action rational...From the standpoint of the present, projected into the future and back again, the future is less important than the present and, given a long enough time span, it is in this scheme of things worthless.
>
> (Adam 1998: 75)

The discovery, and the victory, of clock time has also meant that education became about teaching punctuality. In the industrial model, 'correct time' is valuable, and time is a product that can be bought and sold. As argued by the Blodgett Clock Company in 1896 (quoted in Levine 1997: 68), 'Order, promptness and regularity' became '...cardinal principles to impress on the minds of young people...[And] not better illustration of these principles than this clock can be secured in a school'.

The urgency of punctual behaviour was promoted in school-books, and associated with achievement and success (ibid.: 69–70). The latecomer became characterized as 'a social inferior and, in some cases, a moral incompetent' (ibid.: 69). Schooling based on this temporal template was exported to both local and colonized societies. In the case of the latter, the industrial time template was exported as a 'package':

> The assumptions associated with the linear perspective, New-tonian science, and neo-classical economics, in conjunction with the rationalised time of calendars and clocks, form a powerful, mutually reinforcing conceptual unit. As such, this conceptual

conjuncture constitutes the deep structure of the taken-for-granted knowledge associated with the industrial way of life, creating the by now accustomed semblance of certainty and control.

(Adam 1998: 97)

Not only that, continues Adam (ibid.: 107–108), '[i]t was imposed irrespective of whether or not these temporal innovations were welcomed or rejected there: non-compliance spelt automatic exclusion; it meant being constructed as "other" and therefore in need of "development"'.

While everyone was to learn this promptness, punctuality and what progress was about, there were important differences. Different education was provided for different children, depending on their social positioning. While education was ideally supposed to promote meritocracy, in practice, criteria such as 'merit', various tests and what counts as knowledge were used for streaming and social reproduction of existing social (e.g. class- and gender-based) hierarchies. As this book deals predominantly with issues of culture and gender, I will not discuss the issue of class here, or the ways in which a particular futures discourse was used to reproduce class hierarchies. What will suffice is to say that, throughout western history, education of children from lower classes was always inferior to elite education. This remains one of its main features even today (Angus 1993; Apple 2001; Oakes 1985), despite many educational reformers over the centuries attempting to democratize education according to the ideals of equal opportunity and access. These educational reformers, such as Jean Baptiste de La Salle (1651–1719), Friedrich Froebel (1782–1852), John Dewey (1858–1952) and Maria Montessori (1870–1952), always had improvement and a particular (desired) future in mind. This desired future more often than not included democratization of education as well as the inclusion of other practices (e.g. a 'holistic' approach) that were seen as missing from modern education.

It is also important to note here that there has always been significant dissent in the field of western education itself. During the twentieth century, dissent came from libertarian educators (Shotton 1992), the 'social justice' tradition (Goldstein and Selby 2000), environmental education (Bowers 1997; Orr 1994), peace education, development education, anti-sexist as well as anti-racist education. This book can be contextualized as following this as well as the tradition within critical futures field. Still, while these are important sources of potential change, the dominant linear model more often than not remains defining. Moreover, these approaches to change, based on a linear view of reality, have been founded on 'implementing educational innovations in a rational, systematic manner' (Miller 2000: 146). So, is it possible to provide alternative readings of educational histories which would take into account different, non-linear, views of time?

3 Turn of the spiral: alternative histories

Paradigm shift

I next argue that the paradigm shift has began to occur; thus it is no longer the norm to view indigenous or Eastern approaches to education as primitive, savage, barbaric and so forth. On the contrary, western civilization seems to be seeking ways to rejuvenate itself, to address the dead end (e.g. lack of social and environmental sustainability, the challenge to the idea of progress and development) it currently faces. Thus, the 'discovery' of alternative indigenous histories took place quite recently and connected with a paradigmatic shift, or a 'postcolonial turn'. Partly, this discovery is about writing a more 'accurate' description of those pre-colonization times, as seen from the perspective of contemporary peoples. And partly, this discovery, or 'recovery', is about making choices in terms of whose/which/what kind of history is to inform present choices and decisions of the future. That is, this, alternative, history is often described in terms of what is lost, and could possibly be regained, and in terms of what should be remembered and never repeated.

The following discussion on alternative histories should be seen in terms of the *further exploration of connections between the particular approach to time, vision for the future and educational visions and practices*. However, the connection between the image of the future and the educational system should not be seen in firm deterministic terms, but rather in terms of Polak's (1973) work on how the image of the future informs particular actions of the day. Thus, as suggested by 'layered', critical and civilizational approach within futures studies (e.g. Inayatullah 2002), the worldview level of civilization (which includes type of time and vision of the future) informs the dominant educational system, which then informs the day-to-day lived realities. By challenging the worldview, we can begin to see possibilities for the development of alternative educational systems.

Furthermore, by developing alternative histories, there is no suggestion that they are the 'final story', that historical truth has been discovered. These alternatives, too, are part of the practice of the 'construction' and 'reconstruction' of reality, undertaken from a current perspective – in this case, from the approach informed by postmodernism, feminism and postcolonialism. As argued by Nakosteen, history is always '...a study of ourselves, our problems, our hopes and dreams, our failures and successes, our joys and anxieties. So conceived, history becomes in a wider context the study of [hu]man[s] in the present sense and in the present tense' (1965: 13).

In addition, as argued by Depaepe:

> Because we are biologically situated in a specific spatial (social and cultural) and temporal (historical) context, we can do nothing other than look from a specific standpoint at what lies behind us. And since time always further blurs (and ultimately even erases or wipes out) the past, this looking-back unavoidably implies a 'reconstruction' that attempts to recover 'how it really was'...This 're-construction' inevitably has the character of a 'construction'...in the studying of history, we ourselves construct the story of what is past.
>
> (Depaepe 1998: 16)

Even taking into account the epistemological impossibility of really knowing history, the investigation of alternative histories remains important because they function as resources, as possibilities for the creation of alternative futures. Thus, through destabilizing hegemonic histories, we can also destabilize hegemonic futures. Another crucial point is that educational practices are not a mere consequence of technological development within a particular society, civilization and historical phase, as conceived in mainstream educational history. Rather, these practices are always about what a particular society/culture/civilization considers to be important. Educational practices are *also* about achieving a particular desired future, and are not merely a by-product of the technological development of an era. In fact, the belief that educational practices merely reflect ecological and technological developments of a society and civilization is, in itself, distinctively western.

Dreamtime and the eternal now: an alternative history of indigenous education

As discussed earlier, the recovery/discovery of alternative indigenous histories is quite recent and is connected with a particular paradigm shift. The most recent 'regime of truth' on 'traditional indigenous education' is, of course, totally different from the previous mainstream canon and is part of ongoing negotiation between indigenous and non-indigenous peoples about historical events. Alternative educational histories have only become possible after indigenous peoples were finally allowed to 'speak for themselves' and (possibly) be heard within the context of the mainstream (settler-dominated) society. As this is quite recent, texts written by indigenous peoples about their true history often use materials (texts and visual images) that were collected by (sometimes sympathetic, more often not) westerners. What is different in these alternative histories is not always the described 'traditional' reality, but rather the *interpretation* and *meaning* given to that reality. In that sense, the work of certain contemporary anthropologists (e.g. Lawlor 1991; Voigt and Drury 1997) corresponds with contemporary accounts by indigenous people of 'traditional' indigenous societies and 'traditional' indigenous education (e.g. Bayles 1989; Ilyatjari 1991; Valadian 1991). Both versions are part of the same paradigm shift within the field of history. This shift is, of course, about rewriting history, about writing an alternative story to the western and linear.

The new story does not contest that the traditional education of indigenous peoples was quite different from education brought by European colonizers. What is contested is that this education was somehow inferior, primitive and undeveloped. For example, the western narrative that argues that the indigenous way of life was 'stagnant', 'non-progressive' and 'simple' is replaced with the new narrative that asserts that traditional indigenous societies, in fact, incorporated different approaches to change. That is, change was not seen as linear movement from the past towards the future through the present, but rather as integrating 'past and present, qualities and quantities, objects and process, visible and invisible, sequential and simultaneous' (Lawlor 1991: 321). One interesting example of this traditional (Australian) Aboriginal approach to change is provided by a western anthropologist who performed a series of logic and intelligence tests in the early 1950s, in Australia (ibid.: 320). In the tests, the anthropologist put three matches on the left and two matches on the right, trying to discover whether

'Aborigines were capable [*sic*] of consistently visualizing and identifying the abstract concept of groups' (ibid.: 320–321):

> The Aborigine responded, 'In this place there are three matches and over here there are two matches.' This answer was encouraging to the anthropologist, despite the fact that the Aboriginal subject failed to describe these things as purely abstract, quantitative groups. Next he moved one match from the group of three, placed it in the group of two, and again asked the Aborigine what he saw in this arrangement. A response consistent with western logic would be, 'Now there is a group of two and then a group of three.' The Aborigine's response was, 'I see two groups of three matches and two groups of two matches, and one "three-making" match'
>
> (Lawlor 1991: 321)

Lawlor (ibid.: 321) argues that it is thus western logical habits that cause us to fall into a static, uniform, quantitative interpretation and make us fail to see qualitative process-related differences, such as identifying one 'three-making match' as different from those that are stationary. Brock (1989: xix) also argues that there is now 'much evidence to indicate that Aboriginal society was never static, but was always adapting and changing'. An argument can be made that, in fact, it is non-indigenous societies that resist change. For example, it is in so-called 'early civilization' that we find the first attempts to immortalize those that die – through written records, mummification, creation of tombstones and architectural testimonies to great people who have once lived (Lawlor 1991). And it is now among most 'developed' western societies that frozen bodies and cells of the deceased await to be reawakened in the future, once scientists discover treatments for the diseases to which they succumbed. On the other hand, the traditional Aboriginal worldview not only explicitly forbade the use of names of those that died, it even required the change of the name of an animal if its name was in some way connected to the name of the deceased (ibid.). Life seems to have been lived in full view of change. But it also seems that this view was about acceptance of the organic unfolding of change as the way of nature, rather than trying to control, and even arrest, this organic development. Thus, defining the traditional as static – their society, educational practices – as the mainstream history does, may not be warranted.

Another commonly held view is that indigenous societies are 'simple', while civilizations are 'complex'. The current mainstream narrative still paints a deterministic picture of what happens to education once societies become more 'complex' and 'developed':

> As societies grow more complex, however, the quantity of knowledge to be passed on from one generation to the next becomes more than any one person can know; and hence there *must* [italics added] evolve more selective and efficient means of cultural transmission.
>
> (*Encyclopaedia Britannica* 2001)

This complexity is said to increase historically, especially with western civilization and modern societies. It is assumed that 'there was a "point in time" which was "prehistoric"' (Tuhiwai Smith 1999: 55). It is also assumed that the point at which society moves from prehistoric to historic also represents the point at which tradition breaks away from modernism (ibid.). This implies that traditional indigenous knowledge completely ceased when it came into contact with 'modern' western society (ibid.). This is foundationally problematic from the perspective of contemporary indigenous peoples who base their physical and cultural survival on the idea of (physical and cultural) continuity with 'traditional' indigenous society. In addition, the view of indigenous societies as 'simple' and modern societies as 'complex' can also be challenged by the incredible complexity of the Aboriginal kinship system, languages and mode of perception (as the 'three-making match' example demonstrates).

Time/space, land and relationships

It has now become obvious that pre-colonized indigenous societies would not themselves believe that their educational practices were either 'primitive' or 'underdeveloped'. For example, the traditional (Australian) Aboriginal approach to time and the future does not allow for a distinction between primitive and civilized, 'undeveloped' and 'developed'. According to numerous sources (e.g. Judge 1993; Lawlor 1991; Morphy 1999; Voigt and Drury 1997; Wildman 1997), the traditional Aboriginal worldview did not separate the category of *the future* from the *eternal now*. It is in this eternal now, the Dreamtime,[1] that 'all stages, phases, and cycles were present at once' (Lawlor 1991: 15). According to Voigt and Drury (1997: 27), 'the Dreamtime encompasses past reality and future possibilities in an eternally sacred present':

Thus all of Creation and all Time are contained in a diverse multiplicity of one sacred reality. Irrespective of the particular names ascribed to it, the Dreamtime holds the idea that all aspects of life are eternally interconnected in a vast web of relationship, for all creatures and all things have their origin in the sacred events of the Creation.

(Voigt and Drury 1997: 27)

From the viewpoint of the present, this concept is unique, as it is as much a feature of the future as it is of the past. It is different from the western linear concept of time, as the passage of time and history are not imagined as a movement from the past towards the future, but rather as a passage from 'a subjective state to an objective expression' (Lawlor 1991: 41). It is a movement between external reality, where time is 'absorbed in the circles of birth, growth, decline, and renewal of the living creatures', and the Dreaming, which represents the eternal aspect of time (ibid.: 241). It is also unique because it has 'as much to do with space as with time', referring to origins and powers that are located in places and things (Morphy 1999: 266). That is, both the external reality (the sphere of living and dying) and the eternal Dreaming (the sphere of the Unborn and Death) are materialized in the actuality of space. Space thus becomes the source of knowledge and identities. The stories focus on place descriptions and spatial directions, rather than 'time designations such as when, before, or after' (Lawlor 1991: 239). Thus the movement of traditional indigenous communities was predominately through space, which also incorporated within it a particular understanding of time.

This theme of land seen as 'the core of . . . cultures and the origin of identities' (Goduka 2001) is a common theme across various indigenous traditions. It is not through the passage of time that previous, present and future generations are connected, but through land and space. As argued by Goduka, 'She [the land] connects with the past (as the home of our ancestors), with the present (as nourisher of material and spiritual needs), and with the future (as the legacy they hold in trust for their children and grandchildren)' (ibid.).

Part of western, Christian mythology is that humans have left the perfect place, fallen from grace and so on. All of eschatology, messianism, millennialism and classic utopianism reflect the desire to go back to, or reinvent, the original, perfect place. In Australian Aboriginal cosmology, on the other hand, the land was created perfect by the ancestral beings and it is the role of those that are currently living to keep the world in its original perfection (Lawlor 1991: 87). Therefore, there is no need to project perfected futures 'out there', either as utopia, eupsychia or as the return to the Golden Age, which existed prior to the Fall. The west 'discovered' linear time as primary temporal organizational principle, and, as discussed earlier, western education in many ways reflects this discovery. But education practices remain radically different if time is not projected to be 'out there' but is 'here', not located in some direction 'forwards' but as part of the 'encompassing dream which is [simultaneously] past, present and future' (Wildman 1997: 16).

Consistent with indigenous cosmologies in general, and the Australian situation in particular, indigenous education systems focused on how to build *relationships* – between nature/land, the world of spirits and people, and how to maintain *balance* – transferring knowledge with the purpose of maintaining life and the environment in its original condition (Lawlor 1991; Holm in Parrish 1991). Since it was 'ancestral human and animal beings [that] had moulded the landscapes and their populations' (Council for Aboriginal Reconciliation 1993: 6–7), holistic approaches to teaching and learning cannot exclude 'the vital link between the Land, Language and Culture' (Grant 1997: 56). In common with all known indigenous peoples, existence for Australian indigenous people is seen as 'a living blend of spirit, nature/land, and people' (Goduka 2001); indigenous education draws on the spirit world (intuitive knowledge, myths, divination, prophecy), nature/land and people (oral transmission of knowledge).

The narrative on indigenous educational practices existing prior to colonization outlines that indigenous cosmology and ways of life provided 'more time for the artistic and spiritual development of the entire society' (Lawlor 1991: 165): That indigenous societies were 'child-centred' in the sense that children were not excluded from most adult activities; that there was no 'thing' that was 'nothing', and consequently all aspects and all creatures had their place and their role to play (Voigt and Drury 1997: 26); and that education was aimed at conservationism as well as the maintenance of balance between spiritual, physical and collective aspects of being.

Of course, there were many important differences between the diverse indigenous societies of the past. But there is also agreement among many theorists on indigenous epistemologies (e.g. Battiste 2000; Cajete 1999; Hughes 1987; Semali and Kincheloe 1999; Tuhiwai Smith 1999; Walker 2001) that there are important similarities that can be recovered for the benefits of both indigenous peoples and global human society. I return to this in Part III: *Searching for social and educational alternatives* when discussing the recovery of indigenous traditions in education and the ways the previously outlined alternative history has been utilized to inspire visions for the future.

The cyclical future: an alternative history of 'Oriental' education

The following section provides a different narrative of 'oriental' education to the one previously discussed, and articulated by authors such as Graves (1909), Painter (1908), Laurie (1970), Mulhern (1959) and Macaulay (quoted in Spring 1998). In this section, the connection between underlying views of time, images of the future and educational systems is investigated.

The cyclical understanding of time developed within various cultures and societies, those that are recognized both as western (e.g. Greece and Rome) and as non-western (e.g. Hinduism, Buddhism, Mayan and Chinese civilization) (Taylor 2001). Here, the analysis is limited to approaches to time and education that developed within the Indian episteme. The focus is on the Indian episteme because of its antiquity and the wide historical, as well as more recent, influence it has had on other cultures: the civilizational and global exchange that Galtung (1980), Appadurai (1996), Iyer (2000) and other commentators alert us to.

The Indian episteme is based on a body of knowledge, such as the *Vedas*, that dates back as far as 1500 to 1000 BCE in written form, and approximately as far as 6000 BCE in oral form (Reagan 1996: 93). The Indian episteme is a product of the blending four distinct traditions:

> [t]he religious and spiritual traditions of the original, indigenous people of the subcontinent, whose stone age culture dates back some half million years... [t]he religious and spiritual traditions of the Indus civilization... The religious and spiritual traditions of the Dravidian culture, and... [t]he Vedic religion, which was brought to the subcontinent by Aryan invaders roughly between 200 B.C. and 900 B.C.
>
> (Reagan 1996: 93)

Given this diversity, it comes as no surprise that the notion of time as cyclical was not universally shared by all the philosophical orientations that are part of the Indian episteme. That is, as argued by Sharma (1992: 203), the 'widely, if not universally, held view that the notion of time in Hinduism is cyclical as opposed to the [linear] notion of time in the Semitic religions (Judaism, Christianity and Islam)' is problematic. Sharma (ibid.: 210) concludes that the Hindu notion of time is not a 'monochrome but a mosaic', and is 'too complex to be described as merely cyclical'. Still, the notion of time as cyclical has been an important part of that mosaic, and has often constituted the most dominant discourse within Indian history. However, it is also important to stress here that this notion of time as cyclical is mostly based on the Hindu theory of *Yugas*, *Manvantaras* and *Kalpas*. In particular, the literature known as *Smrti* (e.g. *Ramayana*, *Mahabharata*, *Manu*) contains references to the theory of the *Yugas* which are 'clear, explicit, direct and unequivocal' (ibid.: 207).

The particular educational practices (and theory behind these practices) that I describe in connection to the cyclical understanding of time and the future can probably best be termed as *Brahmanic* education. Brahmanic education was based on the study of *Vedas*, holy texts and scriptures that date back as far as 6000 BCE (Subramuniyaswami 1993: 852). The *Gurukula model* is one way of understanding these ancient texts and is characterized by a spiritual and intimate relationship between the teacher and his students. I say *his* students because, within Indian history, official teachers – gurus – were almost exclusively men. Formal education was almost exclusively the domain of males, and, in addition, the domain of male members of the *Brahmanic* elite.

According to one version of the Hindu timeline, we are now experiencing the *Kali Yuga*, which began at midnight, 18 February 3102 BCE, or in year one according to the Hindu calendar (ibid.: 705). *Kali Yuga* is one of the four *Yugas* (*Satya Yuga*, *Treta Yuga*, *Dvapara Yuga* and *Kali Yuga*) that comprise *mahayuga*, equal to 4,320,000 solar years. Each cosmic cycle – one of the infinitely recurring periods of the universe – comprises one *mahayuga* (4,320,000 years) and 71 *mahayugas*, our current *mahayuga* being the twenty-eighth (ibid.). Each 1000 *mahayugas* constitute a day of Brahma or *kalpa* (or 4,320,000 years) (ibid.: 744). At the end of each *mahayuga*, the physical worlds is destroyed and then recreated, while both the physical and subtle world are destroyed at the end of each *kalpa*. After 36,000 of these dissolutions and creations, there is a 'total, universal annihilation, mahapralaya, when all three worlds, all time, form and space, are withdrawn into Shiva' (ibid.: 705). This period of total withdrawal enables a new universe or life span of Brahma to begin. The entire cycle repeats infinitely (ibid.: 706).

Given the huge length of historical stages – which occur with certainty and are beyond human reach – the individual's supreme duty is to 'achieve his expansion into the Absolute, his self-fulfilment, for he is a potential God, a spark of the Divine [and] education must aid in this fulfilment' notes Mookerji (1960: xxiii). Learning was sought 'as the means of salvation or self-realization, as the means to the highest end of life, viz. *Mukti* or Emancipation' (ibid.: xxi). It was this *mukti* or *moksha* (liberation) that would enable one to break the circle of continuous rebirth. This was partly to be done through education – reading and learning of scriptures.

Apart from scriptures, other traditional vehicles for human perfection included inner zeal and the teacher (Cenkner 1976: 200). Education took 'full account of the fact that Life includes Death and the two form the whole truth' (Mookerji 1960: xxii). Since the physical world is 'transitory, characterized by change, renewal, and decay' (Nakosteen 1965: 38), the permanent pattern of reality that underlies this phenomenon of change could only be realized within 'individual psychic and spiritual unfolding' (ibid.: 25). The notion that basic truths or realities of life and destiny should be realized within intuitive process and realization forms the basic unity of the *Upanishads* – Vedic texts that constitute the theoretical foundations of ancient Indian education. 'The identification of the subject with the object, of the soul with God, of the atman with Brahman, is the fundamental aim of the teachings of the Upanishads' (ibid.).

According to Nakosteen, at its highest peak Brahmanistic education was:

> primarily a system of personal moral disciplines to enable each individual to work out his own by steadily reducing and removing earthly entanglements. It reaches one of its peaks in the moral-educational outlooks of Buddhism, in which the ultimate aim of man's [human] endeavors is not only to save himself from the world but also to be liberated from himself – from illusions of personality, individuality, and selfhood.
>
> (Nakosteen 1965: 39)

Ancient Indian education, however, did not neglect the practical and social aspects of education, but these were defined in the context of the individual's spiritual development:

> There is an outer and external life of man as a member of society which imposes upon it its rules and regulations, conventions

and obligations, ultimately based on morality. But behind this external, social life, there is the inner life of man as an individual, his spiritual life.

(Mookerji 1960: 156)

Embedded knowledge: dharma, karma and moksha

The paths of liberation are many – through faith, knowledge, asceticism, intuition and meditation or service to others – and each individual can choose from these many paths the one for which he is best fitted (Nakosteen 1965: 39). The mode of conduct that is most conducive to spiritual advancement is the adherence to *dharma*, the right and righteous path (Subramuniyaswami 1993: 710).

Given the strict division of the populace into four *varnas* (*castes*), which can be transgressed only in the next life through careful adherence to prescribed *varna dharma* (social duty), there was little need or space left for the development of utopian discourses. Social and other inequalities of human life are explained 'by the doctrines of *karma* and transmigration' (Keay 1959: 11). It is *karma* that determines one's caste, and then it is the caste that provides channels 'for the further progress of one's *karma*, or what one [is] at each point of spiritual evolution' (Nakosteen 1965: 28).

From this perspective, class differences are therefore not so crucial because by fulfilling *dharma* or one's inner destiny and doing good works one can increase one's chances for success (Inayatullah 1997: 183), and achieve a more favourable position in the next life. This also meant, however, that the division between classes, always hierarchical, came to be religiously sanctioned as well as permanent and binding in nature (Reagan 1996: 98). The aim of education here is identical to the aim of life – to provide for each individual the necessary knowledge, arts, skills and values within his own caste (Nakosteen 1965: 38). Obviously this would reflect Brahmanic preferences and their own desired presents and futures.

The formation of particular mainstream futures and educational discourses is always influenced by the domination/knowledge/ authority of a particular social group. In the case of traditional Indian education it is the Brahmans who have been instrumental in creating the system of education which, one would assume, did not necessarily reflect the perspectives and worldviews of other castes. It is also doubtful whether Brahmanic education, which was mostly controlled by men, would reflect the perspectives and worldviews of women within the same caste. But these accounts are largely absent from official recorded history. There is some evidence (Altekar 1957; Keay 1959; Sarkar 1987, 1995) to show that, initially, gender roles were balanced. Over time, as the caste system evolved and the Vedic system hardened, women were excluded from spiritual practices and thus from education. In turn, with the verticality of the caste system becoming hegemonic, the cyclical and spiritual view of life was further reinforced.

Parallel to the above described 'social channels' for the upward realization of the spiritual ideal, 'in a systematic course of duties towards his further conscious evolution' (Nakosteen 1965: 28) the individual was to follow the organization of life within clearly defined life stages. Human life proceeds through four main stages: *brahmachari* (student); *grihastha* (householder); *vanaprastha* (elder advisor); and *sannyasa* (religious solitaire). Each person moves through these phases in pursuit of four human goals: *dharma* (righteousness); *artha* (wealth); *kama* (pleasure); and *moksha* (liberation). Linear and eternal concepts of time coexist parallel to cyclical notions of time, and the notion of time tends to vary between and within these four human goals. Still, the linear conception of time – seen as the ultimate truth within Semitic religions and scientific discourse – is viewed within the Indian episteme as merely a part of one stage, one cycle. Death is but one of those life phases, rich in spiritual potential, when the soul detaches itself from the physical body and continues on in the subtle body (Subramuniyaswami 1993: 708). Linear and cyclical time continue their dance until *moksha*, the final human goal, is obtained. Time then becomes eternal. Depending on the type of liberation obtained, one can find one's self either in *nirvikalapa samadhi*, a state of oneness beyond all change or diversity, beyond time, form and space, or in *visishtadvaita*, a blissful union with God in eternity (Sharma 1992: 211; Subramuniyaswami 1993: 772).

The acquisition of objective knowledge and the focus on the external, outer world is therefore not the chief concern in this system of education. Rather it is to 'directly seek the source of all life and knowledge, which cannot be acquired by piecemeal approach and the study of objects' (Mookerji 1960: xxiii). Education is a process by which the mind is guided from external reality towards the deeper layers which are not 'ruffled by the ripples of the surface, the infinite distractions of the material world' (ibid.: xxv). Knowledge was to be 'in the blood, as an organic part of one's self' (ibid.: xxxi). As such, it is embedded in the teacher, who has obtained a higher level of realization. The close relationship between teacher and student is crucial because 'the pupil is to imbibe the inward method of the teacher, the secrets of his efficiency, the spirit of his life and work, and these things are too subtle to be taught' (ibid.: xxvi).

Thus, education in the classical Indian episteme was: (1) spiritually focused; (2) based on the direct relationship between master and disciple; (3) equated with the goals of life as a whole; and (4) with a view to the ultimate goal, liberation.

This system of education has been challenged in modern times both from outside (by western modern secularism) and from inside (by spiritual education that is integrated, class-caste- and gender-balanced). For example, while twentieth-century Indian educators – Aurobindo, Maharishi Mahesh Yogi, Sathya Sai Baba and P. R. Sarkar – keep spirituality as a basis for their system, they also aim to modernize the Indian educational system, through a focus on science, economic development and gender balance.

On one hand, the Brahmanistic system of education perpetuated and legitimated rigid class division, in particular through a 'nice ideological twist' within doctrines of *karma* and *dharma*. On the other hand, it aimed to provide the liberation of all individuals – not through utopia but through *eupsychia*. Thus, the view outlined by Mulhern (1959) and other western theorists about the inferiority of oriental education, about its deficiency when it comes to values of individual liberty, intelligence and initiative represents a view that would not be *universally* held. The alternative narrative that was provided earlier and was predominantly based on the work of Indian theorists (e.g. Nakosteen, Mookerji) outlines the ways in which the Brahmanistic education system made sense within its own frames of reference. In any case, as will be seen later, this system of education is certainly a far cry from modernist notions of education as essentially practical training for a globalized marketplace. The current spiritual alternative, discussed in Part III: *Searching for social and educational alternatives*, becomes then one of the key disruptive discourses to the modern secularized and the postmodern multiplicity approach. Informed by the Indian episteme, it has been picked up in symbolic and actual forms by the holistic and New Age educational movements. The Indian system thus becomes once again a global historical resource for pedagogical transformation – challenging what is taught, who teaches, the process of teaching and what is true learning – a source of an alternative desired future.

Concluding remarks

Particular understandings of time and the future are the underlying, crucial yet often unrecognized dimensions within educational systems

Table 3.1 Time, future, education – selected education histories compared

	Modern western education	Pre-modern religious education	Indigenous Australian education	Brahmanistic education
Approach to time	Linear Evolution Point of creation (Big Bang) and end for Universe (Big Crash) Time broken into smaller units Clock Time	Linear Creation by God: universe, nature, people	Eternal now, Dreamtime Universe eternal	Cyclical Universe eternal
Future	Progress and development (future improvement of the past and the present; earlier social stages rudimentary and primitive) Utopia	Regress (Fall from the Golden Age) Second coming, Judgment Day	Embedded in the Eternal now	Part of cyclical Yugas Eupsychia Moksha
Ontology and epistemology	Evolutionism, progressivism, utopianism, scientific rationalism and empiricism, anthropocentrism, secularism	Truth of God Faith	External reality and the eternal Dreaming materialized in the actuality of space – source of knowledge and identities, connects present generations with the past, present and the future. All life, all aspects sacramental, interrelated and reflections of each other	Doctrines of karma and dharma Multiple and equivalent ways of knowing: reason, sense-inference, intuition, authority and devotion

Education	For the future	For the afterlife	For the present, past and the future	For the after and next life
	Phases: child, student, worker, retiree	Educated person memorizes given text	For living and being, for artistic and spiritual development	Focus on linguistic and intrapersonal intelligence
	Educational phases: early, primary, secondary, higher	Focus on linguistic and intrapersonal intelligence	Encourages the spatial, bodily kinesthetic, musical, interpersonal, intrapersonal and naturalist intelligences	Elitist education
	Goal: preparation for a productive economic life and responsible nation state citizen	Elitist education	Mass education	
	Values: punctuality, efficiency, linguistic/logical intelligence, reason, inquiry about objective phenomena			
	Mass education			

and practices. It is impossible to educate younger generations without making certain assumptions about the future. The previous discussion showed how these assumptions about the future have varied throughout space and time. In addition, it is important to contextualize particular views of the future within broader civilizational views on time, as these underlying assumptions determine boundaries for change.

Earlier, three main approaches to time were discussed: time as eternal, as cyclical and as linear. Each approach has particular repercussion to how the future is conceptualized and imagined. And each of these three approaches to time has become a resource for imagining alternative futures (see Part III: *Searching for social and educational alternatives*). Table 3.1 summarizes some connections between understanding of time, image of the future and educational practices. In addition, other features such as cosmology and epistemology are added, as these features will be important in the following sections when comparing contemporary – hegemonic, counter and alternative – educational futures discourses.

Table 3.1 outlines just some of the features from discourses on modern, religious and (from alternative histories) 'traditional' indigenous and 'oriental' education. The purpose is not to discover the truth about the past, nor to cement these features as essentialist and inflexible. But, while the previous analysis and the summary contain these and other theoretical risks (e.g. as in theorizing 'other' time and 'other' culture), such an analysis is crucial in destabilizing discourses controlled and managed by dominant social and cultural frameworks of meaning. These histories are important as they enable better contextualizing of current dominant images of the future – namely the vision of globalized and cyber education. For example, they help show the ways in which these 'radically different' futures visions are not entirely new but follow particular (western) civilizational traditions. In Part II: *Destabilizing dominant narratives*, the argument will be made that hegemonic futures visions succeed in capturing the public imagination because they 'make the most sense' from within our current social structures and dominant worldview. That is, these visions arose from within, and are in many ways enhancing the main characteristics of the modern education model, a model that they claim to destabilize, replace and transcend.

Part II

Destabilizing dominant narratives

Globalization and new technologies *are* dominant forces of the future...
– Kellner (2000a)

Things could always be other than they are and what they are is always diverse.

– Edwards and Usher (2000)

Figure 4 Mural painting, *Cosmic Evolution*, by Robert McCall. Used by permission of Foundation for the Future, Bellevue, WA, USA, http://www.futurefoundation.org/[1]

4 The colonization of the future

The current 'Truth' of future I: globalization

During the last decade of the twentieth century, the concept of globalization became 'an all-purpose catchword in public and scholarly debate' (Lechner and Boli 2000: 1). It has become the new 'regime of truth', 'imbued with its own rationality and self-fulfilling logic' (Blackmore 2000: 133). Kelly (1999: 379) states that at the end of the millennium, the word 'globalization' has, together with the 'millennium' itself, become 'the new mantra for our times'. As Robertson and Khondker (1998: 32) argue, the term 'globalization' is therefore in danger of becoming simply a 'slogan' as well as a 'scapegoat for a wide range of ecological, economic, psychological, medical, political, social and cultural problems'. This is further elaborated by Lechner and Boli:

> Government officials could attribute their country's economic woes to the onslaught of globalization, business leaders justified downsizing of their companies as necessary to prepare for glob-alization, environmentalists lamented the destructive impact of unrestrained globalization, and advocates for indigenous peoples blamed the threatened disappearance of small cultures on relentless globalization.
>
> (Lechner and Boli 2000: 1)

The globalization discourse has greatly affected educational policy around the world, to the extent that '..."globalization" (perceived in a particular way) has become an ideological discourse driving change because of a perceived immediacy and necessity to respond to a new world order' (Burbules and Torres 2000: 2).

One of the consequences of this effect is that '...the reconfiguration of pedagogical practices around the globe has taken on a momentum that an earlier generation might well have considered startling and disorienting' (Edwards and Usher 2000: 1). That is:

> In the context of globalization, we can easily see a paradigm shift in public policy and public management toward a financially driven and free-market ideology, whereby education policy change and governance mode have been significantly shaped by market principles and practices. Not surprisingly, discourse of economicism, ideological stance as performativity and notion of neo-liberalism have become increasingly popular in governing educational developments across different parts of the globe.
>
> (Mok and Welch 2003: x)

Within these debates, questions are often raised as to whether globalization is 'a bad' or 'a good' thing:

> Is globalization beneficial to the cause of economic growth, equality, and justice, or is it harmful? Does it promote cultural sharing, tolerance, and a cosmopolitan spirit, or does it yield only the illusion of such understanding, a bland, consumerist appreciation, as in a Disney theme park, which elides issues of conflict, difference, and asymmetries of power?
>
> (Burbules and Torres 2000: 13–14)

What is not questioned is whether the globalized future is *the* future. As argued earlier, while various societies and communities have their own 'regimes of educational truths', assumptions and preferred visions, some of those truths, assumptions and visions have become hegemonic – that is, naturalized and uncontested.

Of course, there are other underlying futures visions that are evoked when the calls for educational reform, in Australia as well as globally, are made. These include, for example, visions of an 'environmentally sustainable', 'multicultural' or 'partnership' society. What distinguishes hegemonic futures narratives from other, counter or alternative, ones is their capacity to convince others of the inevitability of a particular future. For example, compare the 'popularity' of Elise Boulding's vision of a gentle/androgynous society, Riane Eisler's partnership society/gylany or Sri Aurobindo's 'the coming of the Spiritual Age' to the ideas of 'postindustrial' and 'information' society. Hegemonic futures thus *eliminate alternatives* not by contesting them or making them illegal, immoral or unpopular, but by making them invisible and therefore irrelevant (Postman 1993: 48). Alternative narratives become considered possibly 'interesting' and even sometimes 'worth knowing about', but, in general, if looking for the 'truth' about the future, one must turn towards 'dispensers of legitimate knowledge' (ibid.).

Others may assign a dystopian reading to that future, most often expressed in the form of critique. But, as argued by Grosz (1990: 59) earlier, it is by that very act of 'negative or reactive project' that 'the truth' of what is critiqued is reaffirmed. Thus, the dystopian element within these hegemonic narratives is much more prominent than that in alternative futures. Furthermore, it could be argued that it is precisely such dystopian interpretations that make particular visions hegemonic. Unless a vision is seen as a 'real' threat to another future, desired by a different social group/worldview, why discuss it? Why mention it at all? Consequently, the dystopian (critique) elements are much more prominent in globalization and ICT discourses than in those on other marginalized alternative futures.

Of course, given that the processes of globalization are 'deeply asymmetric' (Castells 1996), 'dialectical' (Cvetkovich and Kellner 1997: 2) and 'disjunctive' (Appadurai 1996), it is impossible to determine whether the consequences of globalization are mostly good or mostly bad. There is even disagreement on whether the prevailing discourse on globalization is 'rather optimistic' (Stromquist and Monkman 2000: 19) or mostly about 'unmediated negative effects' (Luke 2001a: 48). But this does not mean that one can step aside from one's own historical and spatial embodiment and theorize from epistemologically neutral 'objective' spaces. Of course, it is precisely these hegemonic discourses which claim to be based on 'the truth' about the future, also implying some sort of 'objective' neutrality. Such is, in essence, the modernist approach which is still powerful enough to influence theorists across the board. For example, Cunningham *et al.* (1997) argue that while there is no shortage of scholarly, journalistic, governmental or institution-specific materials on the intersection of areas such as globalization, information technologies and education, there is, they continue, an 'acute shortage of disinterested, thorough and realistic analyses' (ibid.: 4). Their demand for such an analysis is problematic because, as feminist, postcolonial and poststructural theorists have shown, 'disinterested, thorough and realistic analysis' (ibid.) is an epistemological and ontological impossibility. Rather, the globalization narrative, for example, represents a 'contested terrain described in conflicting normative discourses that provide the concept [of globalization] with positive, negative, or ambivalent connotations' (Cvetkovich and Kellner 1997: 3). Even globalization processes and tendencies 'have a history and geography' (Edwards and Usher 2000: 15). Therefore, the way in which globalization itself is, for example, formulated in policy 'needs to be located as a particular discourse of the contemporary moment that discursively constructs future directions in a particular and often problematic way' (ibid.: 5). If this is missing, so is the acknowledgement that alleged universality is claimed predominantly on the basis of one's own particular experiences and worldviews. Not only does this facilitate the colonization of the future by the dominant worldview, but in addition, such 'far sighted' perspectives are developed 'solely on the basis of one's myopia' (Luke and Luke 2000: 278).

It is important to note here that the discourse of *globalized* education draws on, but then crucially transforms, the previous/parallel discourse of *global* education. Global issues and concerns in the area of education have a long history. As Gough (2000: 80) argues, these global issues and concerns have predominantly functioned as topics or themes in specific learning areas, such as history and geography, or in more recent curriculum areas such as development, industrialization, peace studies and environment. Over the last 25 years, global education predominantly meant dealing with issues such as environment, development and human rights, peace and conflict, race, gender, health and education (Hicks 2001: 413), and was in some ways connected to issues of social justice. Recently, however, 'global/ized education' has come to mean something else. The discourse has been changed, even hijacked, and is increasingly used to denote the need for competition and market-based strategies in education. As described earlier, globalized education has mostly come to mean vocational education necessary for preparation for a competitive market force.

The current 'Truth' of future II: new technologies

Parallel to this development, another ubiquitous discourse emerged:

> At precisely the same moment that the planet is being constructed within the powerful, pervasive all consuming logic of the market, there is a second order language, a fairy tale... that suggests in Utopian terms new possibilities, in particular those presented by the new alchemies of 'the Net'.
>
> (Tracey 1997: 50)

Or, as argued by Burniske and Monke:

> In a mere fifty years the computer has come from being a huge vacuum tube filled machine that counts, adds, subtracts, divides, multiplies, and stores information to a desktop and even a laptop wizard of communication, visualization, entertainment, and work station. Every educator, from those old timers still unsure if they can master and use this new 'machine', to those younger ones for whom the computer was an integral part of their home life and schooling, all know that the computer will (if it has not already) become a major tool of teaching and learning and a ubiquitous feature of daily life in the twenty-first century.
>
> (Burniske and Monke 2001: ix)

So, over the last several decades, and particularly over the last few years, the 'information technology revolution' discourse has 'saturated the media, the marketplace, and the public imagination' (Luke 2000: 69). While the theme of the last decade might have been 'globalize or die' (Inayatullah and Gidley 2000: 9), the current theme appears to be more like 'virtualize or disappear' (ibid.). The implications for education in industrially developed nations have been tremendous. For example, Luke writes that:

> [c]omputer studies have been implemented hastily over the last decade with relatively little teacher or parent resistance. If anything, we have witnessed a tidal wave of financial and in-principle support from federal and state governments for successive initiatives: in the 1980s, to put a computer in every classroom; in the early 1990s to put a computer on every child's desk; and by the mid-1990s, to have every classroom wired.
>
> (Luke 2000: 426)

In addition, not only have computers been embraced with 'fervor' (ibid.), but numerous claims have been made in relation to the revolutionary potential of new ICTs in education. These utopian narratives have been met by equally passionate claims about imminent dangers ahead. So, computers have come a long way from their early days of being 'counting machines'. But, at the same time, computers are also predominantly technological tools; so, why have they been met with so much excitement, 'hype' (Snyder 1997) and 'ecstasy' (Luke 1996a)? Is it because they are 'new'? Is it because every new technology creates passionate responses from people, even love/hate relationships, whenever they are introduced, as Luke (2001a) seems to suggest?

Prediction, determinism and agency

Most importantly, why and how have these two discourses become hegemonic? One common view is that the pressure for current education to change – become more business-like and consumer-oriented as well as information-based – came from major changes that occurred at the global level. The explanations of why and how this happened range in emphasis across various social, economic, technological, cultural, political and historical systemic factors. The most popular, however, are the ones that heavily depend on prediction and determinism. That is, explanations that focus on technological and economic determinism (e.g. Castells 1996; Friedman 1998) seem to have the broadest appeal. As argued by Castells, the most recent technological revolution has originated and diffused during a historical period of 'the global restructuring of capitalism, for which it was an essential tool' (Castells 1996: 13). This did not happen by accident, continues Castells. Rather, the Keynesian model of capitalist growth that earlier brought 'previously unprecedented' economic prosperity and social stability to the western world finally 'hit the wall of its built-in limitations in the early 1970s' (ibid.: 19). Therefore, the capitalist system needed to restructure and rejuvenate and this was made possible by technological innovation and organizational change, focused on flexibility and adaptability. Thus, concludes Castells, 'informationalism is linked to the expansion and rejuvenation of capitalism, as industrialism was linked to its constitution as a mode of production' (ibid.). What finally resulted was a:

> new society emerging from such a process of change [which] is both capitalist and informational, while presenting considerable historical variation in different countries, according to their history, culture, institutions, and to their specific relationship to global capitalism and information technology.
>
> (Castells 1996: 13)

The pressure for current education to change – become more business-like and consumer-oriented – apparently comes from these major global economic and technological changes. Educational institutions are thus to adjust to *the impending future* – variously named as the Global age, Postindustrial society, Global pan-capitalism,

Information and Knowledge society – whose beginnings are already visible today.

In order to constitute the main 'truth' about the future, these hegemonic narratives had to (heavily) depend on prediction and determinism. They continue the type of thinking developed due to the 'combination of science, technology and war [that] fuelled the popular imagination in 19th century Europe' (Slaughter 1996a: xxv). Until the Second World War, futures thinking existed in the west as literary expression (speculative fiction, e.g. that of Jules Verne) and political advocacy (e.g. social prophets Charles Fourier, Henri de Saint-Simone, Robert Owen, Edward Belamy) (Tenner 1998). However, from the end of the nineteenth to the late twentieth century, the focus of futures thinking has moved from utopianism to one of 'scientific' prediction. This prediction about the future usually now takes the form of trend identification and analysis that is, in turn, often based on technological and economic determinism. At other times, determinism is backed by a belief in the ubiquitous character of historical and social structures that leave little space for human agency. And at yet other times, but in now globally marginalized spaces, determinism takes the form of the belief in *karma* or destiny; 'God's mysterious ways', or certain planetary influences, as in astrology. Determinism is, of course, problematic because at any given time there are numerous trends that may impact the future in very diverse, even surprising, ways. In addition, social complexities and human choice outweigh the possibility of truly 'knowing' the future. Of course, the 'push' towards the future (trends) as well as the 'weight of history' (historical and social structures) play very important roles when it comes to issues related to social change and continuity. No present (once future) occurs in a vacuum. But, determinism forgets about the 'pull' of the future, that is, the impact of the desired, hoped for and imagined. It discounts human and social agency.

It is this agency that has also been behind the current push to globalize and virtualize. While proponents of globalization perceive it as a powerful, ubiquitous and 'monolithic force' (Luke 2001a: 32) that is about to engulf us, others point out that globalization is in itself also *governed*, in the spheres of economy and education. As many authors convincingly argue (e.g. Henderson 1999; Weiss 1998), economic globalization depends on the active role of governments and policies that promote deregulation, privatization, liberalization of capital flows, the opening of national economies and so on. Petras and Veltmeyer (2001) assert that 'the origins of globalization as an economic strategy were the consequence of an ideological project backed by state power and not the "natural unfolding" of the market' (ibid.: 43). According to them, the governing of globalization even includes political measures such as military *coup d'état* and support for military dictatorships (e.g. in Latin America):

> Globalists did not merely react to 'failure' or 'crises' of leftist regimes; they vigorously intervened to bring about the outcome they predicted. This active role was massive in scope and involved direct military intervention, ideological and cultural saturation, arms races, and political alliances...
>
> (Petras and Veltmeyer 2001: 47)

The position of the International Labour Organization (ILO 2004) is that problems associated with globalization (i.e. global imbalances) are, in fact, not due to globalization as such, but due to deficiencies in its governance. This poor governance refers to the unfairness of some existing rules for the multilateral trading and financial system (e.g. the 'big bang' approach to market liberalization that was pushed across the board and carried out simultaneously). But, it also refers to the absence of adequate rules in various areas (e.g. for international migration, dysfunctional states, authoritarian governments, poorly functioning boards, deficient auditing and accounting practices, corruption, lack of transparency and accountability, etc.) (ibid.).

Similarly, educational reforms (e.g. curriculum changes, standardized and centralized testing, diverse cultural education and school administration), which were introduced in countries such as the US, Canada, Australia, the UK and New Zealand, were *made* possible through 'the implementation of policy innovation and the adaptation of several reform models' (Davies and Guppy 1997: 435). In addition, argues Ganderton with regard to Australian curricular reforms, there is 'no evidence to suggest stronger pressure from the outside' (1996: 403). Rather, 'much of the pressure is *self-generated* [italics added]' (1996: 403).

That at the beginning of the twenty-first century we find educational systems 'much more attuned with business values and needs than in previous decades' (Stromquist 2002: 38) has not been the result of:

> a natural revolution but rather the result of explicit pressure by the business sectors, on educational systems, a phenomenon

most conspicuous in the United States, the leading force behind the process of globalization.

(Stromquist 2002: 38)

The governing of virtualization included reshuffling of priorities and decisions to spend money on these new priorities. In 1995, in the USA alone, around $3.3 billion was spent on hardware, software, networking and related costs (1.3 per cent of average annual per-pupil spending; or $75 per student) (Cuban 2001: 17). By 1998–1999, spending had increased to $5.5 billion (excluding higher education), or $119 per child (ibid.). Appropriation of substantial funds for sustaining technology in a given district also meant that administrators often left other pressing needs unmet (e.g. smaller class size, higher entry-level teacher salaries, renovation of decayed buildings, responsive school communities, full-day preschool and kindergarten, cross-disciplinary programmes in the elementary schools, another foreign language for middle-school students, etc.) (ibid.: 193).

This governing of virtualization and globalization would, in turn, be impossible without a guiding image of the future towards which such governing aspires. Virtualization and globalization are, thus, terms that are used not only to describe but also to prescribe; they are as much about a prescription as they are about a description. Embedded within this 'push' of the future there is a 'pull' – personal and collective visions and images of the future.

Although they are often discussed together, I have identified the two of these visions, of a globalized and cyber world, and education as two distinct futures and utopian visions. There are, of course, more similarities here than differences, yet these two futures visions accentuate qualitatively different phenomena, characteristics and possibilities. It could be convincingly argued that, taken together, these two visions represent one particular direction for the future towards, for example, the creation of a global network or global information society. This is because the ICT revolution has, of course, been 'the most evident and highly popularized aspect of globalization' (Luke 2001a: 46) and it has, in turn, often been stressed that globalization is made possible predominantly because of the development of new information and communication technologies. However, globalized education and cyber education are discussed separately here because of their emphasis on significantly different material phenomena (e.g. economic vs technological), *and* because of their qualitatively distinctive 'imaginaire' (Appadurai 1996: 31).

I summarize these differences and similarities at the very end of Part II (Chapter 7) and in the concluding Part IV.

To sum up the previous discussion, towards the end of the twentieth century, two dominant, hegemonic visions of the future appeared in the western world. What distinguishes the visions of globalized and cyber world from other futures visions is that these visions manage to convince about their own inevitability, thus eliminating the alternatives by default. The following sections aim at determining why this is so. First, I investigate the continuities and discontinuities of these two visions – how, why and from where they have arisen. Second, I investigate utopian and dystopian elements in them, arguing that their hegemony is in part due to the attractiveness of their projected utopias.

5 Visions I: globalization

Approach to time and the vision of the future

> Quite often, globalization is represented not so much as a historical
> tendency or a complex process, but as an outcome: a 'new order'.
>
> (Dicken, Peck and Tickell 1997: 158)

The new emerging order, or 'Global Age' (Albrow 1997), is in line
with similar theorizing that puts an emphasis on slightly different
phenomena (e.g. postindustrial, postmodern, information or knowledge society). The Global Age has become the new image for the future
and a globalized world, the new 'imagined community' (Anderson
1983). This new image encompasses previous metaphors of postindustrial and postmodern society, becoming a new phase, a new
direction towards progress, development and linear evolution. This
clearly locates it within the western 'imaginaire' – 'a constructed
landscape of collective aspirations' (Appadurai 1996). In addition, as
Albrow writes, the new 'Global Age' is also sometimes referred to
using the following metaphors: 'age of automation', 'atomic age',
'electronic age', 'solar age' (1997: 1). This, too, locates the global age
within concerns, priorities, desires and experiences within industrially
developed societies. Although represented as a radically 'new' phase
of human and social evolution, the globalization discourse is more
premised on the continuities of the current world than on the
discontinuities and radical change.

Not surprisingly, compressed, globalized time does not follow
the tradition of so-called 'event time' of cultures and individuals that
perceive human activity 'as a measure of time and not the other
way around' (Szalai, quoted in Levine 1997: 60). Neither is it
women's 'glacial', 'shadow' or 'rhythmical' time (Adam 1995: 52; Fox
1989: 127; Urry 2000: 439). It does not allow for time to be seen as

'intergenerational' (Urry 2000: 429), or as existing in the 'eternal present' (Judge 1993; Lawlor 1991; Levine 1997: 94; Voigt and Drury 1997; Wildman 1997). Rather, it is the 'instantaneous time' of a 'three-minute culture' (Urry 2000: 432–433), an 'evolutionary progression from a "time surplus" to a "time affluence" to a "time famine" society', which is how most developed countries could now be characterized (Levine 1997: 13). It is only possible where there is a 'mechanical approach to human beings' rather than a focus on people and their collective well-being, argues Levine (ibid.: 18–19, 74). As 'people are prone to move faster in places with vital economies, a high degree of industrialization, larger populations, cooler climates, and a cultural orientation toward individualism' (ibid.: 9), compressed globalized time reflects time understood and lived in the affluent west. Globalized time is thus not only about the 'shrinking of space and time'. It also reflects how time is experienced and how this experience is perceived and conceptualized within the industrially developed west. Perhaps needless to say, this experience is neither universal nor 'global'.

While Levine argues that globalized time follows in the tradition of the industrial linear one (see Figure 4), others (Nowotny 1994; Tyrrell 1995; Urry 2000) argue that compressed globalized time is radically different from the more conventional linear one. That is, globalized time is 'instantaneous' and 'simultaneous' (Nowotny 1994; Tyrrell 1995; Urry 2000). It is not linear. Digital clocks and watches are different from the conventional watch that indicates that time, indeed, is passing:

> Digital clocks and watches convey no such context [indicating time passing]. Impaired instruments that they are, they are unable to comprehend more than one instant at a time, with nothing to hint that there is a process going on that includes what went before and what comes after. A digital timepiece resembles a highly trained specialist who has learned to do only one thing, to do it very well, and to ignore all surroundings and relationships. Digital watches and narrow visions fit together very well, and both are signs of our time.
>
> (Meeker 1987: 57)

Still, globalized time is based on 'contemporary technologies and social practices', which are themselves based 'upon time frames that lie beyond conscious human experience' (Urry 2000: 433). As such, it is based not on measuring time by human activities or environmental changes, but on clock time. In addition, it is founded on Anglo-American cultures, and their addiction 'to rapid and perpetual change' (Levine 1997: 44). Globalized time is still seen as a commodity, a product, even money; as something that passes, that can be wasted, that can be saved and bought (Evans-Pritchard, in Urry 2000: 417). Inactivity still equates with 'doing nothing', signalling 'waste and void' (Levine 1997: 41). Within the Anglo-American cultural context, Levine argues, inactivity is dead time:

> Even leisure time in the United States is planned and eventful. We live in a culture where it is not uncommon for people to literally run in order to relax, or to pay money for the privilege of pacing on a treadmill. It sometimes seems as if life is constructed with the primary goal of avoiding the awkwardness and sometimes the terror of having nothing to do.
>
> (Levine 1997: 41)

Like industrial time, globalized time also continues to be exported and forced upon individuals and societies that may have different relationships to time. Globalized time demands the compression of education processes – the need to be perpetually available, around the clock, without an 'excuse to [ever] be away from e-mail for more than 12 hours at the time' (Dator 2002, personal communication). Those that are, still risk being called slow and incompetent. But this attitude continues to devalue the future, as argued earlier by Adam (1998). So, while education is to prepare children for the future, the future itself is devalued, and immediate gratification promoted. Concerns both for future generations and for the environment are missing from such a 'compressed', instantaneous approach to time. Also missing are concerns and priorities raised by women's movements and those coming from non-western traditions (as will be seen in Part III).

However, this approach to time remains necessary if it is a materialistic, pan-consumer-oriented, uni-chronous future that is desired. The call to 'globalize' the world and the call to globalize education are both most often made by evoking the futures image of an economically developed global society in which everybody benefits, eventually. Behind this, there is also an assumption that 'a single culture and society will, in time, come to occupy the planet' (Little 1996: 427). Globalization is seen as 'the highest and last stage in history in which all countries and economies are linked together through the capitalist market' (Petras and Veltmeyer 2001). At the same time, this image of a globalized future is understood and described mostly in terms of the future becoming (even) more competitive, challenging, with risk professionally managed. Given the 'victory' of economic globalization, in this future world there is little space left for alternative ways of living and doing things. That globalization continues to be influenced mostly from 'above', by multinationals and states, is implicit in this future. The world is populated by the global consumer, social order is profit-oriented, and the focus is on 'wants' and instant satisfaction of needs. To fulfil these 'wants', there are ever-increasing material products and material choices. Intellectual development and property remain paramount and only rational aspects of knowledge are still valued. This reflects the current situation in which most '... knowledge that has circulated in global spaces to date has continued to exhibit the core rationalist attributes of secularism, anthropocentrism, scientism and instrumentalism' (Scholte 2000: 185).

The main role of education, then, is to adapt and adjust rather than to focus on future possibilities. Education is mostly seen to be market-led, suggesting a 'utilitarian future curriculum that would be narrowly vocational' (Ganderton 1996: 395). The assumption behind this is that 'competition is necessary to increase educational standards, improve efficiency, and reduce costs' (Stromquist 2002: 38).

Globalization as the pull of the future

While the mainstream paradigm (informed by techno and economic determinism) argues that globalization is a result of unprecedented technological and economic innovation, it is possible to outline the ways in which these innovations were guided by a desired vision of a (globalized) future. Material processes that are usually attributed to be the drivers of globalization, such as communications and other technological innovations, markets and finance, prototypical global organizations and migrations, have been current for many centuries if not millennia (Hirst 1997; Hopkins 2002; Pieterse 2000; Robertson 1992, 2003; Schirato and Webb 2003; Tomlinson 1999). Most importantly, the imagining of the world as 'one place' *preceded* the development of more substantive social relations and technologies of globalization (Scholte 2000: 62).

This imagination has been current for many centuries and was most obviously apparent among, but not exclusive to, world religions (ibid.: 64). Furthermore, this imagination of the global is also connected with western expansionism, as argued by O'Sullivan:

> Before 1492, cartographical procedures for mapping commerce routes were flat. For Europeans, Columbus moved the mapping systems for commerce from a flat surface to a globe. The globe is a mapping device made for commerce today. The language of globalization is first and foremost for commercial purposes.
>
> (O'Sullivan 1999: 194)

O'Sullivan further argues that, while often used interchangeably, the terms 'planetary' and 'global' actually imply two different things (ibid.). While 'a planet' implies 'organic totality ... [that] we are one species living on a planet called "Earth"', 'globe' implies 'a cartological map [and] is a construct of human artifice' (ibid.). As the notions of 'globe' and 'global' were invented to help expand European markets, these concepts are, in essence, connected to European colonization and imperialism. The desire for the 'global' thus precedes the most recent 'take' on globalization processes, as in the hypothesis of globalization. It also precedes the most recent 'awareness' that the world is becoming 'one place'. Rather, it came out of a particular view that has, in turn, created desire and the need for particular technologies, now seen as the sole force behind 'globalization'.

It is also important to note here that a distinction between globalization processes and globalization discourse needs to be made. While, depending on one's interpretation, the history (or histories) of globalization(s) might go back several hundred or even thousand years, globalization as a particular discourse, as a hypothesis and as a vision of the future that currently dominates can be more easily located geographically and temporarily. Geographically, the globalization hypothesis originated in western societies, the vast majority of its theorists being USA or western European male academics. That is, globalization has been predominantly theorized from the western spatial location as well as from the perspective of male embodiment. This means that, so far, globalization has itself 'been analysed from a very un-global perspective' (Massey 1994: 166).

More relevant to the argument in this book is the temporal location of how globalization is hypothesized. Historically, the globalization hypothesis coincided with the coming of the Christian millennium, emerging in the 1980s and increasing in influence during the last decade of the twentieth century. It has coincided with a period in western history that can be characterized by a certain void in socio-economic futures visions. As narratives on progress and development were weakened by postmodern, postcolonial and feminist discourses, the space opened and the need arose for another guiding image of the future to appear. Globalization – as process and theory – became a useful replacement for these old narratives. It has helped name more concretely the vaguely described 'New World Order'. It has also helped replace more problematic terms such as 'monopoly capital' or 'world capitalism', conveniently neutralizing anti-capitalist rhetoric. The globalized future has not, therefore, come to represent the victory of 'the Right' in the historical ideological battle with 'the Left'. More conveniently, it has come to represent a whole new system with a new set of rules that can potentially benefit all humanity. While, arguably, this may be the case, this globalized future can clearly be identified as a new phase within western and patriarchal under-standings of time and social change. As Cvetkovich and Kellner write:

> In many mainstream social theories, the discourse of the global is bound up with ideological discourses of modernization and modernity, and from Saint-Simon and Marx through Habermas and Parsons, globalization and modernization are interpreted in terms of progress, novelty and innovation, and a generally beneficial negation of the old, the traditional, and the obsolete. In this discourse of modernization, the global is presented as a progressive modernizing force; the local stands for backward-ness, superstition, underdevelopment, and the oppressiveness of tradition.
>
> (Cvetkovich and Kellner 1997: 13–14)

To summarize, the currently dominant vision of a globalized world that emerged in the west at the end of the twentieth century: (1) imagines a pan capitalistic competitive world; (2) is based on under-lying narratives of progress, development and linear evolution, with industrial time further compressed into even smaller units; (3) is informed by neo-liberal, anthropocentric, materialistic and secular worldviews; and (4) is likely to result in a narrowly vocational future curriculum.

Why is it that this vision has been so influential? What lies in its broadly spread appeal? Is it just because it was propagated by dominant social groups or are there elements in this vision that might be more universally appealing?

Utopian and eutopian versions

The globalized world is essentially a vision of a utopian society, or at least a eutopian society. As I argued earlier, it should not be seen only as an argument for opening up national markets, as a push of the future, but as a compelling pull of the future.

According to its proponents, although the negative consequences of globalization are certainly regrettable, they are either seen as minimal or justified as something that needs to be endured so that humanity as a whole can benefit in the end. As Martin (2000) passionately argues, globalization is 'the best thing that has happened in the lifetime of the post-war generation', including those residing in non-western countries (ibid.: 12–13). This is because:

> It [globalization] will lead to an irreversible shift of power away from the developed countries to the rest of the world...[It]...is simply untrue, both in relative and in absolute terms...that there are many more losers than winners from globalization... It is sometimes said that free trade must cede precedence to more elevated values. Surely there is no more elevated values than delivering billions of people from poverty, creating opportunities for choice and personal development, and reinforcing democracy all round the world? The liberal market economy is by its very nature global. It is *the summit of human endeavor* [italics added].
>
> (Martin 2000)

Here, Martin not only advocates globalization but also promotes a particular desired vision for the future, that of a neo-liberal global democracy. For Francis Fukuyama, too, the common evolutionary pattern for all human society is in the direction of liberal democracy (Fukuyama 1992). Such a desired future – that of universally spread liberal capitalism and democratic nation states – incorporates a belief in the 'Western forms of government, political economy and political community...[as]...the ultimate destination which the entire human race will eventually reach' (Burchill and Linklater 1996: 28). Fukuyama's *The End of History* thus assumes a globalized world in which 'markets, democracy and prosperity had put an end to conflicts, authoritarian regimes and the reign of necessity' (Petras and Veltmeyer 2001: 42).

While not everyone is as enthusiastic as Martin and Fukuyama, most authors mention at least some positive aspects of globalization, which often include a shift towards the understanding of human differences within the unified view of humanity, increased ecological consciousness, higher cultural interchange, more consumer and employment choices, and the opening up of possibilities in travel, communication and business (Kofman and Youngs 1996; Lechner and Boli 2000) – an authentic eutopia.

This is true as well for education:

> At its most visionary, the ideal of global[ised] education is one of a movement away from the bounded classroom, seen as a haven from the world, self-contained and static, to a dynamic synergy of teachers, computer-mediated instructional devices, and students collaborating to create a window on the world. Interaction with learners on a global scale leads to an increased awareness of the extraordinary complexity of interrelations and a relativistic comprehension and tolerance of diverse approaches to understanding.
>
> (Mason 1998: 6)

Expansion, choice and quality

Globalization is, therefore, marked by the disruption of modernist educational practices that in many ways constitute previously mentioned spaces of enclosure (Lankshear, Peters and Knobel 1996). Thus, it is argued that it can open up some spaces for critical emancipatory education (Edwards and Usher 2000: 154), and the possibility to creatively re-imagine educational practices. According to Cogburn (2002), this re-location created by globalization will influence the creation of a new system of knowledge, education and learning that will include many components that do not currently exist. This new system of knowledge, education and learning could, and according to Cogburn (ibid.) *should*, include the following key components: a focus on abstract concepts; a holistic, as opposed to linear, approach; enhancement of the student's ability to manipulate symbols and to acquire and utilize knowledge; production of an increased quantity of scientifically and technically trained persons; blurring of the distinction between mental and physical labour; encouragement of students to work in teams; and the use of virtual teams around the world. In addition, there is the emergence of 'an agile and flexible system' that effectively 'breaks the boundaries of space and time' (ibid.: par. 31).

The benefits of a global student body are connected with the creation of a network that has the ability to energize, diversify and deepen what is thought (O'Donnell, in Mason 1998: 4). Globalization, in fact, argues O'Donnell (ibid.), mitigates against the usually dominant western worldview.

Another compelling educational justification for globalized education is that of access:

> Whether potential students be geographically remote, time constrained, financially constrained, house-bound, disabled, or simply unable to find a course on the subject they want locally, there exist large un-met educational needs which every research report, policy study and educational analysis shows are increasing.
> (Mason 1998: 4)

Another purely educational rationale for promotion of global courses is that:

> the expertise of the few can be made available to the many, such that those in remote areas can have the same access to educational resources, specialist courses and renowned experts as those located in large cities and developed parts of the world.
> (Mason 1998: 4)

A global curriculum can provide students with a much broader perspective than a course presented by a single lecturer or developed by a single institution (ibid.: 6). While neo-Marxist and other similar ideologies might not look favourably on the trend towards student-as-consumer, Edwards (1995, in Mason 1998) argues that this, too, can have positive outcomes. Knowledge is exchanged on the basis of the usefulness it has to the consumer, '...effectively empowering the learner and forcing the providers of education to concern themselves with students' needs, rather than with the transmission of a pre-established canon of knowledge' (ibid.: 7).

Courses demanded by the global consumer will become flexible, adaptable, portable and interactive, and all this could promise great benefits for the student body. Even for the traditionally disadvantaged social groups within education, such as women, globalized education (e.g. the corporate university) could potentially increase their chances in the job market. As potential customers, women could influence changes in both learning environments and curricula. For example, in the area of higher education, educational institutions might decide to compete for female students by making studying more accessible and more flexible for women, allowing re-entries, providing childcare, and more effectively addressing sexual harassment issues. These educational institutions could also be motivated to shift curricula towards inclusion of women and women's perspectives as well as to diminish gender bias in most disciplines (Milojević 2000: 177–178). Some of these developments are already occurring in many places, but they can also gain new momentum. Globalization thus represents a sign of hope, of the transformative future that can be.

The dystopian version

The dystopian version, however, seems equally compelling. The negative consequences that are mentioned most often include the widening gap between rich and poor globally and within nation states, further environmental degradation and the continuation of cultural colonization. The educational, culturalist and social science discourses on globalization have produced 'volumes of scholarship' that present the negative effects of globalization:

> Among these are the obliteration of local cultures, the demise of nation-states, the erosion of cultural identity and tradition, the loss of sense of place and home, the technologising of everyday life and concomitant compression of space and time and loss of 'authentic' communications, a global sameness of desires and consumption patterns, and a dramatic blowout of social inequalities and unequal capital accumulation.
>
> (Luke 2001a: 48)

According to Garate (2002), globalization is a process of transnational domination grounded in:

> Technologies that contaminate and ravage our resources; the penetration of the market into our politics, culture, human rights, and spirit; a pedagogy of oppression by gender, race, beliefs, and hierarchies; a reduction of our human condition to that of mere consumer.
>
> (Garate 2002)

It is a force that 'emphasizes material over spiritual growth, corporate ties over family ties, competition over cooperation' (Feffer 2002: 16). And it is a force that is 'running out of control', creating negative consequences for future generations (Hedley 2002). This includes the growing global instability and terrorism (Hedley 2002; Scruton 2002) as a single global system is more vulnerable to unforeseen risks.

The restructuring of societies for corporate capitalism has been increasingly life-destructive on 'almost every indicator of social and ecological life – from health protection, literacy development and future vocations for the young to maintenance of biodiversity and the planet's security of air, water, soil and climate' (McMurtry 2002: 5).

Rather than being the 'wave of the future', 'a more appropriate ocean metaphor for globalization... is an undertow pulling working people back into an ignominious past' (Petras and Veltmeyer 2001: 45). The notion of inevitability of globalization is akin to messianic messages that:

> patent medicine makers attributed to their produces and itinerant preachers vowed would affect non-believers: if it is not here, it is coming; if it is not visible, it is just over the horizon; if you are experiencing pain, prosperity and well-being are 'around the corner'.
>
> (Petras and Veltmeyer 2001: 45)

All this masks the reality that is very different from the promised benefits of globalization: the future for most of the young generation looks insecure and fearful, it is a future of 'a prolonged work life with declining wages and without job security or social assistance' (ibid.). We are witnessing havoc on democratic practice and the re-emergence of imperial relations (ibid.: 71). Rather than being the wave of the future, globalization is, in fact, reverting social conditions on the eve of the twenty-first century to those of the nineteenth century (ibid.: 45). Globalization is the wave of the future only for speculators and financiers (ibid.).

Furthering consumerism and colonization

Dystopian reasoning to a large extent focuses on the undesirability of consumerism in general and the concern that education is becoming 'a product to be bought and sold, to be packaged, advertised and marketed' (Mason 1998: 8). There is also a concern that globalized education might support the further breakdown of the community by offering a much less substantial substitute in the form of virtual communities (ibid.). There are concerns about colonization, imperialist attitudes, the loss of indigenous cultures and the relentless imposition of western values (ibid.). Global educators are seen as the new colonizers, insensitively spreading their own views of the world to developing nations in the mistaken belief that they are actually helping people (ibid.: 7). Globalized education will thus weaken national initiatives to develop local educational provisions for local needs; globalization is likely to help create the potential for a postcolonial dependency on another 'developed' nation (Evans 1995, in Mason 1998: 10). Analysing dominant discursive practices in international education markets, Sidhu (2002) concludes that they are both neo-liberal and neo-colonial. The three major 'producers' of international education – the United States, the United Kingdom and Australia – assume a particular version of an 'educated subject', an international student:

> a passive 'other' to be tutored into the ways of the West, an elite 'other' whose allegiances are to be cultivated and an economic subject steeped in competitive individualism who holds an instrumentalist orientation to education.
>
> (Sidhu 2004)

Another comprehensive study encompassing essays on universities and the academic profession in Mexico, Argentina, Brazil, China, Malaysia, Singapore, Korea, the Arabian Gulf, Nigeria, South Africa and India, edited by Altbach (2003), concludes that the conditions of academic work have deteriorated everywhere due to 'the central realities of higher education in the 21st century – massification, accountability, privatization, and marketization' (Marien 2003: 18).

Increasing conformism, decreasing quality and equality

Focusing on the 'hardest' definitions of both globalization and learning, Anthony Sweeting concludes that the prospects presented for the globalization of learning 'would seem to many a very dire, nightmarish one' (Sweeting 1996: 384):

> Instead of the line-workers (teachers and students) having to sacrifice individual styles and idiosyncratic enthusiasm in order to satisfy *national* criteria, they would have to make the same and, perhaps, additional, sacrifices in order to meet *global* criteria. The opportunities for bureaucratic rigidities to smother all forms of creativity as, for example, officially authorized check-lists were utilized, would be legion. Lock-step progress towards publicly pre-announced 'key-stages' or 'targets' would become the major item on the hidden agenda of all schools. The worst, repetition-riddled, aspects of mastery learning would be in the ascendant in most schools that feared dropping in status. And in the

populist name of 'parent power' and the econometric name of 'accountability', efforts would probably be made via techniques of behaviour modification to ensure a docile, hard-working, conformist group of students.

(ibid.)

From a Foucauldian perspective, this may not be anything new, as the creation of docile and conformist group of students is inherent in how education has been practiced within most societies and throughout most historical periods. Still, Sweeting argues that one very probable outcome – whenever the expression globalization of learning is taken to mean a deliberate effort on the part of one group of people to globalize the learning of the majority – would be nothing short of an 'Orwellian nightmare' (ibid.).

While globalization has increased the need for education, Stewart argues, it has also made it 'more difficult for many countries to provide it in sufficient quantity or quality' (1996: 332). The problem, of course, is that globalization is being inextricably linked with the neo-liberal emphasis on increasing the role of the market and reducing that of the state, which also involves a downward pressure on government expenditure (ibid.). But it is unrealistic to expect improvement in quality and access with little or no increase in public expenditure (Vaidyanatha Ayyar 1996: 348). Not surprisingly, in about two-thirds of the countries of sub-Saharan Africa and Latin America where educational expenditures were significantly cut (e.g. 30 per cent in Argentina and about 60 per cent in Nigeria and Zambia), pressures to 'globalize' have not improved access but have instead resulted in reduced school attendance (Stewart 1996: 332). In addition to reduced school attendance, other consequences of reduced public funding include a worsening in the quality of education and a negative impact on gender equity (McGinn 1997: 43; Stewart 1996: 332). This means that unless the critical importance of education is recognized, the forces of globalization will have dire results, '...the uneducated within and among countries will become an underclass, with low and often falling incomes, large families, poor nutrition, and acute gender imbalances since where education is poor it is invariably girls who suffer most' (Stewart 1996: 333).

In addition to the negative impact on gender equity in education, there is a compelling argument that restructuring caused by the extension of global capitalism will impact negatively on women in other areas as well. Since in both 'Second' and 'Third' world societies women provide and are expected to provide services that buffer the negative aspects of this restructuring (e.g. Afshar and Barrientoes 1999; Heyzer, Kapoor and Sandler 1995; Spar 1994; UN 1999; UNIFEM 2000), they will have to cope with additional pressures to care for the family and community. All reforms have hidden costs, but the costs of globalization are passed discriminatorily and disproportionately onto women. The reality and tendency of global-ization is towards:

> forcing more women into 'informal' sector jobs as mainstream employment opportunities fade; promoting export crops which men tend to dominate; disrupting girls' education; increasing mortality rates and worsening female health; more incidents of domestic violence and stress; and an overall increase in the work load of women both inside and outside the home.
>
> (Ellwood 2002: 105)

The benefits that may result from national economic restructuring, such as more job opportunities and greater consumer choice, will continue to be reserved for younger and educated professional women; it will be only some women who will benefit from these processes, and the majority will be left behind. For women, the globalization process, at best, presents a mixed picture:

> On one hand, there are more opportunities than ever before for individual and social action in the economic, educational, and political spheres. At the same time, there are serious constraints for emancipatory action, both because of the weakening welfare responsibilities of the state and because of the depoliticization of culture. The sexual division of labor has not been altered under globalization, and the feminization of poverty continues unabated.
>
> (Stromquist 2002: 154)

Contrary to the eutopian version of globalized education potentially benefiting either some or maybe even the majority of women, there are concerns here that this would occur in an environment that is, in general, increasingly hierarchical, unequal and insecure. Globalization, even while benefiting some women, will thus fail to radically transform gender relationships, the nature of education and the patriarchal character of our societies (Milojević 2000: 178). The transformation of the patriarchal character of our societies is the main priority within feminist alternatives, discussed in Part III (Chapter 8). But before focusing on narratives counter and alternative to the mainstream discourse of the futures of education, I first investigate another hegemonic futures vision, that of the 'information society' and cyber education.

6 Visions II: cyberia; the information age

The WebNet vision of the world

> I have a vision for the year 2020; I like to call it the 20/20 vision.
> Think of everyone at screens: A billion around the planet. And
> each person at a screen will be able to extract from a great com-
> mon pool any fragment of whatever is published, with automatic
> royalty and no red tape.
>
> (Nelson 1992: 44, quoted in Snyder 1997: 130)

The mainstream paradigm argues that the WebNet vision of the
world originated from attempts to 'make sense of the profound
transformation wrecking industrial societies since the mid-1950s'
(Nelson 1996: 479). To describe this shift, various terms have therefore been used, such as 'postindustrial society', 'service society',
'technological society', 'computer society' and 'knowledge society'.
The term 'postindustrial' seems to be one of the oldest, as it first
appeared in print in 1917, but the earliest widely read book to
appear on this subject was Bell's (1973) *The Coming of Postindustrial
Society* (Nelson 1996: 479). The term 'information society' appeared
in 1968, the 'service society' was the preferred term in the 1970s, and
the earliest reference to 'knowledge society' apparently dates from
1969 (ibid.). The OECD adopted the term 'information society' as early
as 1975, and by the early 1980s it had started to come into common
use (ibid.). Finally, in 1982, John Naisbitt gave the final verdict by
saying that 'it is now clear that the postindustrial society is the information society' (ibid.). But the idea of the information age/society is
now as obsolete as 20 year-old computers (Koelsch 1995). It is therefore
claimed that we have now embarked on a new era. Schneider (1999:
77) argues that this era is so distinctively different that a whole
history can be divided into periods BC (before computers) and AC

(after computer). We are now getting the first taste of 'Cyberia', argues Sardar (1996), a taste of a new civilization emerging through our human–computer interface and mediation. Koelsch (1995) argues that the engine of the emerging new world economy will be *infomedia* industries – computing, communications and consumer electronics. Kellner (1998: par. 23) agrees, and attempts to describe this change by coining the slightly clumsy term 'infotainment society'. Glenn (1996) uses the term '*post*-Information age', as does Negroponte (1995). Castells (1996), however, moves from the term 'information society' that he has previously used, to describe *The Rise of the Network Society*. Whatever term is used, there is very little disagreement on what is emerging. For example, Glenn argues:

> Today, *advanced* [italics added] nations are completing the transition from the industrial to the information age. The early signs of the post-information age are barely visible, but do point to the emergence of a new age and civilization that can be anticipated. Technological trends in micro-miniaturization, communications, voice recognition and synthesis, artificial intelligence, human interactivity with software, biotechnology, genetic engineering, bionics, and manufactured object with build-in intelligence should continue and become increasingly and mutually reinforcing. The social trends in public participation, globalization, democracy, lifelong learning, and the rate of scientific inquiry and curiosity should also continue and become increasingly and mutually reinforcing. The interaction of these social and technological trends over the next century will create the post-information age.
>
> (Glenn 1996: 744)

Human and machine interface

Other characteristics of this new, post-information age include the integration of humans with technology to the point where distinctions between humans and machines will begin to blur until humanity and intelligent technology become an interrelated whole (ibid.). This means a strong trend towards the 'cyborganization of humanity' (ibid.). In addition, the built environment will become alive with artificial intelligence, communications, and voice recognition and synthesis. In sum, the main product of this age is 'linkage' (as opposed to food, machine and info-service of previous ages). Power has moved from religion (agricultural age), state (industrial age) and corporation (information age) towards the individual. Wealth in the post-information age becomes the quality of one's experiences, life and being. It is no longer based on land (agricultural), capital (industrial) or access (information age). The central place is neither that of a farm, factory nor office, but 'motion'. This means that people will conduct their livelihood 'anywhere, with anyone, at any time' and therefore be viewed by others as constantly in motion (ibid.: 745). Our sense of time is equally altered; it has moved from cyclical (agricultural), linear (industrial) and relativistic (information age) towards the invented (ibid.).

Similar descriptions can be found among the writing of other futurists and theorists of the post-information or 'AC' age. For example, this is how Castells describes the rise of the Network Society:

> The twenty-first century will be marked by the completion of a global information superhighway, and by mobile telecommunication and computing power, thus decentralizing and diffusing the power of information, delivering the promise of multi-media, and enhancing the joy of interactive communication. In addition, it will be the century of the full flowering of the genetic revolution. For the first time, our species will penetrate the secrets of life, and will be able to perform substantial manipulations of living matter... Prudently used, the genetic revolution may heal, fight pollution, improve life, and save time and effort from survival, so as to give us the chance to explore the largely unknown frontier of spirituality.
>
> (Castells 1998: 335, 353)

And:

> A new world is taking shape in this end of the millennium. It originated in the historical coincidence, around the late 1960s and mid-1970s, of three independent processes: the information technology revolution; the economic crisis of both capitalism and statism, and their subsequent restructuring; and the blooming of cultural social movements, such as libertarianism, human rights, feminism, and environmentalism. The interaction between these processes, and the reactions they triggered, brought into being a new dominant social structure, the network society; a new economy, the informational/global economy; and a new culture, the culture of real virtuality.
>
> (Castells: 336)

Technology: changing lives and societies

In the area of futures studies, the mainstream discourse is predominantly concerned with forecasting emerging technologies. For example, at issue is 'competition and cooperation among fibre optics, cellular radio, and satellites in meeting communication and transportation needs' for the twenty-first century (Kurian and Molitor 1996: 124). The way new communication technologies will change our lives is often described with catchy titles such as *The Cyber Future: 92 Ways Our Lives will Change by the Year 2025* (Cornish 1996). Other forecasts include a future in which a new generation of personal computers will be able to download millions of megabytes in nanoseconds, or that almost all information will be in cyberspace by 2047. The latter is argued by Bell and Gray (1997) of Microsoft, who further state that 'it is safe to predict that computers in the year 2047 will be at least one hundred thousand times more powerful than those of today' (Marien 1997a: 2). Apparently, even this might be an understatement. The editors of *Future Survey* argue that, using straight extrapolation, Moore's Law and present rates of improvement, 'at 1.60/year, computers would be ten billion times more powerful' (ibid.). It is also consistently predicted that the infomedia industries such as computing, communications and consumer electronics will be the engine of the new world economy (Koelsch 1995). To sum up, via the title of an article which argues that around 2005 the number of mobile telephone subscribers will exceed fixed lines, we are informed that 'The future is bright, the future is mobile' (Minger, Mannisto and Kelly 1999).

According to this discourse we can 'safely' assert that in the future people will routinely use virtual reality to gather knowledge and experience from far-away countries and events. Or that we will be able to control computers with our voices, movements and even thoughts, and reach anyone anywhere through a personalized phone link. The movement of people will be revolutionized with the development of new means of transport, which will be more economical, faster and safer, and possibly less polluting. The variety and enormity of technological inventions will have implications in the entertainment industry and the media, changing the way we work or shop, and revolutionizing everything from space research to everyday life.

This view of the future has been heavily popularized in science fiction. Almost every single blockbuster movie that is based 'in the future' brings similar images. Because they are visual, these images are even more powerful than futures visioning in either academic journals and books or popular magazines. The images are part of the deeper myths that organize our worldviews and, eventually, educational policy. They help define reality. Quite clearly, they make techno-narratives and ideas even more popular: 'Popular culture industries have a way of harnessing the public imagina[tion] and turning technology into narratives of consumption... and narratives of the fantastic, the futuristic, and the anarchic, all of which generate their own social dynamics' (Luke 1997: 15).

The WebNet vision of the world is described, predicted, imagined and visualized in a meticulous fashion. It is now commonly accepted as 'the truth' about the future; possibly even to an incomparably greater level than other visions, including the previously described vision of a globalized society. Not surprisingly, it is this 'truth' that demands urgent changes in educational policy and strategy. But, while futurists are mostly concerned with forecasting, educators often take these forecasts for granted, focusing on how education should adjust to the emerging changes. Interestingly, while social rhetoric overall demands that importance be given to *education*, the reality is that not only education but also the *social* and *cultural* too often *remain invisible* in the WebNet vision of the world. True to this general trend, science fiction either does not describe/portray education in the future at all or, alternatively, presents it as effortless, instantaneous and technologically mediated (as in, e.g. the films *The Matrix* or *Battlefield Earth* wherein information and knowledge are instantly downloaded). True to its hegemonic status, the WebNet vision of the world and education has inspired both a utopian and a dystopian 'take'. Even though the utopian take was present in previous descriptions of the vision of the future, the following section discusses this more explicitly.

Utopian and eutopian versions

> Pick up any newspaper or magazine, or turn on a television, and you will see endless advertisements and news items suggesting that the latest digital phone, palm computer, minidisk player, or chip-implanted credit card will yield increased productivity, enlivened leisure time, and enhanced communication – not to mention social harmony, economic stability, and democracy.
>
> (Trend 2001: 17)

For those of us in the developed world the future holds a cornu-
copia of brilliant possibilities, as life-long education becomes a
reality, easily available at low cost to everyone in forms that are
adapted to the way people learn best.

(Ravitch 1993: 45)

There is no race. There is no gender. There is no age. There are
no infirmities. There are only minds. Utopia? No, Internet.

(MCI WorldCom, in Trend 2001: 33)

If the post-information society utopia could be described in only
two words, these would be 'Libertarian Utopia' (Kinney, in Sardar
1996: 9). In this utopia, the digital age removes limits imposed by
time and geography. It includes 'less and less dependence upon
being in a specific place at a specific time, and the transmission of
place itself will start to become possible' (Negroponte 1995: 165).
The relativism of time is connected with the increased personal
power to invent reality, to the point where 'time itself will seem an
invention' (Glenn 1996: 745). Other limitations – that of a physically
less-abled body, disadvantage due to race or gender – also cease to
exist. This also means that the Internet enables new means and

Figure 5 Leading the way in higher education. Further education billboard,
Caboolture, Australia, July 2002. Photographed by the author.[1]

opportunities for the formation of identity. Because there is no obvious framework of constraint, the individual is free to become the 'author of meaning' (Kenway 1996: 222). As there is not yet real censorship in cyberspace, totalitarian societies stand less chance of controlling information. Being a new medium, the Internet tends to be in the hands of more creative, ambitious, and usually younger, members of society. Here lies its potential to provide support for pro-democracy social groups. As a new medium that is presently beyond censorship, it is distinct from traditional means of communication that are mostly dominated and controlled by those with political power. The potential for freedom of expression is also limitless. The Internet decentralizes and therefore democratizes. It will enable more democratic polity and new models of social and economic organization (ibid.). New technologies liberate us not only from space and time but also from totalitarian regimes. Eventually, they will also free us from repetitive boring tasks, whether in the office or at home, thereby giving us more time for leisure.

Harmony, abundance and empowerment

In addition to its libertarian aspect, the digital age is also 'harmonizing' (Negroponte 1995: 229). Digital technology has the potential to be 'a natural force drawing people into greater world harmony' (ibid.: 230). New ICTs provide the means for resolving many of the world's problems. Problems become more visible thanks to global media, enabling quick and committed responses. New ICTs also provide a means for addressing hunger and illness among the world's poor, as we can now globally produce more food than ever, better prevent and cure certain illnesses, and more quickly transfer and provide for the victims of natural catastrophes and social conflicts. These capacities can have harmonizing effects in addressing the issue of the gap between the rich and the poor, predominantly by improving conditions for the world's poor. New ICTs also allow for ever-increasing access to tools of ever-increasing productivity, and those that adopt technology later will actually benefit by acquiring advanced technology created by entrepreneurs, avoiding the mistakes of the trailblazers (Gates *et al.* 1995). Adequate and quick communication and, most of all, the opportunity to learn about and understand others are probably the most necessary conditions for conflict resolution. Technology has enabled the creation of links between many diverse civilizations, nations, groups of people and individuals. The possibility of learning about and understanding others is increasing; for example, through personal inter-cultural contacts made easier and cheaper, with the help of new means of transport, the Internet and even information that we gather from television. New ICTs can help individuals to find their soul mates on other continents. New technologies have helped create conditions in which the world can see itself, can imagine itself, as one global community. In addition, while many intellectual movements are 'distinctly driven by national and ethnic forces...the digital revolution is not' (Negroponte 1995: 204). Rather, its 'ethos and appeal are as universal as rock music' (ibid.). New ICTs can also help harmonize people with nature, by resolving current environmental problems (e.g. fixing the ozone hole with a layer of scientifically/technologically created ozone replacement).

Two more crucial utopian aspects of new ICTs are the creation of abundance, and individual and group empowerment. The post-information society promises more jobs and new economic opportunities, 'a bountiful harvest of information and entertainment, and new prosperity in a computopia that would make Adam Smith proud' (Kellner 1998: par. 7). The choices are virtually limitless, whether in buying products, being entertained, improving health or acquiring education. Information will be easily accessed and will create numerous benefits for the person who seeks it. The easy acquisition of information helps in numerous areas, '...[in] creating ideas, finding directions, acquiring skills, getting support or confirmation, getting motivated, calming down or relaxing, getting pleasure or happiness, and reaching goals' (Bruce and Candy 2000: 3).

The main or root metaphor of the digital age is 'network'. This metaphor implies 'new, non-hierarchical, democratic and reciprocal model of human relationships' (Kenway 1996: 222). As opposed to the pyramid metaphor of the industrial and agricultural ages, we are now living in a phase of multiple and shifting centres (ibid.). In the words of Appadurai:

> The crucial point...is that the United States is no longer the puppeteer of a world system of images but is only one node of a complex transnational construction of imaginary landscapes... The new global cultural economy has to be seen as complex, overlapping, disjunctive order that cannot any longer be understood in terms of existing center-periphery models (even those that might account for multiple centers and peripheries).
>
> (Appadurai 1996: 31–32)

Previously excluded social groups now have a medium through which they can participate, promote their politics and agenda and make their issues visible. The Internet provides subordinated groups with 'new opportunities to represent themselves in their own voices and own ways' (Kenway 1996: 222). The anonymity of the Internet allows other political opportunities, such as 'fluid identity games' (ibid.: 223). These games are possible because people can '…live parallel lives, use nicknames or false names, conceal their identity and have multiple identities – including multiple gender and sexual [racial] identities' (ibid.).

Individual empowerment is said to be in the following areas:

> The gains of electronic postmodernity could be said to include, for individuals, (a) an increased awareness of the 'big picture,' a global perspective that admits the extraordinary complexity of interrelations; (b) an expanded neural capacity, an ability to accommodate a broad range of stimuli simultaneously; (c) a relativistic comprehension of situations that promotes the erosion of old biases and often expresses itself as tolerance; and (d) a matter-of-fact and unencumbered sort of readiness, a willingness to try new situations and arrangements.
>
> (Birkerts 1994: 27)

To summarize, the post-information or digital age is liberating, democratizing, harmonizing and empowering in many ways. Similar gains are to be obtained in education. They include liberation from the limits of time, geography, class, race and gender; improvements in access to and quality of education; individual-centred education; pedagogical abundance; and general improvements in teaching and learning.

Access, flexibility and interconnectedness

Because the Internet removes almost all constraints of time and space, its potential is in allowing 'individuals to take courses at their own pace, and to choose from all possible courses in the world those which best meet their learning needs' (Skolnik 2000: 57). With constraints of space and time removed, the benefits are obvious:

> If Little Eva cannot sleep, she can learn algebra instead. At her homelearning station, she will tune in to a series of interesting problems that are presented in an interactive medium, much like video games. First the learning program will identify her

level of competence and then move her to the appropriate level of challenge; algebra, she will discover, is presented as a series of brain-teasers, puzzles that she wants to solve.

Young John may decide that he wants to learn the history of modern Japan, which he can do by dialing up the greatest authorities and teachers on the subject, who will not only use dazzling graphs and illustrations, but will narrate a historical video that excites his curiosity and imagination. When he decides that he wants to learn Japanese, he may enter into a program of virtual reality, learning the language in conversation with Japanese speakers.

(Ravitch 1993: 40)

Other benefits that result from removing geographical boundaries include improved access to top-quality education: 'For every student who gets into a Harvard or a Princeton or a Berkley there are probably a hundred who could handle the work. Why should they be denied the opportunity?' (*Forbes.Com* magazine 2000, par. 12).

Limitations of class, race and gender are also removed. The new technological era in education promotes greater equity of access for those previously excluded. This argument is implicit in the previous quote, and more explicit in the following:

Before, when schooling was limited to traditional buildings and managed by a state bureaucracy, poor children usually got the least-experienced teachers and the poorest quality of instruction. In the new era, technology makes it possible to provide exactly the same quality of instruction to every child. Using the new technologies, all children will have access to exactly the same electronic-teaching programs, learning at their own speed and in settings of their own choosing, at home or at school, in a community learning center or at a friend's home. Regardless of her race or her parent's income, little Mary will have the same opportunity to learn any subject, and to learn it from the same master teachers as children in the richest neighborhood.

(Ravitch 1993: 40)

While educational institutions will initially resist these trends towards democratization, they will eventually 'give in':

Students will be able to shop around, taking a course from any institution that offers a good one. Degree-granting institutions will have to accommodate this. They will resist at first, but eventually society will realize that anyone is entitled to the best courses, and barriers will fall. Quality education will be available to all. Students will learn what they want to learn rather than what some faculty committee decided was the best political compromise. Education will be measured by what you know rather than by whose name appears on your diploma.

(*Forbes.Com* magazine 2000, final paragraph)

The democratization of education will occur because new ICTs are making education less costly, more accessible and flexible. They will enable student-centred lifelong learning and faster acquisition of skills than that in any period before. This means that disadvantaged social groups who lack financial resources and unlimited free time for study will still be able to obtain education. For example, a single mother living in a remote, impoverished rural area can improve her lot in life by enrolling on courses that do not cost too much and do not last too long. She can study after putting her children to bed, before they wake up or at any time that suits her. She can afford these courses with a greater ease than financing three to four years of study at a traditional institution of higher learning.

Another important utopian promise lies in the emerging 'pedagogical plenty' (Ravitch 1993: 40). Cyberspace is about the creation of webs of knowledge with unlimited access to information, with a potential to provide access to 'everything'. All the knowledge and all the existing information exist 'at the fingertips'. This knowledge is available 24 hours a day, 365 days of a year. There is no longer any need to memorize, use rote learning or focus on the acquisition of data. All this will help improve the quality of education because, as argued by Negroponte, the major part of learning does not come from such teaching but from 'exploration, from reinventing the wheel and finding out for oneself' (1995: 199). Computers allow yet again approaching *learning by doing*:

> Learning for more information is unnecessary because it is becoming increasingly possible to retrieve specific information when needed…students can substitute learning to find what they need to know for the impossible task of learning everything they may need to know.
>
> (Grabe and Grabe 1998: 5)

Technology-assisted pedagogy is oriented towards 'self-directed, but collaborative learning that is resource-based and problem-oriented'

(Kapitzke 1999: 4). This would help educators to be 'more able to reach children with different learning and cognitive styles' (Negroponte 1995: 198). The approach to education has become 'constructivist', while the focus on 'abstract and meaningless numbers' (ibid.: 200) and on data is gone:

> We are finally moving away from a hard-line mode of teaching, which has catered primarily to compulsive serialist children, toward one that is more porous and draws no clear lines between art and science or right brain and left...Personal computers will make our future adult population simultaneously more mathematically able and more visually literate. Ten years from now, teenagers are likely to enjoy a much richer panorama of options because the pursuit of intellectual achievement will not be tilted so much in favor of the book-worm, but instead cater to a wider range of cognitive styles, learning patterns, and expressive behaviors.
>
> (Negroponte 1995: 220)

All this will bring back excitement and motivation into learning. Picking up on such promises, information technology corporations like AT&T and Apple have 'increasingly drawn on the rhetoric of education to market their products' (Dimitriades and Kamberelis 1997: 138):

> Their advertisements promise a utopia, a shrinking world where information is available at the touch of a finger and exotic peoples can be accessed with a click of a mouse. These images are replete with wonder, enchantment, and awe. They promise a generation of young people capable of dealing with both the challenges and the possibilities of a radically shrinking world, a world increasingly constituted by and through rapidly developing technological apparatuses.
>
> (Dimitriades and Kamberelis 1997: 138)

Other promises of cyber education highlight increased student independence, curiosity and autonomy. In the 'networked classroom', the traditional distribution of students' bodies in rows and the unobstructed gaze of the teacher are disturbed (Kapitzke 1999). Instead of being atomized as in traditional 'teacher-centered classrooms, students work collaboratively, pooling knowledge and skills in the search for information' (Luke 1997: 31). Overall, teaching becomes subordinated to learning, enabling teachers to become mentors, guides, even friends to their students. Teachers themselves will be liberated from the expectation that they know 'everything' and can start enjoying their new role as facilitator of learning. Networked classrooms will finally help realise 'the utopian dream of an equitable sharing of classroom authority' (Faigley 1992: 167). And, just as the authority of the teacher is de-centred, the authority of the written text and the pedagogy founded on the linearity of print-based textbook learning can meet a similar fate (Faigley 1992: 185; Luke 1997: 31). It is also suggested that unlimited technology in the classroom 'leads to better problem solving ability, less truancy and greater collaboration between students' (Berston and Moont 1996: 43).

Beyond the networked classroom is the promise of virtual reality. For example, students can now safely conduct chemistry experiments, visit virtual galaxies, walk through a factory and even visit historical events or enter into a novel and interact with its characters (Briggs 1996). Disciplinary boundaries are also shattered, facilitating more productive approaches to learning.

The list of potential benefits and improvements in education does not stop here. Some writers go so far as to suggest that we are at the beginning of a learning revolution, with children themselves becoming agents for change at school (Papert 1996). Or that the advances in knowledge are such that the information age could more appropriately be termed the 'Innovation Age' (Pitsch 1996) revolutionizing everything. Old dreams and utopias can now finally be fulfilled:

> The promise of the Information Age is the unleashing of unprecedented productive capacity by the power of the mind. I think, therefore I produce. In so doing, we will have the leisure to experiment with spirituality, and the opportunity of reconciliation with nature, without sacrificing the material wellbeing of our children. The dream of the Enlightenment, that reason and science would solve the problems of human kind, is within reach.
>
> (Castells 1998: 359)

But not everyone is convinced.

The dystopian version

'Without attention to social justice, critical literacy and social change, our students will know how to send an email, but have nothing to say in it' (Brabazon 2002: xiii). The dystopian version can be summed up in two words: 'Corporatist Dystopia' (Kinney, in Sardar 1996: 9). This dystopia is based on a continuation of traditional relations of power and control (ibid.). According to Drahos (1995), the evolution of the information society can best be characterized as *Information Feudalism*. Vast amounts of information have fallen into private hands and private databases, information is excludable and fee-based, the info-rich have found new ways of robbing the info-poor, and consumption is rampant. This situation is similar to European feudal society which was characterized by a profound weakening of the state, especially when it came to its protective capacity, and by rigorous economic subjection of the many to a powerful few (Drahos 1995). In a similar fashion, Johnson (1996) describes *The Information Highway from Hell*. In this 'worst-case scenario', choice is greatly limited by the formation of monopolies; the network and most of its services are controlled by only a few companies. Most of the traffic is recorded and analysed for commercial use, freedom of speech is restricted and advertising is ubiquitous (ibid.). Advertising has triumphed and become not just a central institution, but the central institution, creating the new culture of Adcult, argues Twitchell (1996). He stresses that by 1993 American companies already spent more than $140 billion per year on advertising, while an average adult saw some 3000 ads every day (ibid.).

The information superhighway has not only degraded into a corporatist tool for extracting profits, but there is a substantial lack of privacy and ubiquitous surveillance. The introduction of the new information technologies initially resulted in the demise of the surveillance state and in 'Big Brother' being laid off (Whitaker, quoted in Marien 1999: 5). But the panoptic tendencies in modern society have gained immeasurably in scope and efficiency, the shift towards the surveillance society has occurred, and 'Big Brother is being brought back as an outside consultant' (ibid.). The concept of privacy has come and gone (ibid.). Because 'everything you do could be known to anyone else and recorded forever the basic principle underlying the mechanism of democracy is undermined' (Chaum, quoted in Kenway 1996: 224).

Unlike prior utopias, which were brought about by philosophical reflection, social amelioration or proletarian revolt, cyber utopia seems to be new because it is a version of the future that is 'a product of different sort' (Trend 2001: 17). In this case, a perfected existence comes from multinational corporations – as a by-product of 'the purchase of the[ir] appropriate products and services' (ibid.). But this vision is also not so new; it too comes from a particular tradition:

> Throughout history, business interests have cloaked their agendas in a rhetoric of social betterment. General Electric's familiar 'better

living through technology' mantra of the 1950s was really just
another way of focusing consumer attention on the added
convenience of electric frying pans, blenders, and dishwashers –
and away from the specters of industrial pollution, nuclear
annihilation, and the forces of predatory market capitalism.

(Trend 2001: 17)

There are other arguments about why the information age does not
provide democracy but is, instead, based on elitism. These are
predominantly founded in arguments about the 'info-rich and info-
poor' or the 'haves and have-nots' (e.g. Haywood 1995; Wresch 1996).
To highlight this issue, Ebo (1998) uses the term 'Cyberghetto', and
contrasts it with the more commonly used term 'Cybertopia'.

Stress, impoverishment and mono-culture

Other authors focus on data smog, or 'infoglut', phenomena which
no longer add to the quality of life but instead begin to 'cultivate stress,
confusion, and even ignorance' (Shenk 1997). Putting a computer in
every classroom is not unlike putting an electric power plant in
every home (ibid.). Information overload threatens peoples' ability
to educate themselves, leaves them more vulnerable as consumers
and diminishes control over their lives. Social cohesion as well as truth
are also threatened; 'in our increasing distraction and speediness,
the lies will move so much faster than the truth, they will too often
become the truth' (quoted in Marien 1997b: 4).

Other arguments about the dystopian character of the impending
digital age include *temporal and cultural impoverishment*. This is
because the intrusiveness and overbearing character of technology
leaves us with 'no moments of silence, less time to ourselves, and a
sense of diminished control over our lives' (Norman 1998). There is
a general loss of meaning and non-verbal expression. Imagination is
impoverished:

Technology is taking away our ability to speculate, and from
speculation comes imagination. From imagination comes origin-
ality and inventiveness; the kaleidoscope of visions one has
before them. Technology has slaughtered the lost substance of
newness and novelty. There is no longer any need to come up
with new ideas in new ways, when chances are some computer
can do it all for us.

(Bohen 2001: 55)

The dystopian digital age is characterized by the future being devalued. Long-term thinking is virtually non-existent. As summarized by Frank Ogden (quoted in Marien 1996: 4), 'today, my idea of long-range planning is lunch'. In a similar manner, an advertisement in *Wired* magazine '...depicts an anxious-looking twenty-something man, dripping wet, peeking from behind a shower curtain, with the caption 'A lot has happened while you were off-line' (Trend 2001: 19).

Culturally, cyberspace is a desert. To start with, the Internet is an outcome and expression of (only) male culture (Kenway 1996: 227). One language dominates, which will not help reverse the trend towards the extinction of languages – 'at least half of the world's 6,000 or so languages will be dead or dying by the year 2050' (Ostler 1999). The appearance of English as a global language is not a benign phenomenon, but a form of linguistic colonization. As the world's dominant language, English creates certain forms of thinking and suppresses others. It cannot replace or fully express words and phrases from other cultures, which have centuries of meaning behind them. The English language is the 'invisible technology' (Postman 1993: 123) of the Internet and, like any other language, has an 'ideological agenda that is apt to be hidden from view' (ibid.: 124). The language of the Internet is not only the language of the most powerful nation but also the language of the dominant form of knowledge: technical rationality. Only one culture of expression is possible and other ways of knowing and experiencing the world are suppressed. New ICTs aid and abet the process of communication that engages with nature through domination and the need to suppress and conquer. Nature and cultures that respect nature are also silenced.

Sardar (1996) argues that techno-utopian ideology distracts western society from the actual increase in spiritual poverty, meaninglessness and inhumanity in everyday lives. While the west focuses on colonizing yet another 'frontier', it does so to forget its problems at home. Cyberspace is 'an emphatic product of the culture, world-view and technology of Western civilization' (Sardar 2000: 734); it did not appear from nowhere. Rather 'it is a conscious reflection of the deepest desires, aspirations, experiential yearning and spiritual *Angst* of Western man' (ibid.). Cyberspace is the 'American dream' writ large; it marks the dawn of a new 'American civilization'. It is a place where the white man's burden shifted from the 'moral obligation to civilize, democratize, urbanize and colonize non-Western cultures, to the colonization of cyberspace' (ibid.: 735). European authors such as John Gray and Enrique Gil Calvo agree. For Gray, the Internet is not only a product of neo-liberal ideology that reduces the complexity of human interactions to the model of the market interchange, it is also a pure mimicry of American culture (Gray, in Gil Calvo 2000). For Gil Calvo, Americans have created the Internet to replace the emptiness resulting from a lack of authentic interpersonal bonds. Americans are always fleeing from something, argues Gil Calvo: its European origins, the Indians of the prairies, the blacks of the urban ghetto, its poorer fellow citizens (Case 2001; Gil Calvo 2000). They lack the place, the locality and a closely binding public culture, traditionally identified as the 'agora'. Europeans, especially Mediterraneans, are still comfortably integrated with their primary networks of community solidarity and only resort to secondary associations for 'utilitarian convenience, and not for existential therapy' (Case 2001: 29; Gil Calvo 2000). Americans, on the other hand, connect themselves to a network to redeem their own lack of place.

Not only were cultural factors important in creating the Internet in the first place, but the culture of the Internet helps maintain and promote historical relationships of domination and submission between ethnic, racial and cultural groups. Nakamura (2000) argues that race is either erased or exoticized and can find no discursive space outside those two options. For example, the stereotypes of Asian-ness deployed are those of either martial arts experts and Samurai or sexualized, docile, submissive Geishas. The invisibility of race is seen as a necessary requirement for harmony. Those who choose to describe themselves in racial terms as Asian, African American, Latino, or as members of other oppressed and marginalized minorities are often seen as 'engaging in a form of hostile performance, since they introduce what many consider a real life 'divisive issue' into the phantasmatic world of cybernetic textual interaction' (ibid.: 712–720).

The cyber age is also dangerous because it threatens local communities. As cyber communities increase in popularity, the atomization of society increases, and the weakness of local, immediate communities deepens. While some hail the ability of cyber communities to provide more support and understanding than local ones, virtual communities can never provide as much caring, support and protection. They are based on selfishness rather than on realities of everyday existence where relating to others in meaningful ways is required.

Even Negroponte (1995: 227) talks of the dark side of the digital age. For him, the main dangers lie in intellectual property abuse, invasion of privacy, digital vandalism, software piracy, data thievery, the loss of many jobs to wholly automated systems and the disappearance of the notion of lifetime employment.

To conclude this section on the dystopian character of the digital age, what follows are two lists that summarize the problems of the digital age. According to Marien, a 'top 10' list of the dark side of the information technology revolution includes:

> greater social gaps, speeding the pace of life, more privacy invasion, less democracy, a distraction from building a sustainable society, vulnerability to infowar and infoterrorism, cybercrime, negative influences on futures thinking, and – above all – the problem of infoglut (leading to specialization, devalued information, boredom, stress, and sleeplessness).
>
> (Marien 1997a: 4)

In a similar fashion, Birkerts writes:

> In the loss column, meanwhile, are (a) fragmented sense of time and a loss of the so-called duration experience, that depth phenomenon we associate with reveries; (b) a reduced attention span and a general impatience with sustained inquiry; (c) a shattered faith in institutions and in the explanatory narratives that formerly gave shape to subjective experience; (d) a divorce from the past, from a vital sense of history as a cumulative or organic process; (e) an estrangement from geographic place and community; and (f) an absence of any strong vision of a personal or collective future.
>
> (Birkerts 1994: 27)

Interestingly, while some authors argue that technology in itself is neutral and that the main issue is how a particular technology is used, others believed that the 'danger' lies in the very essence of technology. This is because, among other things, it forces human beings to think in purely instrumental terms (Mayers and Swafford 1998: 155–156). As we move into the sphere of hyper-reality we inevitably lose touch with our body, with nature, with other people and with focal things and practices (Kellner 1998). In sum, new technologies are technocratic by nature and potentially dominant – the main threat is a totalitarian nightmare (Snyder 1997: 129).

The costs to education

All these negative aspects are also reflected within the educational discourse. As approaches to knowledge, learning, relationships and so on are affected, so too is education. Technological change is neither additive nor subtractive but ecological, argues Postman (ibid.): 'one significant change generates total change' (ibid.: 18). For example, in a technocracy, tools play a central role in the thought world of the culture and everything must give way to their development: 'Tools are not integrated into the culture; they attack the culture. They bid to become the culture. As a consequence, tradition, social mores, myth, politics, ritual, and religion have to fight for their lives' (ibid.: 28).

Technopoly is, continues Postman (ibid.: 48), a totalitarian technocracy that redefines what is meant by religion, family, politics, history, truth, intelligence and so on. In concrete terms, computers carry with them the banner of private learning and individual problem solving, not unlike the print medium that stresses individualized learning, competition and personal autonomy (ibid.: 17). Orality, on the other hand, stresses group learning, cooperation and a sense of social responsibility (ibid.). In technopoly, the main focus in education is to improve 'learning technologies' (ibid.: 171). Education is reduced to being an instrument of economic policy, teaching children about 'progress without limits, rights without responsibilities, and technology without cost' (ibid.: 179). It is about teaching that technological innovation is synonymous with human progress. It promises heaven on earth through the conveniences of technological progress, telling a story of a life of skills, technical expertise and the ecstasy of consumption (ibid.).

What is the point of connecting children to the Internet, others ask? It can only breed 'a cop-out society by feeding fantasy, escapism and nostalgia' (Kenway 1996: 226). As Postman argues, the information superhighway is unnecessary because we already have an over-abundance of information (Postman 1993: 48, 179). In addition, there are concerns that the Internet provides one more tool for sexual predators to find new victims, creating a reverse civil society, a community of the predatory violent. It is also feared that the Internet is becoming yet another tool for the spreading of pornography, thus communicating a 'distorted view of sexuality' (Milojević 2002a: 101). While pornography existed earlier, the new technologies facilitate its spread and will continue to do so. For example, *Time* magazine recently reported, 'As of July 2003, there were 260 million pages of pornography online, an increase of 1,800 per cent since 1998. Porn amounts to about 7 per cent of the 3.3 billion Web pages indexed by Google' (Paul 2004: 75). And, 'it is estimated that the cyber-sex industry constitutes 60 per cent of the current Internet economy' (Gomez-Pena, in Stromquist 2002: 149).

Lastly, as is the case with the dystopian discourse on globalization, there are concerns with mechanical approaches towards nature. In the not-so-distant cyber future, nature is replaced incrementally until it disappears altogether. This, in turn, threatens the very survival of humans and other living beings.

To conclude, in this section I have engaged with utopian and dystopian thinking rather than dismissing either. Of course, the particular position taken depends on, for example, one's own position in the world society in economic, education, gender, cultural and ethnic background, and worldview terms. As well, it is affected by one's own preferred vision of and for the future. In short, whether new ICTs are seen to be more beneficial or more detrimental to our societies and education is not only a matter of pure intellectual reasoning, it is also a matter of a belief system, backed by historical and contemporary myths, metaphors and other meta-narratives. These are summarized in the following section.

In Part II, it has been argued that, although visions of globalized and cyber society and education are often seen to be realistic discourse of the 'imminent future', discourse analysis shows that these visions are also constituted by desire and imagination, by what is hoped for. In addition, the CLA analysis (see Chapter 7) shows that these desires and hopes are still firmly based on western and patriarchal worldviews. Another crucial argument here is that dominant futures visions succeed in capturing the public imagination because they 'make the most sense' – are easily intelligible – from within our current social structures and dominant worldview. The globalized and cyber world concepts are succeeding in the modern world not because they challenge its basis, but because the assumptions of their worldview fit perfectly with it. Globalization and the information society continue the linear stage-like history of the west. Indeed, both processes rescue capitalism from its stagnation. Thus, while globalization and the WebNet supersede modernity, they do so not by destroying the basis of modernity but by continuing it – its linear view of history, its exclusion of the Other, its patriarchal bias. These visions not only arose from within but also in many ways enhance the main characteristics of the modern education model, a model that they claim to destabilize, replace and transcend.

7 Contextualizing global dreams and nightmares

Causal layered analysis of globalization and WebNet visions

This section presents an analysis, using tables, to sum up the main points of Part II. Tables 7.1 and 7.2 present selected features of both the globalized world and the WebNet vision of the world respectively. These features include: (1) the approach to time; (2) the vision for the future; (3) the utopian promise; (4) dystopian dangers; and (5) social eutopia. For example, the vision for the future for the globalized world is the alternatively global pan-capitalism, post-scarcity society and postindustrial society. The utopian promises are material benefits, instant satisfaction of material needs, global international democracy and more consumer and employment choices. Other features are shown in Tables 7.1 and 7.2.

Tables 7.3 and 7.4 summarize educational futures – globalized education and cyber education respectively. This is done by answering the following questions: (1) What is the underlying vision of the future? (2) What is the utopian promise? (3) What are dystopian dangers? (4) What is the social eutopia offered? (5) What are the worldview and approach to knowledge? (6) What is the epistemology? (7) What is the educated subject? (8) What is the educational content? (9) What is the educational process? and (10) What is the educational structure?

For example, for cyber education, the underlying vision for the future is the interconnected world. The utopian promise is improved access and quality. The dystopian dangers are, among others, linguistic colonization and the suppression of other forms of learning. The educational eutopia is expansion in approaches to teaching and learning. The worldview consists of scientism, instrumentalism, secularism, empiricism and technological determinism. The

Table 7.1 Globalized world – social futures

Approach to time	Vision for the future	Utopian promise	Dystopian dangers	Social eutopia
Linear/compressed Time as product – it can be bought, sold and saved Time of 'project and history' Instantaneous Simultaneous	Global pan-capitalism Post-scarcity society Postindustrial society Global age	Material benefits Instant satisfaction of material needs Pushing towards international democracy globally More consumer and employment choices	Gap between haves and have-nots/rampant poverty Increase in gender inequality Single culture and society dominating the planet, global sameness, western imperialism Environmental degradation Hierarchical, unequal and insecure social environment	Potential for global transformation, international/ transnational government and cooperation Potential to move away from the 'tyranny of the local community'

Table 7.2 WebNet vision of the world – social futures

Approach to time	Vision for the future	Utopian promise	Dystopian dangers	Social eutopia
Linear/compressed	Post-Information society	Cyber democracy	Digital divide, info-rich and info-poor	Potential environmental benefits
Time replacing distance	Knowledge society	World harmony	Formation of Cyber-ghettos	Increased efficiency
	Network society	Environmental crisis resolved	Electronic surveillance, total lack of privacy	Increased possibilities for intercultural exchange within the discourse of rationalism
	Digital age	Freedom to create new virtual identities and communities – invent reality	Information feudalism – network controlled by few companies	
	Electronic age		Adcult – advertising ubiquitous	
	Age of automation	Freedom from repetitive boring tasks – more time for leisure	Infoglut – information overload – cultivates stress, confusion and ignorance	
	Atomic age	Liberation from the limits of time, geography, class, disability, race, gender	Temporal and cultural impoverishment	
	Cyberia			

Table 7.3 Globalized education – educational futures

Underlying vision for the future	Utopian promise	Dystopian dangers	Educational eutopia
Globalized world	Dynamic synergy of teachers, computer-mediated instructional devices and students collaborating globally	Education a product to be bought and sold	Benefits from globalizing student body and globalizing curriculum
	Transnational and transcultural dialogues and learning	Commercialization and corporatization of education	Improvement of access to educational resources and expertise
	Deepening what is thought, expansion of knowledge	Westernization	
	Student-centred education, students' needs central	Sacrifice of individual styles and idiosyncratic enthusiasm to satisfy global criteria	
		Increase in bureaucratic rigidities	
		Smothering of all forms of creativity	
		Creation of docile, hard-working, conformist students	
		In non-OECD countries decrease in both quantity and quality	

Table 7.3 (Continued)

Worldview and approach to knowledge	Epistemology	Educated subject
Neo-liberalism	Rationalism	Measurable technical production of skilled, flexible, movable global worker
Anthropocentrism	Instrumentalism	
Focus on growth	Secularism	Students as consumers
Economic determinism	Scientism	
Market liberalism and social conservativism		

Educational visions/futures		
Content	Process	Structure
Vocational	Focus on skills	Connection between traditional educational institutions
Pragmatic and token multiculturalism and gender equality	Standardization	Privatized – voucher system
	Focus on achievement and success	Agile and flexible system
	Centralized testing	

Table 7.4 Cyber education – educational futures

Underlying vision for the future	Utopian promise	Dystopian dangers	Educational eutopia
Interconnected world	Improved access and quality, education less costly and more flexible	Linguistic colonization	Expansion in approaches to teaching and learning
	Student-centred lifelong learning	Suppression of other forms of learning (e.g. oral)	Powerful method that can meet the needs of some students the best
	Self-directed, collaborative learning	Too much stress on individualized learning and personal autonomy leads to competition	
	Learning by doing	Education teaches about progress without limits, rights without responsibilities and technology without cost	
	Increase in students independence, curiosity and autonomy		
	Faster acquisition of skills than ever before		
	The era of 'pedagogical plenty'		
	Equitable sharing of classroom authority – authority of the teachers decentred		
	Knowledge available 24 hours a day, 365 days of a year		

Table 7.4 (Continued)

Worldview and approach to knowledge	Epistemology	Educated subject
Scientism	Rationalism	Computer-literate
Instrumentalism	Techno-scientific approach to knowledge	Operational skills and expertise
Secularism		
Empiricism		
Technological determinism		

Educational visions/futures		
Content	Process	Structure
Computer and multimedia literacy	Focus on skills	Networked classroom
Gender and cultural issues seen as irrelevant	Flexibility, adaptability, interaction	Individualized learning

epistemology employed is rationalism and the techno-scientific approach to knowledge. The education subject is computer-literate and has operational skills and expertise. In terms of educational content, computer and multimedia literacy is primary. The process is skills focused and the structure is the networked classroom and individualized learning. These and other features are summarized in Table 7.3.

Table 7.5 summarizes the key words used to describe the globalized world and education, and Table 7.6 the WebNet vision and cyber education. For the globalized world, these include terms such as choice, freedom, opportunities and competition. For interconnected and cyber education, these include terms such as interactivity and multi-directionality.

Tables 7.7 and 7.8 restate the analysis conducted earlier in the text. Table 7.7 divides the future into four levels. The first is the litany. In terms of the globalized world, the litany is the statement that globalization is dramatically changing education and our world. The second is the social cause level. Social causes may include, depending on one's worldview, neo-colonialism, patriarchy or capitalism. At the deeper level, underlying assumptions are individualism, modernity and rationalism. The myth/metaphor level that underlies this is, alternatively, the Land of Cockaygne (land of milk and honey), the Golden Age and Evolution. The bottom line for education is that education is about the provision of skills for human capital formation, education as economic investment and as providing skills so as to compete in the global economy.

In terms of the interconnected world and cyber education presented in Table 7.8, the litany consists of the statement: computers and the Internet are revolutionizing education. The social causes of this are the development of ICTs and economic decisions that support cyber education. The worldview beneath this is based on instrumental rationality as well as on linear progress and technology. The myths and metaphors that describe this are those of the global brain, the new world, the new frontier and, of course, the network. For education, the bottom line is that education is about increased access to information.

The globalized and the WebNet world are deconstructed in Tables 7.9 and 7.10 respectively. The questions asked are: (1) Who gets to speak? (2) Who and what is silenced? (3) What is missing from the discourse? (4) What is the continuity? and (5) What is the discontinuity? For the globalized world, government and consumers speak. The individual, the family, the community, NGOs and the

Table 7.5 Globalized world and education – key words

Change	Future	Society	Education	Other key words
Rapid and perpetual	Already given, more of the same	Globalized	Human capital	Choice, freedom, opportunities
Need to adjust to change, trends unstoppable		Rationalization	Achievement success	Competition
		Healthy economy		Opening of national economies
		Deregulation, privatization, liberalization of capital flows		

Table 7.6 Interconnected world (WebNet) and cyber education – key words

Change	Future	Society	Education	Other key words
Rapid and perpetual	Already given, more of the same	New information technologies	Access	Interactivity
Exponential			Potential	Interconnectedness
Irrevocable			Networked classroom	Multi-directionality
Need to adjust to change, trends unstoppable			Digital library – cybrary	Flow and seamlessness

Table 7.7 Globalized world and education – causal layered analysis

Litany	Social cause	Discourse/worldview	Myth/metaphor	Education bottom line
Globalization is dramatically changing education and our world	Capitalism Patriarchy Neo-colonialism and imperialism Governance of economic globalization (social and educational policy)	Individualism Rationalism Modernity (movement towards the modern form of schooling)	Land of Cockaygne (land of milk and honey), Golden Age Western world at the top of development ladder Darwinian paradigm/evolution and survival of the fittest Free market World as 'one place'	Education mainly about providing vocational skills in order to achieve and compete Education as investment in economy Education as human capital formation

Table 7.8 Interconnected world and cyber education – causal layered analysis

Litany	Social cause	Discourse/worldview	Myth/metaphor	Education bottom line
Computers and Internet are revolutionizing education	Invention and development of new information and communication technologies Economic investment and policy decisions that support cyber education	Internet a representation of instrumental rationality Focus on individual and her/his interface with technology Sense-based education privileged Linear progress and development	Global brain World mind New world New frontier Discovered but not yet fully colonized space Network	Education mainly about increased access of information

Table 7.9 Globalized world – deconstruction

Who gets to speak	Who and what is silenced	What is missing from a discourse	Continuity	Discontinuity
International cooperation Government Consumers	Individual, family, community and environmental concerns and NGOs	Concern with social and environmental sustainability Concern with social justice issues and ethics Development of critical thought Slow time	Western civilization, patriarchy Imagination about the world as 'one place'	The fall of communism in eastern Europe, 1980s in the west Postmodernism

Table 7.10 WebNet world – deconstruction

Who gets to speak	Who and what is silenced	What is missing from a discourse	Continuity	Discontinuity
Those that have the access and knowledge	Majority of the world; their issues and concerns	Emotional and spiritual aspects of the self Respect for silence and reflection (seen as inactivity) Non-verbal expression	Thousands of years of human attempts to improve lives through development of various tools and technologies	Cold War 1950s USA Transformation in 1970s capitalism

environment are silenced. Sustainability is thus missing from the discourse, as is a concern for social justice, slow time and critical thought. The main continuity is with the west and patriarchy, as well as with the imagination of the world as one place. Discontinuity is needed with the new vision that appeared in the 1980s and 1990s, and coincided with both 'the end of Millennium' and a collapse of socialism (as a genuine futures alternative to the western capitalism).

For the WebNet world, those who have access and knowledge get to speak. The majority of the world is silenced: their issues and concerns are lost. Emotional and spiritual aspects of the self are missing from the discourse, as are silence and non-verbal expressions. This world continues humanity's techno-evolution development. The discontinuity is the Cold War, 1950s USA and the transformation of 1970s capitalism.

Concluding remarks

The purpose of the tables has been threefold. First, they summarize the main arguments. Second, they unpack the levels of reality underneath the claims of realism for each image of the future; these are derived from specific social and technological causes as well as worldviews and myths. Third, they enable us to question these images of the future, to ask questions that disrupt – who and what is silenced, what is missing from the discourse and who gets to speak, for example – so that space for alternatives can be created.

As I have previously discussed, discourses on globalization and new ICTs argue that the main task of contemporary educators is to prepare students for a future where global technology dominates. It is not to contest – make these futures problematic – or to search for alternatives. Another argument is that these external changes have already started to destabilize educational systems and practices, that is, many analysts assert that they are simply describing existing changes; that globalized and cyber trends are not so much a vision of and for the future but an accurate description of how things 'are'.

On the other hand, I have argued that these two visions have been behind policies and actions that enabled some of the earlier techno-logical developments. As well, these two visions continue to inform our present, the actions that are taken today, which then further govern/enable/privilege particular futures.

Interestingly enough, many now question the claims of dramatic changes in education due to relentless processes of globalization and virtualization. For example, Mason (1998) argues that, despite all the talk about the dramatic impact of globalization, so far very little effort has been put into globalizing educational context, structure and practice, along multicultural and transnational lines. Most efforts towards globalized education are therefore currently organized along 'piecemeal operations' lines consisting of:

> a good deal of flag-waving from senior staff, or idealistic visions of new educational paradigms from educational technologists, or financial officers rubbing their hands in expectation, but at the end of the day, a very few academics and trainers are actually delivering something that could be called global in parts.
>
> (Mason 1998: 15)

Many attempts to privatize education (e.g. in the USA, voucher system, charter schools, etc.) have also not lived up to their promise of providing quality education for all. And it is questionable whether it is possible to (ever) implement a vision of a fully privatized education, because:

> For this to happen, the economy would have had to operate so as to allow all parents to earn enough to pay for the full cost of their children's education. No marked economy has yet reached the stage where this has occurred, and various mixes of private and public provision apply as a compromise.
>
> (Regan 2002: 144)

The argument has also been made that, even in the industrially most developed countries, computers have not significantly transformed educational content, process and the structures within which it takes place (Figure 6). As Riffel and Levin (1997: 51) argue, it seems that information technology is at best an 'adjunct' to existing educational practices, 'not yet integrated into people's thinking about teaching and learning'. Despite all the 'hype' (Snyder 1997) and 'ecstasy' (Luke 1996a), it seems that, in practice, things have indeed changed very little. One report (USDE 1996) estimates that even in the United States, students' use of computers for learning is, on average, only a few minutes a day.

Billions of dollars invested in technologies over the last decade have yet to produce the worthy outcomes, concludes Cuban (2001: 197) in his research on the use of computers in classrooms. Even in Silicon

Figure 6 'New look for e-classroom', but in which ways have computers changed the industrial model of schooling? Photo by Winston Hamilton and reprinted by permission of UK Foreign and Commonwealth Office.[1]

Valley schools – where there is an abundance of technological wealth – teachers made infrequent and limited use of computers in classrooms (ibid.: 59, 171). That is despite the astonishing success of educational reformers in wiring schools and equipping them with computer stations in the USA: '…in 1981 there were, on average, 125 students per computer in U.S. schools. A decade later, the ratio was 18 to 1. By 2000 it had dropped to 5 students per computer' (ibid.: 17).

An Australian-based report links this to previous promises of radio, film and television, which have 'all been put to work in the classroom, with the intent of enriching the instructional experiences for students' (Meredyth *et al.* 1999: 11). But, despite promise, 'these technologies have remained marginal to the educational process' (ibid.). So, although currently '…the idea of an information technology driven revolution of social and economic life is commonplace, both in Australia and elsewhere…the use of information technology in classrooms is the exception rather than the rule' (ibid.: 13).

Frustrated by the slow introduction of 'everything digital' in contemporary schools, Negroponte writes:

> Seymour Papert tells the story of a mid-nineteenth-century surgeon magically transported through time into a modern operating theater. That doctor would not recognize a thing, would not know what to do or how to help. Modern technology would have totally transformed the practice of surgical medicine beyond his recognition. If a mid-nineteenth-century schoolteacher were carried by the same time machine into a present-day classroom, except for minor subject details, that teacher could pick up where his or her late-twentieth-century peer left off. There is little fundamental difference between the way we teach today and the way we did one hundred and fifty years ago. The use of technology is almost at the same level. In fact, according to a recent survey by the U.S. Department of Education, 84 percent of America's teachers consider only one type of information technology absolutely 'essential': a photo copier with an adequate paper supply.
>
> (Negroponte 1995: 220)

It seems that new ICTs have failed to live up to their promise, and numerous futurists and other authors in general express their frustration and disappointment at the lack of expected changes. For example, as early as 1967, Watson Davis, who was, according to Rossman, fully supportive of H. G. Wells's World Brain idea:

> expressed his frustration over why it was taking so long to materialize four important concepts that had promising beginnings right after World War II: one big global library; on-demand publication; one global scholarly journal; and the World Brain – a system to manage human knowledge.
>
> (Rossman 1992: 77)

A decade ago, in the article *Megatrends or Megamistakes? Whatever happened to the Information Society?*, Forester (1992) wondered what happened to promises such as: dramatic reductions in the quantity of paid employment; large increases in the amount of forced and unforced leisure time; the paperless office and so on. Instead, argues Forester, the vast majority of people in the workforce appear to be working harder than ever, while junk mail and surface mail have not only remained strong, but are constantly growing in volume. The information technology 'revolution' in education seems to have somehow failed to satisfy predictions of exponential, irrevocable and unstoppable trends. As well, the central contradiction of the emerging ICTs remains the disconnection between 'the often-professed intentions of digital culture (utopian, democratic, universal) and the resulting social consequences (regressive, inegalitarian, exclusionary)' (Trend 2001: 39). Not only had the simple additions of new devices had little chance of producing real change, even in the country that has led this innovation, the USA, but 'we are now seeing the unanticipated effects of new technologies, ways in which they do both more and less than we had hoped' (Bruce 2003: 192).

All this should come as no surprise, argues Cuban (2001). While a 'good' school has, by definition, become 'a technologically equipped one' (ibid.: 159), technological changes take far longer to implement in formal education than in business because schools are citizen-controlled and non-profit (ibid.: 153). In addition, 'As systems, they [schools] are multipurpose, many-layered, labor-intensive, relationship-dependent, and profoundly conservative' (ibid.).

Although 'eventually' teachers will increase 'the frequency, breadth, and integration of advanced information technologies into their classroom routines' (ibid.: 152), this has to happen in a context where teachers have more say over how technologies are being used and designed. Thus ICT is not a panacea in itself – good teaching still remains crucial to good education (Fallows and Bhanot 2002).

In any case, it can be concluded that, while the impact of globalization and new ICT processes has so far been uneven, complex and discriminatory, the impact of the future these discourses envision has been more unified. This future has influenced authors and educators across the board, whether opposing or championing it. There is a general agreement about the new emerging social and educational order – a prediction about a certain future to which everybody will have to adjust, eventually. Because of these 'predictions' – for example, in regard to new ICTs – it has become very hard to '...avoid encountering the avowedly evangelical predictions about the educational implications of the digital "this" and the electronic "that", and the triumphalist announcements of the optimists introducing the education superhighway here and the virtual university there' (Mason 1998: 3).

Even 'critical' education theorists have been 'affected'. For example:

> As we enter a new millennium, most people are by now aware that we are in the midst of one of the most dramatic technological revolutions in history that is changing everything from the ways that we work, communicate, and spend our leisure time. The technological revolution centers on computer, information, communication, and multimedia technologies, is often interpreted as the beginnings of a knowledge or information society, and therefore ascribes education a central role in every aspect of life. This Great Transformation poses tremendous challenges to educators to rethink their basic tenets, to deploy the new technologies in creative and productive ways, and to restructure schooling to respond constructively and progressively to the technological and social changes that we are now experiencing.
>
> (Kellner 2000b: 245)

And, 'There can be little doubt that new technologies are helping to bring into effect a new economic order, call it what you will' (Kenway 1996: 227).

Thus, the way these hegemonic futures operate in the contemporary discourses on social and educational change is one example of the creation of a particular regime of truth and of putting epistemological power into action (Foucault 1982). But, as maintained in the Introduction, the Foucauldian take on power also implies that the process of normalization is never complete, and that resistance is always possible. Things could always be other than they are (Edwards and Usher 2000) and other than they appear to be/are becoming. That is, there are many possible sites of subversion and resistance – sites of imagining and envisioning different futures.

Part III

Searching for social and educational alternatives

> Opposition is not enough. In that vacant space after one has resisted there is still the necessity to become – to make oneself anew.
>
> (hooks 1991: 15)

> You must have a positive alternative, a vision of a better future that can motivate people to sacrifice their time and energy towards its realization.
>
> (Alcoff 1988: 418)

Introductory remarks

While there are many alternatives challenging both the modernist and the globalized and cyber vision of/for education, I analyse feminist visions, the recovery of indigenous education and spiritual education in detail. These alternatives offer foundational challenges to the hegemony of the modernist vision.

The feminist alternative in education is crucial because it is the approach that has so far thrown out the deepest challenge to patriarchal interpretations of time, history, future and knowledge. Further, the recovery of indigenous traditions in education and spiritual education challenge the way time, history, future, knowledge and education have been understood and framed within the mainstream western intellectual tradition. They are not mere add-ons that can be incorporated into the modernist paradigm through incremental change.

While these (and other) alternatives do overlap in some ways, I here discuss feminist, spiritual and indigenous alternatives in terms of their main *core*; that is, in terms of what stand out as *fundamental* issues, concerns and strategies within each of these discourses – alternative

Figure 7 Millennium Tree © Josephine Wall. www.josephinewall.co. uk.
Used under license from Art Impressions, Canoga Pk., CA.[1]

visions. For example, there are basic similarities in spiritual, holistic
and eco-centric visions of education. Holistic education is spiritual
as spirituality is an integral part of the whole. Spiritual education is
holistic in that it is 'encompassing all of life' (Erricker and Erricker
2001: xi). The environmental, ecological education vision is close to
holistic and spiritual alternatives in its 'deep ecology' approach. At
the same time, these three alternatives, while having many similarities, still have their own sets of 'educational truths' – the fundamental

core of what they are about (Milojević 2002b: 306–310). As well, their 'legitimacy' within the mainstream differs. Of these three alternatives, it is the ecological discourse that has managed to capture the public imagination most successfully. Similar to the globalization discourse (Burbules and Torres 2000: 2), 'ecology' too has become a catchword, an ideological discourse driving change because of a perceived immediacy and necessity to respond to a particular order, in this case, environmental degradation. Indeed, many assert that ecology is the emerging new grand narrative (Myerson 2001). But others warn that this discourse, too, is currently being coopted by, for example, being interpreted in terms of 'more politically acceptable forms of education' (Fien 1992: 9) that do not go far enough. That is, they do not incorporate a new environmental paradigm that views people and nature as interdependent (ibid.), but implement mostly ameliorative approaches that dilute what environmental education is/should be about. This incorporation has taken place in relation to feminist discourses as well; for example, when 'boys' failure' is attributed to too much feminism in education. Analysis of the core of feminist alternatives, as will be seen later, shows that girls' success at the expense of boys is as far removed from the feminist ideal of 'partnership' society/feminist pedagogy as is the previous success of boys at the cost of girls' exclusion. Thus, the recovery of these and other 'forgotten' aspects of various alternatives is important in reclaiming them as legitimate discourses for the future.

In addition to the radical 'otherness' of feminist, indigenous and spiritual alternatives, and the mainstream educational model, there is a range of educational futures. Along with the holistic and environmental and the globalized and cyber are the humanistic, global (not globalized), multicultural, peace, back-to-basics, elitist, religious and nationalist models. Thus, there is a range of alternatives – from the Left to the Right, past to the future, elite to populist, secular to religious – all vying for legitimacy and, indeed, hegemony. These alternatives express themselves differently according to location and history.[2]

The point in mentioning these alternatives is first to acknowledge that there *are* alternatives to the present. There is not one future. Second, that certain alternatives fit better into the modernist template and thus are considered more realistic. It is this point that is crucial: these alternatives are considered more plausible because some of their dimensions can be better appropriated by the modernist. Third, to acknowledge how societies put 'into operation an entire machinery for producing true discourses' (Foucault 1980: 69), including what visions of and for the future are to be legitimate. For example, the globalization discourse can be used to justify both 'new Right ideologies of market liberalism and social conservativism' (Blackmore 2000: 135), or demands for a more inclusive and multicultural world. This discourse can inform both those who demand the return to 'good old fashioned' values in education and those who demand that the curriculum should be radically transformed and more inclusive. But, while various social groups use the same discourses for their diverse strategies, some discourses become normative, or 'the truth' about the future (e.g. globalization, globalized education), others dissenting or 'utopian' (e.g. vision of global education). Analysis of various dominant and alternative visions for the future shows the ways in which certain regimes of educational truths – at the end of the twentieth century and the beginning of the twenty-first – emerged in the west as a product of particular discursive practices.

The alternatives I have chosen for further analysis allow us to remark, rethink and challenge the foundations of modernist education, and the alternatives considered the most real and relevant (globalized and cyber). While I use a similar template to that already applied in Part II, the focus here is on three main questions: (1) In which ways, if at all, are these alternative visions different from the hegemonic futures visions, and to what degree? (2) What is their main approach to time, how is history interpreted and what is the guiding (desired, implied) vision for the future? and (3) What is the connection between these guiding futures images and educational visions for the future?

8   Visions III: feminist alternatives

Feminism and education: introductory remarks

The twentieth-century feminist movement, ideology, theory and philosophy produced a wealth of social and educational visions for the future. Feminist writings on the futures of education, and the subsequent development of alternative educational models, fundamentally disrupted the many givens in futures and educational discourses. The Golden Age of feminist visioning belongs to the second wave of feminism, starting in the west in, roughly, the 1960s and culminating in the 1980s. This section analyses the feminist visioning that developed in the 1980s and continued into the 1990s, in particular, visioning based on the distinctiveness of 'women's ways of knowing', doing and being. This phase, however, needs to be firstly contextualized within a history of the feminist movement and theory and feminist engagement with education.

Arguments for the distinctiveness of women's ways of knowing have been based, as Ferguson (1993: 61) argues, on approaches either within *praxis feminism*, which focus on the distinctiveness of what women are said *to do*, or on approaches within *cosmic feminism*, which focus more on what women are said *to be*. More concretely, female experience has most often been defined by '…mothering and reproduction; by the political economy of the gendered division of labor; by the arrangements of the female body; by women's connection to non-human nature; by spirituality and contact with the divine' (ibid.).

Numerous authors (e.g. Annas 1978; Hartsock 1983; Jaggar 1983) also argue that women's ways of knowing are not only different from the dominant perspective (of the white, male, middle- or upper-class social group), but that a feminist perspective is, in fact, more 'accurate' and 'complete'. Standpoint epistemology, developed by these authors, implies that less powerful members of society have the potential to form a more complete view of social reality because they are aware and of sensitive to both the dominant worldview of the society and their own (Nielsen 1990: 10). As argued by hooks:

> I [am] not speaking of a marginality one wishes to lose, to give up, or surrender as part of moving into the center, but rather as a site one stays in, clings to even, because it nourishes one's capacity to resist. It offers the possibility of radical perspectives from which to see and create, to imagine alternatives, new worlds.
>
> (hooks 1990: 34)

Because of the ability to incorporate a more complete view of social reality, such 'double vision' means that less is assumed and more examined and that, therefore, the appropriate metaphor to describe such a shift is the 'turn of a spiral, not the flip of a coin' (Thiele 1986: 41).

Similar arguments have been developed in the area of futures studies. Masini (1993b, 2002), for example, has repeatedly argued that women have a better-developed capacity to create alternatives for the future than that men have. She argues that this is because of certain women's individual capacities and social capacities that are well documented by empirical work (ibid.: 255). Influential 'pop futurists', such as Aburdene and Naisbitt, in their *Megatrends for Women* (1992), argue along similar lines. According to them, successful human beings, now and even more so in the future, will need to possess a combination of traditional masculine and feminine traits; to be, for example, competitive and compassionate, goal-oriented and nurturing, intuitive and risk-taking (ibid.: 262). This means that the 'cardboard, one-dimensional females and males alike are doomed to failure' (ibid.). While the struggle to become a gender hybrid seems to rest on the shoulders of each individual, Aburdene and Naisbitt go further to argue that, as a social group, women have absorbed positive masculine traits more successfully than most men have integrated desirable female characteristics; women have therefore evolved into 'a more complex state of wholeness' (ibid.). This is because patriarchal societies have for a long time devalued feminine characteristics, so that men had 'little incentive to integrate them until recently' (ibid.).

In terms of their politics and visionary input, insights by authors such as Masini, Aburdene and Naisbitt, and the arguments developed by standpoint epistemology are crucial. But, it is also important to note that the arguments of the distinctiveness of 'women's visions' fail to completely satisfy academic rigour. That is, given the diversity among the world's women, in-group differences can be as big as differences between the two genders. Even within the same (e.g. western) culture, and even within a reasonably unified social movement, such as feminism, there is a myriad of perspectives and worldviews. The introduction by Putnam Tong to *Feminist Thought* (1998), for example, identifies eight distinctive positions within feminism – from older liberal, radical and Marxist/social feminist to the more recent, psychoanalytic/gender, existentialist, postmodern, multicultural/global and eco-feminist perspectives. In addition, at least three more perspectives need to be included as completely distinct rather than being discussed within the previous positions – for example, lesbian, cyber and spiritual feminism. This variety demonstrates that while politically there may be a consensus on where priorities, seen in futures visions, are, epistemologically it is impossible to identify even *a* feminist vision for the future, let alone 'women's'. As any universalist statement about woman/women can easily be challenged from the position of epistemological (and group) minorities, it is impossible to assert what 'women's approaches to time' or 'women's visions of the future' might be.

Still, I here argue for the distinctiveness of 'feminist' or 'women's' visions and perspectives – as developed by western feminists – on several grounds. First, as Putnam Tong (1998) and hooks (2000) maintain, the diversity within women's visions and among feminists that is *heard* nowadays is one more argument that supports the claim about the women's movements' strengths rather than weaknesses. They testify that feminist thought, 'like all other time-honored modes of thinking...has a past as well as a present and a future' (Putnam Tong 1998: 1). The diversity within women's visions therefore does not annul the existence of such visions (feminist, women's), albeit it does make a singular utopia an impossibility. Second, it has been repeatedly argued by feminists themselves that, despite all differences within feminism and various other women's movements that refused to be identified as such, there is a core (of beliefs, values, epistemological positions) that is rarely challenged. This widely accepted core commonly incorporates acknowledgement of the following:

- gender issues are important, the influence of gender is pervasive;
- knowledge is socially constructed;
- there are deep structures but there is also the possibility of change;

- current imbalances in the world exist partly because women's perspectives, experiences and knowledge are marginalized;
- feminist and women-centred theories and approaches provide a basis for understanding every area of individual and social lives; they are not just a laundry list of 'women's issues';
- the main goal is the reorganization of the world based on sex (gender) equality/partnership in all human relations;
- there is a commitment to struggling against racial, class, sexual and heterosexual oppression, as well as against other oppressions based on a hierarchy of differences;
- feminism (and other women-centred approaches) is political theory, practice, social movement, worldview and way of life; and
- the feminist (women's) perspective can affect the world politically, culturally, economically and spiritually, and bring about significantly different futures.

Third, while acknowledging various differences, it is also possible to develop a position of 'strategic essentialism' (Spivak 1985) that both argues for the distinctiveness of women's perspectives and positions, and is aware that these are predominantly socially constructed discourses. This strategic essentialism is also used and applied in discourses created by other disadvantaged groups (e.g. 'non-western' people). In any case, whether presented as an essentialist or socially constructed discourse, feminist engagement with education theory and practice has always relied on narratives that assumed the existence of social groups such as 'women', 'girls', 'men' and 'boys'.

Four feminist turns... and the backlash

Of course, feminist discourse has evolved, changed and transformed during the course of the last four decades. Since the 1960s, feminist intervention in the area of education took at least four main 'turns'. These include: (1) liberal feminist; (2) gender and education research; (3) radical/women's ways of knowing; and (4) a poststructural/ diversity phase. More recently, post-feminist and 'what-about-the-boys' phases have come to mark discussions around gender and education issues.

Initially, during the liberal feminist phase, feminists campaigned for equal access to education for women and argued against the separate acquisition of feminine skills (Humm 1989: 60). The focus was to reverse/transform patriarchal history, wherein women's exclusion from formal education or inclusion within a context that sharply polarized genders was the norm. What was sought was equality and equal inclusion of women into existing social and educational institutions.

The second phase focused on the critique: the ways in which education functions as the major vehicle for the reproduction of gender inequality. The most often criticized aspects of modern education include:

- existence of 'hidden curricula', i.e. different treatment for boys and girls in such a way that existing gender inequalities are maintained;
- fragmentation of knowledge into discrete specializations where everything has to be classified, measured, categorized and presented in terms of higher and lower achievements;
- lack of topics of interest for women (e.g. childbirth, housework, sexual abuse, family relationships, peaceful management of our species through history, daily life and work);
- bias against women in most textbooks; and
- concentration on 'big' names and 'big' events, as well as on teachings about the conquest and domination of the Others (including nature) (Milojević 1998: 87).

In the area of education, much of the feminist work through the 1970s and early 1980s could be characterized as 'gender and education' research (Luke and Gore 1992: 8; Kenway and Modra 1992):

> Throughout that period [1970s and 1980s], the results of gender and education research filtered through to state and federal commissions and inquiries into girls and schooling and subsequently into educational policies and curricula. Policy texts prescribed the need for gender-inclusive curricula and for girls' greater access to and participation in maths and sciences, sports and physical education. Curricular texts began to give girls equal representational space. More textual illustrations of and reference to girls became evident...Equal classroom time, equal numerical participation, and equal curricular presence were the main aims and outcomes of the 1970s and 1980s gender and education research.
>
> (Luke and Gore 1992: 8)

The third turn has been inspired by, but has moved away from, the critique. It has focused on the development of alternative educational models that transcend previous limitations while including women's experiences and 'ways of knowing': 'Reflecting the separatist move of much feminism of that period [1980s], the construction of feminist pedagogy in Women's Studies gave limited attention to male-authored constructions of pedagogy, with Paulo Freire's work the only significant exception' (ibid.). The main impact of this approach was the further development of Women's Studies, as an alternative to current education, informed by alternative visions for the future:

> Women's Studies, diverse as its components are, has at its best shared a vision of a world free not only from sexism but also from racism, class-bias, agism, heterosexual bias – from all the ideologies and institutions that have consciously or unconsciously oppressed and exploited some for the advantage of others... The uniqueness of Women's Studies has been its refusal to accept sterile divisions between academy and community, between intellect and passion, between the individual and society. Women's Studies... is equipping women to transform [society].
> (Charter document of the National Women's Studies Association 1977, quoted in Kenway and Modra 1992: 149)

Since it was introduced in the late 1960s and early 1970s, Women's Studies programmes and courses have expanded 'dramatically' (Hoffmann and Stake 1998). They can now be found not only in the majority of universities in the west but in universities throughout the world.

The fourth turn is consistent with this expansion, and is mostly characterized by the widening of feminist analysis and (predominantly internal) critique. First, those critical of Women's Studies in general started to question the legitimacy of pedagogic approaches used. The main argument is that feminist education in fact discourages independent thinking, overemphasizes students' personal experience, is overly politicized, promotes anti-intellectualism and intolerance, replaces inquiry with ideology, and free expression with dogma (ibid.). Second, those coming from the education field questioned the distinctiveness of pedagogical approaches within Women's Studies (e.g. Gore 1993; Kenway and Modra 1992). The third critique was by representatives of group minorities, especially lesbians and women of colour (Gunew 1990: 29–31). These theorists (e.g. Adrienne Rich, Gayatri Spivak, bell hooks) questioned the unifying and universalist approach that characterized much of the visioning developed in the previous phase, and challenged some of the most common assumptions that underlie feminist visions of transformative education. For example, bell hooks raised the issue of literacy as pertinent to people of colour, the issue of covert racism, the inability to be heard or of being put in the spotlight to speak for their whole race in the feminist classroom:

> In a feminist classroom, especially a Women's Studies course, the black student, who has had no previous background in feminist studies, usually finds that she or he is in a class that is predominantly white (often attended by a majority of outspoken young, white, radical feminists, many of whom link this politic to issues of gay rights). Unfamiliarity with the issues may lead black students to feel at a disadvantage both academically and culturally (they may not be accustomed to public discussions of sexual practice). If a black student acknowledges that she is not familiar with the work of Audre Lorde and the rest of the class gasps as though this is unthinkable and reprehensive, that gasp evokes the sense that feminism is really a private cult whose members are usually white...Suddenly, the feminist classroom is no longer a safe haven, the way many [in] Women's Studies imagine it will be, but is instead a site of conflict, tensions, and sometimes ongoing hostility.
>
> (hooks 1994: 113)

The fourth critique came mostly from the poststructural, postmodern orientation, and has highlighted inherent inconsistencies and contradictions within feminist thought, such as issues of power, control, authority and so on. For example, Janice Raymond argued that non-hierarchical practices can, in effect, prevent women from '...discovering and using their own individual strength and can also encourage them to endeavor to achieve their goals through the exercise of indirect power or even manipulation within a group' (quoted in Kenway and Modra 1992: 162). And, '...no real power emerges from a group that silences its best and brightest voices for a false sense of group equality. And certainly no strong friendships can be formed among women who have no power of being' (ibid.).

Perhaps because of this internal critique, or perhaps because of the ongoing backlash against feminism, the current 'fifth' turn emerged, marked by a pronounced weakening of the feminist discourses in education. As well, as the 'what-about-the-boys' debate testifies, the success of some feminist intervention in education seems to have annulled the need for these very interventions for 'this day and age'.

In these debates, some go as far as to suggest that educational establishments are now so thoroughly infused with feminist ideals and ideology that we are in fact in the midst of *The War Against Boys* (Hoff Sommers, Simon and Schuster 2000). Alternatively, it is argued that it is 'the feminisation of curricula and assessment systems' (Commonwealth of Australia 2002), together with other factors such as absence of fathers and male teachers, the declining status of men and the prevalence of negative, violent hypermasculine stereotypes in the media (ibid.), that may be 'guilty' for placing boys on the weaker side of the education gender gap. But, have feminist visions really been fulfilled – in most western societies and/or in the educational system? And, is the failing 'achievement' of boys truly due to feminist goals now being realized?

In the following section, I argue that while girls currently 'thriving' in schools may satisfy liberal feminist visions, the current education system is still a far cry from educational goals as developed within feminist eutopias based on the distinctiveness of women's ways of knowing. Furthermore, the previous 'what-about-the-boys' discourse forgets that such gendered analysis would not have been possible prior to the invention of the very category of gender by feminists. As well, it ignores that this educational hierarchical system, even while favouring girls, is as far from the feminist desired model as the previous system within which the girls were disadvantaged. It is, of course, the hierarchy itself that radical feminists sought to dismantle – partly by acknowledging the pervasive influence of gender. These connections will become more obvious, once feminists' preferred visions for the future are discussed.

To summarize, so far I have outlined the context of feminist educational alternatives. I next investigate the connection between educational and futures visions developed by women who are influenced by feminist theory. To do so, I investigate an alternative approach to time and vision for the future that is argued to be 'women's'. These alternatives were mostly developed in a particular historical moment – the 1980s in OECD nations in response to radical feminists' demands to go beyond liberal concerns with inclusion, but prior to the general increase in popularity of postmodern theory amongst the Left. I then analyse the worldview, epistemology and approach to knowledge behind these visions, and ask how they are connected with particular educational visions. Finally, I investigate feminist utopian promises and apply CLA to feminist writing on the futures of education and the subsequent development of alternative educational models.

Approaches to time and visions for the future

Feminism originally developed within an exclusively western, linear approach to time arguing for further 'progress' and development, which predominantly meant women's inclusion within already existing institutions. Then, various approaches that argued for the distinctiveness of *Women's Ways of Knowing* (Belenky *et al.* 1986) 'discovered' that women's approach to time differs from the dominant, linear, instrumental, industrial, patriarchal 'clock' time.

For example, authors in *Taking Our Time: Feminist Perspectives on Temporality* (edited by Forman and Sowton 1989) argue that to think about time within patriarchal history is to think within man-centred epistemologies (O'Brien 1989: 14). They introduced the concept of a patriarchal time, which is an 'abstract time', 'time out of mind', for example, in Hegelian dialectics (Forman and Sowton 1989: ix). Women's time as historical time is a contradiction, argues Deeds Ermarth (1989: 37), because the discourse of historical time exists 'in the first place by means of the crucial exclusion or repression of women'. This linear time, which Kristeva (1981: 17) calls 'the time of project and history', is now taken for granted, as a given, as 'natural'. Women's time does not fit within the time of the project and history because, 'Like their personal lives, women's history is fragmented, interrupted; a shadow history of human beings whose existence has been shaped by the efforts and the demands of others' (Elizabeth Janeway, quoted in Deeds Ermarth 1989: 42).

The best way to define women's time is, then, to look at the past within more gender-balanced matrilinear societies, where 'time itself was considered female' (Forman and Sowton 1989: xii). Here, we move to viewing time predominantly as 'event time', or 'cyclical like the seasons', 'spiral', 'dialectical', 'chaotic', 'contradictory', 'knowing no beginning and no end' and 'life as it is lived'.

It is important to note here that it is often argued, predominantly by postmodernists in general and postmodern feminists in particular, that one should stay away from locking women's and men's differences within binary approaches because these not only lack epistemological justification but in effect disempower women themselves. For example, by fixing women's time as 'cyclical' – the particular experience of some women during a particular era (the past, agricultural one) – time is essentialized and romanticized. While aware that women's approaches to time and their preferred vision for the future vary along the political and epistemological continuum, I suggest that it is crucial to look at the 'essential core' among these various approaches. The main argument here, for example, is not to assert that so-called 'women's time' applies to all women at all times of their lives (Adam 1995: 94), because it does not. Rather, it is to argue that 'women's time' can be used as 'an exemplar for times lived, given and generated in the shadow of the hegemony of universal clock time' (ibid.). The main purpose here is not to establish 'new dualisms and dualities' but to 'sensitize us to a complexity largely untheorized and left implicit in social science analyses that focus on some aspects of time to the exclusion of others' (ibid.). In addition, when we compare multiple times, we can 'begin to see that not all times are equal' and that some times are 'clearly privileged and deemed more important than others' (ibid.). This is, of course, the case not only for the various approaches to time but also for various approaches to the future, including those that focus on educational issues. Outlining various alternatives, in this case, women's, serves the purpose of both challenging hegemonic futures visions and making present decisions about the future more informed.

In any case, compared with 'historical time', 'women's time' is not abstract or time out of mind, but 'experienced time', 'species time', 'common time' (O'Brien 1989: 14):

> Men have used mind for the sorts of understanding of reality embedded in the history of the conquest of time, men's history. Women 'mind' the children. The obvious thing that is wrong with this is the failure to realize that the first is destructive of history, a quest for Nirvana, the periodization of abstract heroes arrogantly symbolized in the cyclically insignificant death of the deified individual: the second – coping all the time – is the absolute condition of a human existence in time. Human history has meaning only in species time, a reality dimly recalled by 'remembering' our individual birthdays while forgetting the cyclical integrity of species life.
>
> (O'Brien 1989: 14)

Nothing can be more distinctive of 'women's experiences' than giving birth to children, and this theme is also used to argue for the distinctiveness of women's approaches to time. As previously argued by O'Brien, the main difference is in the shift from 'a death-determined future to a birth-determined one' (Forman and Sowton 1989: 7). While not all women give birth, those that do become intimately aware of the difference between time that follows the motion of the clock and organic, event time:

> the woman in labor experiences herself not as moving with time [of the clock] but as moving in it. For her, time stands still, moments flow together, the past and the future do not lie still behind and before her. In place of sequence, and linear relation, there is an overwhelming richness of sensation, which pulls her attention from the outer world. She is immersed in the immediacy of her experience. Her body is no longer a neutral background for her consciousness.
>
> (Fox 1989: 132)

Because most women spend time caring, loving, educating and managing a household, and because most experience female times of menstruation, pregnancy, childbirth and lactation, women are familiar with times that operate according to non-economic principles, argues Adam (1995: 95). These times, of caring, loving, education and so on, can neither be 'forced into timetables, schedules and deadlines nor allocated a monetary value' (ibid.). They are open-ended, not so much 'time measured, spent, allocated and controlled as *time lived, time made and time generated*' (ibid.). These time-generated and time-giving activities have '...no place in the meaning cluster of quantity, measure, dates and deadlines, of calculability, abstract exchange value, efficiency and profit' (ibid.).

Because currently all work relations are touched by clock time and tied up with hegemony and power, women's time is rendered invisible and outside normative time as well as outside basic assumptions and categories of classical social science analysis (ibid.: 94–95). As mentioned earlier, Adam (1998) also argues that the problem with industrial/patriarchal time is in discounting both nature and the future. Nature is discounted on the grounds of assumptions that view the earth as 'a man-made machine', and the future by being given less value than the present (ibid.: 74, 79). Because they stayed in 'the shadow of the hegemony of universal clock time' (Adam 1995: 94), women are more closely aware of the existence of now-devalued 'natural' time – event time or 'species time' and 'generational time'.

This particular theme, of time as generational, has best been developed by Elise Boulding in her concept of the 200 year present. Boulding (1990: 3) argues that the time frame used to both make foreign policy and live our personal lives is too short and narrow.

In many cultures – for example, within the traditional Indian approach to time discussed in Part I – the sense of time and history is much broader; it is also sometimes *so large* as to make individual human events seem insignificant. On the other hand:

> Between these extremes there lies a medium range of time which is neither too long nor too short for immediate comprehension, and which has an organic quality that gives it relevance for the present movement. This medium range is the 200 year present. That present begins 100 years ago today, on the day of birth of those among us who are centenarians. Its other boundary is the hundredth birthday of the babies born today. This present is a continuously moving movement, always reaching out 100 years in either direction from the day we are in. We are linked with both boundaries of this moment by the people among us whose life began or will end at one of those boundaries, five generations each way in time. It is our space, one that we can move around in directly in our own lives and indirectly by touching the lives of the young and old around us.
>
> (Boulding 1990: 4)

The gender-balanced society

This approach to time is important within what Boulding (1977: 221) calls 'gentle society'; a society situated within a decentralized and demilitarized, yet still interconnected and interdependent world. This 'gentle' society is predominately androgynous, and will be created by androgynous human beings. Like Aburdene and Naisbitt (1992), Boulding argues that these androgynous human beings combine qualities both of gentleness and of assertiveness in ways that fit neither typical male nor typical female roles. The gentle society will be created through three main leverage points. These points are education, particularly in the early-childhood school setting of nursery school and early elementary school; family; and community.

Another theorist who has destabilized the usual approach to time and history is Riane Eisler. Eisler (1987, 1995, 2000) has developed a cultural transformation theory that includes gender theory as transformation praxis (Inayatullah 1998b: 44). She argues that the best way to understand our past, our present and the possibilities for the future is by 'charting the dynamic interaction of two movements' (Eisler 1997: 141):

The first is the tendency of social systems to move toward greater complexity, largely because of technological breakthroughs of phase changes. The second is the movement of cultural shifts between two basic organizational forms or 'attractors': the dominator and partnership models.

(Eisler 1997: 141)

One main difference between these two models is that the templating of the dominator models 'gives high priority to technologies for domination and destruction', whereas the templating of the partnership model 'gives high priority to technologies that sustain and enhance life' (ibid.). Eisler's two basic models describe systems of belief and social structures that either nurture and support or inhibit and undermine equitable, democratic, non-violent and caring relations. At one end is the partnership model that embodies equity, environmental sustainability, multiculturalism and gender-fairness. At the opposite end of the continuum is the dominator model, which emphasizes control, authoritarianism, violence, gender discrimination and environmental degradation. Most importantly, they represent two basic underlying alternatives for human relations, irrespective of technological and economic change.

Eisler draws on the work of Marija Gimbutas and other women archeologists who assert that there is enough evidence to support the claim that the partnership model existed before being swept away by androcratic and patriarchal societies. But while androcracy has been the dominating model for millennia, Eisler also argues (in common with Aburdene and Naisbitt) that our era is characterized by a renewal of partnership with a strong movement towards more balanced societies already underway in some places. The *partnership society is clearly the desired future*, not only for Eisler but also for almost all other women futurists, visionaries, theorists, feminists and women's movements' social activists. Given the homogenous, corporatist and patriarchal tendencies within the currently dominant globalized and cyber vision for the world, it is questionable whether this future is likely to emerge as another hegemonic ideal. But clearly, for Eisler and many others, if it does not, what is at stake is nothing less than the survival of the human species. In this nuclear/electronic/biochemical age, concludes Eisler, transformation towards a partnership society is a necessity, but whether it will occur or not is far from certain. The difference between such a view of history and the future, as opposed to hegemonic futures visions that argue about the inevitability of certain futures, is the difference between choice and determinism. As argued previously, one of the core beliefs of feminists and women's movements is that while patriarchy is ubiquitous there is, indeed, a possibility of change. This possibility of change exists at the micro level (the level of the individual, personal, immediate community) and also at the macro level (broader society, nation states, international society).

While arguments about diversity among women abound, similar visions emerge wherever they are claimed to be distinctively 'women's'. For example, in *The Fabric of the Future* (Ryan 1998) and the 1997 special issue of *The Futurist* on 'What Women Want' (Wagner 1997), as well as in *Women of Spirit* (Jones 1995), the majority of women envision futures inclusive of gentle ways of organizing human affairs. The preferred futures outlined in *The Futurist* focus on the following issues: the breaking of glass ceilings; establishment of representation of the sexes at all levels of government; creation of human-scaled institutions; establishment of equal education for women throughout the world as well as adequate community- and business-based childcare; demilitarization leading to less war, crime and violence in general; maintenance of the clean environment based on principles of sustainability; and creation of inclusive futures that benefit all of humanity, including men. The perspectives outlined in *Women of Spirit* are best summarized by Pregaluxmi Govender, who argues that:

> The struggles to transform human relationships are the most difficult and they are at the core of the transformation of the world. The struggle to change ourselves, the struggle to change our relationships and the struggle to change the world seem to be exclusive of each other, yet they go hand in hand.
>
> (in Jones 1995: 6–7)

The thrust of the previous two compilations is slightly different: focused on external change – as in the case of *The Futurist* – and focused on internal change – as in the case of *Women of Spirit*. This distinction is, however, challenged by authors in *The Fabric of the Future* (Ryan 1998). This compilation incorporates visions by both western and non-western women – both groups coming from strong spiritual, eco-centric perspectives. While *The Fabric of the Future* compilation, previously mentioned, is too broad to be summarized here (500 pp., 38 authors), what will suffice is to say that the main themes follow two key arguments previously made. These are: first, humanity is 'at the crossroads', living between the old and a new emerging path; and second, this new emerging path is questing for wholeness where possible/desirable futures are 'co-created'.

One of the rare texts that summarizes 'Third World Women's Perspectives' is a vision expressed by Gita Sen and Caren Grown for the project Development Alternatives with Women for a New Era (DAWN). Written in 1984, this summary is important because it is these perspectives that are most commonly invisible and marginalized – even within feminism. The paragraph which summarizes DAWN's vision is worth quoting at length:

> We want a world where inequality based on class, gender, and race is absent from every country, and from the relationships among countries. We want a world where basic needs become basic rights and where poverty and all forms of violence are eliminated. Each person will have the opportunity to develop her or his full potential and creativity, and women's values of nurturance and solidarity will characterize human relationships. In such a world women's reproductive role will be redefined: child care will be shared by men, women, and society as a whole. We want a world where the massive resources now used in the production of the means of destruction will be diverted to areas where they will help to relieve oppression both inside and outside the home. This technological revolution will eliminate disease and hunger, and give women means for the safe control of their fertility. We want a world where all institutions are open to participatory democratic processes, where women share in determining priorities and making decisions.
>
> (Sen and Grown 1984: 80–81)

Feminist science fiction and utopian visions

The visions outlined in this and previous compilations, in the work of Boulding, Eisler and other women futurists such as Henderson (1999), Sahtouris (2000) and Marx Hubbard (1998), are in many ways similar to the visions that exist in feminist utopian and science fiction. As argued by feminist utopian and science fiction critics (e.g. Bartkowski 1989; Halbert 1994; Sargisson 1996), the common themes in most feminist novels are:

> future societies tend to live in 'peace' with nature and have some sort of sustainable growth, they are generally less violent than present ones; families seldom take a nuclear form but are

more extended (often including relatives and friends); communal life is highly valued; societies are rarely totalitarian; oppressive and omnipotent governmental and bureaucratic control is usually absent, while imagined societies tend to be either 'anarchical' or communally managed.

(Milojević 1998: 90)

As further elaborated by Marge Piercy:

One characteristic of societies imagined by feminists [in feminist science fiction] is how little isolated women are from each other. Instead of the suburban dream turned nightmare in which each house contained a woman alone and climbing the walls, or the yuppie apartment house where no one speaks but each has perfect privacy in her little electronic box, the societies women dream up tend to be long coffee klatches or permanent causal meetings. Everybody is in everybody else's hair...[there is] freedom from fear of rape and domestic violence...society is decentralized...nurturing is a strong value...communal responsibility for a child begins at birth.

(Piercy 2003: 137)

Feminist science fiction has now grown to such an extent that there are numerous compilations (e.g. Bartkowski 1989; Sargisson 1996) and countless web pages discussing it. Preliminary research suggests that, contrary to mainstream/malestream science fiction that either does not portray education at all, or where learning is technologically mediated and instantaneous, the worlds imagined within feminist fiction are quite different. Not only are current gender relationships challenged – this is the most common theme – but education and parenting are extremely respected and sometimes the main purpose for the existence of these imaginary worlds (Milojević 1998: 90).

To sum up the previous discussion, feminist alternatives still have a common core that provides a reasonably unified vision for the future. The main characteristics of this vision include a shift from death, power, competition and hierarchy-based glorifications to a vision where life, love, caring and equality are more valued. There is an emphasis that the future in front of us depends on our actions today, rather than solely on some universal, omnipotent and irreversible 'objective' processes. In addition, while hegemonic futures visions claim to be about 'the real', feminist alternatives are unashamedly utopian.

Given that feminism is predominantly western, it could be expected that it has focused mostly on eutopian and external measures when it comes to social change. However, feminist alternatives do, perhaps unintentionally, take into account the concept of eupshychia, the development of the 'good' self. This is because feminists argue for the expansion of 'one-dimensional', emotionless, 'cardboard' humans – an image central to industrial, patriarchal and modern society. As argued by Nielsen:

> The fact that Descartes's ontological reality (his sense of existence of being) was grounded in thinking rather than, say, feeling or loving – he did not say 'I feel (or love); therefore, I am' – illustrates an extraordinary trust in rational thought.
>
> (Nielsen 1990: 2)

Feminists have therefore argued for an ontological reality that incorporates not only the rational but also the emotional aspects of one's being. While in general staying short of including spiritual aspects of one's self, feminists have made important steps towards arguing for the inclusion of internal psychological processes in education. This change is not always seen to be about external outcomes (performance, skills) and cumulative rational effects; rather, what becomes equally important is how one is transformed through education (towards empowerment).

These previously outlined (utopian) futures visions are implicit in educational alternatives developed by feminist theorists and activists – in particular, within the development of 'Women's Studies'. This field is one of the more concrete manifestations of the feminist educational 'ideal model'. Most significantly, the previously outlined approach to time and vision of the future changes not only education from within – that is, educational content, structure, process and subject – but also, more importantly, how education as a whole is situated within society. In short, these visions imply a prioritizing of parenting and education, a world where 'education, welfare, and eldercare [are] getting all the money they need, and the military would have to hold bake sales' (Walker 2000: 361).

Educational visions

As is the case with broader futures visions, there are many tensions in terms of what feminist education should be about. However, I argue here that – in keeping with the previous discussion – it is possible to identify a common core of what constitutes (ideal) feminist education or more specifically, feminist pedagogy. As McDonald and Canchez-Cazal write:

> The feminist pedagogical principles that guide our classroom strategies – decentering the authority of the professor, developing and foregrounding subjugated knowledges, legitimizing personal identity and experience as the foundation of authentic and liberatory knowledges (especially marginalized identities and experiences), discussion-based classes, emphasis on student voice – have enormous power to democratize knowledge production in the classroom...
>
> (McDonald and Canchez-Cazal 2002: 5)

Similarly, Arnot (1994: 84) asserted that while the variety of 'educational moments' – feminist interventions and visions – seen separately may appear inconsequential, when put together they comprise a pattern that is qualitatively different. The following discussion identifies this qualitatively different pattern, or the core of feminist visioning and alternatives in education. The representation will be consistent with feminist epistemology that focuses on the collaborative efforts of many writers. That is, particular themes are followed here, rather than particular authors and their approaches. The texts from which I draw themes include Belenky *et al.* 1986, Bignell 1996, Boulding 1990, Bright 1993, Bunch 1983, Bunch and Pollack 1983, Clark *et al.* 1995, Cohee *et al.* 1998, Cohen *et al.* 1999, Coffey and Delamont 2000, Culley and Portuges 1985, De Francisco 1996, Eisler 2000, Friedman 1998, Gore 1993, Greenberg 1982, Gunew 1990, hooks 1994, Hoffmann and Stake 1998, Marx Hubbard 1998, Kramarae 1996, Lather 1991a,b, Leck 1987, Lewis 1993, Looser and Kaplan 1997, Luke and Gore 1992, Mackinnon, Elgquist-Saltzman and Prentice 1998, Maher 1987, Maher and Tetreault 1994, Manicom 1992, Milojević 1996, 1998, 2000, Nielsen 1990, Parry 1996, Rich 1979, Robertson 1993, Roy and Schen 1993, Sandell 1991, Scanlon 1993, Shrewsbury 1987, Stone 1994, Tierney 1989–, Weiler 1988 and Weiner 1994. Of course, not all these authors could possibly agree on all the details I further discuss. However, I argue that there is a common enough understanding among these authors about the ways in which feminist educational alternatives are different from mainstream education and about feminist education's main concerns. This common understanding represents the core of the feminist educational project for the future; this, in turn, influences the educational practice of those influenced by feminist theory to varying degrees. This core consists of the following elements:

- *Importance of gender* If another criterion for describing what feminist education is about is either not 'new' or not specifically feminist, this characteristic alone would suffice in describing the distinctiveness of feminist education. This distinctiveness means incorporating awareness that gender issues are important, or at least that they *could be* (Houston 1994: 122). Feminist pedagogy insists that all human experiences are gendered that they are essentially shaped by our being either men or women and, as such, subject to social prescriptions associated with either sex (Maher 1987: 197). Feminist education is about developing a gender-sensitive education versus a gender-free one (Houston 1994: 122). Gender is seen as social practice, as something people *do* (rather than as something people *are*). But feminist pedagogy is not only concerned with gender justice, but rather it seeks to remove oppressions inherent in the 'genderedness' of all social relations and, consequently, of all societal institutions and structures (Sandell 1991: 180–181).
- *Themes of nurturing and caring* Feminist education is about the '3 C's of caring, concern and connection' (Luke and Gore 1992: 153). The traditional rigid, unquestioned *authority* of the teacher is transformed. Ideally, feminist education is supposed to practice horizontal power relationships, flatten existing hierarchies and social structures, and focus on egalitarian pedagogical processes and power-with instead of power-over. Dialogue is encouraged; there needs to be mutual growth and learning between students and teachers. The learning is experiential, collaborative, participatory and relational. The focus is on relations between students and teachers, among students, and students and their course material. Classroom interaction is to be promoted. *Feminist pedagogy* is, therefore, based on cooperation not competition, on reducing divisions between people by flattening, transcending traditional notions of hierarchy and equalizing power between teachers and students. All involved are seen as both learners and teachers, at the same time. Ideally, feminist pedagogy emphasizes 'connection over separation, understanding and acceptance over assessment, and collaboration over debate' (Iskin, in Bunch and Pollack 1983: 183). Consciousness-raising is its quintessential expression.

- *Education and knowledge are 'holistic'*   This means that (artificial) divisions between thought and action, theory and practice, knowledge and politics, reason/rationality and emotion, mind and body, self and other, caring and self-expression, communal concerns and independent judgement, private and public spheres are removed. Feminist education intends to integrate these elements. It adopts the development of interdisciplinary 'connected knowledge' – knowing in relationship – as opposed to separate abstract knowing. This connected knowing is implicit in the empathetic understanding of the world of others. Connected knowledge incorporates public and private issues, cognitive, emotional/affective and intuitive. The *environment* needs to support both emotions and the intellect because being able to grow and change is seen as a basic precondition for learning. For example, it is important to deal with emotions like fear, anger, anxiety and pain when women 'first face their own feelings of being oppressed, powerless, and immobilized' (Sherman, in Bunch and Pollack 1983: 132).
- *Knowledge is created through 'methodology' that is eclectic*   The eclectic approach is reflected in the choice of research methods adapted to the specific demands of each individual research project. But qualitative methodologies are especially valued. Feminist education transforms traditional disciplines into perspectives that can be used as approaches to problems, with the goal of solving problems in accordance with the best interests of today's peoples and futures generation.
- *Personal experience is valued*   Knowledge should not be only about abstract categories and information but about experiential and participatory learning. Knowledge is experiential as it emerges from 'first hand experience' (Iskin, in Bunch and Pollack 1983: 132). Knowledge structures need to correspond to the real world. Empirical, concrete knowledge is valued as much as knowledge built up from abstractions. Theory needs to be meaningful and contextualized within lived experiences. Personal experience and everyday-life issues are validated. Personal experience is highly valued, if not equal to (or even more important than) what is thought 'officially'. An awareness needs to be there that knowledge is always embedded – knowledge from and about the body is also knowledge about the world (Grumet, in Stone 1994: 149). But, most of all, feminist education is about a balanced and con-textualized exchange of insight and information, experience and expertise (Hoffmann and Stake 1998).

- *Critical thinking and active participation are promoted* Teaching and learning are interactive. This includes a critique of authority and affirmation of diversity of perspectives. Critical thinking is crucial because it encourages social understanding and activism. The focus is on empowerment (of student) and not domination (by teachers and official knowledge). Knowledge should be knowledge *for* instead of just knowledge *about*. The main skill to be developed is open-mindedness. Students are to be involved in the negotiation of meaning and the production of knowledge. Ideally, critical thinking should be applied to feminist theory and teaching practices as well. That is, feminist educators need to attend to contradictions and discontinuities in the field and be open to self-critique. Knowledge is always 'provisional, open-ended and relational' (Luke and Gore 1992: 7); it is holistic, not separated from politics, and it is important to encourage social understanding and activism (Hoffmann and Stake 1998).
- *Focus on difference and diversity, multiplicity* Diversity is valued. Incorporating views and knowledge from marginalized social groups – because of their race, nationality, age, sexual preference, disability, class – is to be encouraged. There is an awareness that the classroom is not ideologically neutral, but is embedded in a web of social relationships, and that feminist educators as well as students are variously positioned within this web. As everyone is invited to 'speak out' and is 'listened to', students from diverse backgrounds should be empowered to voice their own difference without being put in the 'spotlight'. Constant efforts are to be made to include the perspectives of the powerless/marginalized.
- *Concern with ethics* Promoting values – of community, communication, equality, mutual nurturance, shared leadership, participatory decision-making, democratic structure, interdependence. This is a concern with moral education, but ethics is relational.
- *Concern with the future* Because of the link with future generations (Grumet, in Stone 1994: 152). The image of a desired future is implicit in the focus on transformation, liberation, empowerment, emancipation of oppressed/subjugated/marginalized social groups. Feminism also requires 'optimism because the basis of feminism is a belief that things can change, that we are not entirely caught in a deterministic trap which allows us simply to shrug our collective shoulders and avoid responsibility for the shape of the world' (Hawthorne 2002: 4). Sometimes, the concern with the desired future is also explicit, for example, Bunch's (1983) teaching model includes not only description

(of what exists) and analysis (why such reality exists) but also vision (which determines what should exist) as well as strategy (how to change to what should be). Concern with the future is also present when the importance of students' perspectives and students' issues are stressed or when it is imagined that children should have a more prominent role in the public sphere (Boulding 1990).

- *Curricula are transformed*   Previous biases (exclusion and degradation of women and girls) are removed. The crucial focus throughout each discipline is gender. Overall, curricula are interdisciplinary, flexible, problem-oriented, knowledge-based, holistic and practical.

- *Education is about transformation*   Education is not only about skills but also as a means to transform and change the very societies within which learning takes place. It is also about inner transformation, awareness of one's oppression leading to insight, and to inner and outer transformation. Feminist alternatives seek to be useful in improving the conditions of women's lives and teaching activities aimed at changing patriarchal characters and cultures. Education for transformation is a liberatory practice (hooks 1994).

- *Empowerment*   Feminists tend to view power as repressive; it is used to dominate, oppress, coerce and deny (Gore 1993: 120). At the same time, in the notion of empowerment, feminist pedagogy embodies 'a concept of power as energy, capacity, and potential rather than as domination' (Shrewsbury 1987: 8). Empowerment means developing strategies that allow students to find their own voices, discover the power of their own authenticity, develop their thinking about the goals and objectives they wish and need to accomplish, as well as their independence, skills of planning, negotiating, evaluating and decision making, and to increase their self-esteem (ibid.: 8–9).

- *Community-based learning*   The boundaries between educational institutions and the community are obliterated and the active participation of community members is encouraged. Community is both local and broad – as in a global sisterhood.

- *New technologies are seen as tools*   Contrary to the general belief that the feminist vision is technophobic, there is a place for technology but a refusal to worship it (Marx Hubbard 1998: 166). The focus is on politics, on creating women's own information networks, computerized mailing lists and political alert systems (Tierney 1990).

Summary: analysis of feminist alternatives

'Feminism pedagogy is still defining itself, largely through a process of questioning long-standing beliefs and practices in education' (Brown 1992: 52). The following tables indicate that feminist priorities differ from the mainstream vision of the future. As seen in Table 8.1, the predominant vision is that of a gender partnership in the context of a gentle society. What is important is to create an inclusive society based on the principles of social justice and equality. To be able to do this, feminists rethink time, transforming it from the linear time of modernity and the hypertime of the information society to a range of alternative temporalities, including cyclical, eternal and glacial. Especially important in this context is Elise Boulding's notion of the 200 year present, where the life of the grandparent and the grandchild co-exist.

Educational futures also differ from hegemonic ones. They are focused on the removal of gender bias and prejudice in education. Nowhere in these visions is there an unbalanced educational system and unbalanced society that favours girls. Rather, the current efforts to improve the educational outcomes for boys who are 'lagging behind' – even though often assuming feminist backlash and anti-feminist rhetoric – should be seen as distinctively feminist. The vision of an inclusive, partnership society implies abolition of gender hierarchies, even those that favour women and girls.

The utopian promise lies in 'truly holistic education' oriented towards bringing about positive social and personal change. Dystopian dangers include the bias against boys' and men's issues and concerns. As feminist education is political and aims to produce 'empowerment' and particular social change, other dystopian dangers mentioned most often lie in the possibility of feminist education becoming overly ideological, anti-intellectual, intolerant and dogmatic. As well, the possibility for domination by the perspectives of white, middle-class women exists. While the circular classroom is celebrated as a symbol of the removal of hierarchies between students and teachers, the dystopian interpretation sees this educational setting as part of the Panopticon which, in fact, results in hierarchies becoming even more intrusive.

Educational content, process and structure are also radically transformed, as presented in Table 8.2. For example, the content includes both personal experience and theory; the process is cooperative wherein everyone is both student and teacher; and the structure ideally breaks the division between public and private spheres. Table 8.3 summarizes key words used by feminist visionaries and

Table 8.1 Partnership society – social futures

Approach to time	Vision for the future	Utopian promise	Dystopian dangers	Social eutopia
Linear (as in progress)	Partnership society	Everyone able to fulfil potential irrespective of their gender, race, ethnicity, religion, ability, culture, sexual preference	Dystopia developed by feminists as a method to critique patriarchy	Improvement in women's lives, more choices and opportunities
Cyclical (women's biological rhythm)	Gentle society		Critique mostly internal-symphatetic	
Eternal (as during labour)	Inclusive society based on principles of social justice and equality	Survival of the human race	Disturbance of the 'natural' order of things	
Glacial/generational			Boys and men becoming second sex	
Time lived, made and generated	Education itself (together with parenting) being at the core of the future society			

Table 8.2 Gender-balanced education – educational futures

Underlying vision for the future	Utopian promise	Dystopian dangers	Educational eutopia
Partnership, gender-balanced society	Truly holistic education	Neglect of boys' and men's issues	Removing of gender bias and prejudice in education
	Education bringing about positive social change	Feminist education ideological, anti-intellectual, intolerant, dogmatic	
	Positive effects on personal lives and relationships	Inhospitable classroom for those outside of the feminist 'private cult' (e.g. women of colour, poor women)	
		Circular classroom arrangement replicates Panopticon – students visible to an all-seeing eye, self-surveillance of each other also promoted	

Worldview and approach to knowledge	Epistemology	Educated subject
Knowledge integrated, based on everyday experiences, for cooperation, connected	Incorporation of the cognitive and the emotional	More complete, balanced individual
Women's ways of knowing	Double standpoint epistemology	More informed, politically active, in charge of one's own life
		Empowered with developed critical thinking skills
		Outcomes: critical thinking, raised consciousness, active participation in public life

Table 8.2 (Continued)

Educational visions/futures

Content	Process	Structure
Interdisciplinary, flexible, problem-oriented, knowledge-based, holistic, integrated, practical, experiential curricula	Cooperative, non-hierarchical, focus on connection, collaboration, understanding and acceptance	Flattened, as in circular classroom
Includes both personal experience and theory	Caring, nurturing, networking	Most within (slightly transformed) traditional educational institutions
Recognition that knowledge is constructed	Interactive teaching and learning	Also in range of alternative educational settings, e.g. local communities and national and global (civil) society
Various perspectives are included	Participatory learning and classrooom practices	Ideally, would break division within public and private spheres – education in 'private' sphere, 'private' issues in education
	Horizontal power relationships, power with	Children participating in public life
	Democratic, group cooperation	
	Promotes critical thinking and open-mindedness	
	Promotes political-social activism	

Table 8.3 Partnership society, gender-balanced education – key words

Change	Future	Society	Education	Other key words
Need to create, bring about change Personal and social change	Different future (to the extension of the present, to the patriarchal one) possible	Cooperative Nurturing Gentle Caring Inclusive	For transformation To encourage social justice, equity, inclusion, diversity	Love, relationships, body, reproduction, life, caring, equality, diversity

Table 8.4 Partnership society, gender-balanced education – causal layered analysis

Litany	Social cause	Discourse/worldview	Myth/metaphor	Education bottom line
Women's concerns and issues missing from traditional education	Patriarchy Industrialism Mass education	Empowerment of marginalized social groups Equality Progress	Matriarchy Giving birth	Education for social transformation Education for creation of more (gender) balanced societies
Women's involvement in educational process is increasing				

Table 8.5 Partnership society, gender-balanced education – deconstruction

Who gets to speak	Who and what is silenced	What is missing from a discourse	Continuity	Discontinuity
Feminists Women's activists and theorists	Other groups and epistemological minorities	Economic growth Negative aspects of human nature Expertise	Women challenging patriarchy throughout history Women's liberation movements, especially starting from nineteenth century	1960s social movements in the west

educational theorists. These, too, are radically different from the key words used when discussing globalized and cyber visions. This is so across all five categories. Change is to be created rather than passively accepted; society is described in terms of qualitative social indicators rather than in quantitative economic and technological terms, and education is for social justice and equity rather than for achievement and success.

The main goal within the feminist movement, as presented in Table 8.4 on CLA, is to educate for social transformation instead of preparing students for a competitive globalized world. Education is neither an investment in the economy nor predominantly about information access. Rather, it is about the creation of more balanced and inclusive societies. The main myths and metaphors used are based on women's experiences of giving birth as well as on narrative, 'reconstruction' of history that implies once-egalitarian gender relationships. The purpose of this reconstruction is to inspire, because what has existed is seen to be possible (Boulding and Boulding 1995), and can be created again.

The final table (Table 8.5) in this section deconstructs the partnership society, answering questions of who speaks, who and what is silenced and what is missing from the discourse. The development of the feminist movement and vision was made possible by both continuity, such as women challenging patriarchy throughout history, and by the main discontinuity, the second wave feminist movement.

Together with the mass education of women, it was the second wave feminist movement, which started in the 1960s west, which was most influential in enabling the articulation and development of feminist visions.

The tables, as well as the summary they provide, make the discrepancy between current/emerging educational and social praxis and feminist visions more obvious. While small (and significant) gains have certainly been made over the last four decades, the society and education envisioned by feminists still remain in the domain of the utopia. To paraphrase Sandra Harding (Harding 1986: 141), we will thus have a feminist education (curriculum, pedagogy) 'only when we have a feminist society'.

9 Visions IV: indigenous alternatives

Recovery of indigenous traditions in education: introductory remarks

> The Western ignorance of indigenous knowledge holds profound consequences for everyone.
>
> (Semali and Kincheloe 1999: 39)

> is the study of indigenous peoples and their knowledges in itself a process of Europeanization? In some ways, of course, it is, as Western intellectuals conceptualize indigenous knowledge in context far removed from its production.
>
> (Semali and Kincheloe 1999: 39)

The above comments represent the main dilemma non-indigenous people encounter in regard to the recovery of indigenous traditions in education. On one hand, there is a demand for inclusion. For example, 'It is important that this [indigenous] knowledge be recognized and valued at the level of the school curriculum, and that it be incorporated into the teaching/learning process' (George 1999: 90).

> Particularly I think the appropriate education ensures that Aboriginal perspectives are included across the curriculum and ensures that community members are playing an important role in the education of not only Aboriginal students, but all students.
>
> (Davison 1999: 22)

On the other hand, there is an acute awareness that the very process of incorporation of indigenous knowledge into teaching/learning processes by non-indigenous educators carries the great risk of the intrinsic 'western gaze', in the appropriation, commodification and essentializing of indigenous knowledge. An obvious solution is to enable higher participation of indigenous educators in schools and in academia. However, that too is not without problems. First, due to the generally marginalized status of indigenous peoples in colonized societies, there is, unfortunately, an acute shortage of indigenous educators. Second, because of a 'history of hurt, humiliation, and exploitation that has been perpetrated by some institutions and academics' (Smith 2000: 213), some indigenous communities have adopted an 'often strident anti-intellectual and anti-academic stance' (ibid.). Third, many indigenous educators are, rightfully, becoming increasingly impatient with the lack of awareness of indigenous issues within mainstream communities. Some feel that they are repeatedly asked to teach mainstream communities for free and may express their frustration as: 'here we go again – educate another whitefalla' (Craven 1999: 52).

After several decades of recovery of indigenous traditions at the global level, marked by indigenous activism, knowledge production and various educational initiatives, non-indigenous people are increasingly expected to 'do their own homework' and educate themselves about indigenous issues, perspectives and ways of living and knowing. These two sets of issues present as almost an unsolvable dilemma: How is a non-indigenous educator to 'know', be informed about and learn about indigenous knowledge without 'gazing' into it? And, how is the non-indigenous educator to 'talk' and teach indigenous knowledge without being accused of appropriating, speaking for and in the name of indigenous peoples? As Semali and Kincheloe further argue:

> Western scholars and cultural workers concerned with the plight of indigenous peoples and their knowledges are faced with a set of dilemmas. Not only must they avoid essentialism and its accompanying romanticization of the indigene, but they must sidestep the traps that transform their attempts at facilitation into further marginalization. Walking the well-intentioned road to hell, Western scholars dedicated to the best interests of indigenous peoples often unwittingly participate in the Western hegemonic process. The question: how can the agency, the self-direction of indigenous peoples be enhanced? must constantly be asked by Western allies. What is the difference between celebration of indigenous knowledge and an appropriation? Too often Western allies, for example, don't simply want to work

with indigenous peoples – they want to transform their identities and become indigenous persons themselves.

(Semali and Kincheloe 1999: 20)

Because of these difficulties, most non-indigenous educators stay away
from dealing with issues of indigenous knowledges and education.
Some work closely with local indigenous communities, which is the
most preferred model of cooperation. But what of theoretical work?
Could and should a non-indigenous person study indigenous
knowledges, education and pedagogy?

Semali and Kincheloe argue that in this respect western intellectuals
have 'little choice':

> if they are to operate as agents of justice, they must understand
> the dynamics at work in the world of the indigene. To refuse to
> operate out of fear of Europeanization reflects a view of indigenous
> culture as an authentic, uncontaminated artifact that must be
> hermetically preserved regardless of the needs of living indigen-
> ous people.
>
> (Semali and Kincheloe 1999: 20–21)

They also argue that:

> as complex as the question of indigeneity may be, we believe
> that the best interests of indigenous and non-indigenous
> peoples are served by the study of indigenous knowledges and
> epistemologies. An appreciation of indigenous epistemology,
> for example, provides Western peoples with another view of
> knowledge production in diverse cultural sites. Such a perspective
> holds transformative possibilities, as they come to understand
> the overtly cultural processes by which information is legitimated
> and delimited.
>
> (Semali and Kincheloe 1999: 17)

By embracing indigenous knowledge, the whole of society should
benefit. This is most commonly argued in view of current and
projected future ecological problems. For example, 'The western
arrogance and ignorance not to embrace a culture whose harmonious
existence nurtured a co-existence with the land, its habitat and its
people, remains a puzzle to me and many of my people' (Smallwood
1995: 13).

You [who call yourselves Australians] must now accept the full
responsibility for the many inequalities and injustices of 20th
Century Australia. You are responsible for the continued
destruction and desecration of my people's culture and the
natural environment...So in the interest of our children and all
future generations, in the interest of the survival of the human
race, we must all become a part of the solution and stop being
part of the problem.

(Bayles 1989: 6)

There are two different points at issue here. The first is the right
of Aboriginal peoples to exercise their own culture; the second
is the benefit that the Western world can derive from this
culture. Western scholars are gradually realizing how important
Aboriginal knowledge may be to the future survival of our
world.

(Battiste 2000: 194)

The argument has been made in some of these texts that, while there
are certain areas of indigenous knowledge that should only be studied
and taught by the indigenous peoples concerned, the study of indigenous knowledge, education and visions for the future are topics
that could be studied and thought about by non-indigenous
researchers and educators as well. As I have already mentioned,
Semali and Kincheloe argue that it is through the study of indigenous
knowledge and epistemology that the best interests of indigenous
and non-indigenous peoples are served. In addition, Craven,
d'Arbon and Wilson-Miller (1999) develop a set of guidelines in terms
of the types of knowledge that could be taught by non-indigenous
educators and those that should only be taught by indigenous people;
this can perhaps be applied to theoretical research as well. According
to them, the topics that should be taught only by indigenous people
(if they deem it appropriate) include ceremonial life (sacred symbolism,
ritual, mystic language, sacred stories); languages; spirituality;
information about sacred artefacts and men's business; women's
business (Craven *et al.* 1999: 240). There are, however, some topics
that can be taught by non-indigenous educators. These topics include:
'*contemporary issues* [italics added]; economic, political and social
relationships; about belonging to the land; land rights; *educational
pedagogy and historical practices; futures perspectives; gender roles* [italics
added]; historical events; about kinship; land and water usage and

management; conservation and technology' (ibid.: 240). They also stress that 'whenever possible, activities should be developed, implemented and evaluated with consultation and participation of the local Indigenous community' (ibid.).

Local/global tensions

There is yet another set of issues, best described as local/global tensions. Originally, indigenous societies were firmly based in their own localities. After colonization, indigenous issues were also debated at the nation state level. More recently, indigenous issues have moved to the global level. This has taken place because the social context has changed and indigenous peoples now must further grapple with two worldviews, two epistemologies and two consciousnesses in order to survive in the world of capitalism and global economy (Semali and Kincheloe 1999). While the mainstream discourse on globalization and globalized education represents globalization as 'a new phase' within indigenous alternatives, globalization is theorized as being part of a continuous project:

> To the extent that 'indigenous' has meaning today in a global context, it is derived from an historical colonial relationship between indigenous peoples and European conquerors. The European project of incorporating resources into a global economic system controlled by nation states has necessitated programs aimed at the cultural assimilation of indigenous peoples – their cultural destruction and subsequent 're-education'.
>
> (Semali and Kincheloe 1999: 12–13)

> For indigenous peoples, the beginning of a new century is really a continuation of a struggle that began five centuries ago. The optimism that prevails is based on the belief that now more than ever before in the last 500 years indigenous peoples are better able to respond...indigenous peoples [have]...re-position strategically around international alliances in ways which have reinforced a sense of movement towards a positive future. But that is an optimistic view. The pessimistic view is that we are dying and that the legacy of the presence of indigenous peoples on earth will be obliterated. Indigenous peoples are positioned along both ends of that continuum.
>
> (Tuhiwai Smith 1999: 104)

In this context, globalization remains part of a broader process of 'dis-indigenization', or assimilation of indigenous peoples into Western culture (Maurial 1999: 62). Dis-indigenization (assimilation) of indigenous peoples into western culture occurs through various processes. These processes may be quite different from each other, but still result in dis-indigenization because they attempt to assimilate indigenous peoples and cultures within western goals and historical projects. Indigenous peoples then 'become *workers* for industry, *consumers* for the markets, *citizens* for the nation and *humans* for mankind' (Sbert, quoted in Maurial 1999: 62). As a response to this continuing and now global colonization, indigenous issues and identities have moved from the contextual and local, to become part of the global problematique:

> In indigenous studies, such as the Native American academic programs, emerging new political awarenesses have been expressed in terms of the existence of a global Fourth World indigeneity. Proponents of such a view claim that Fourth World peoples share the commonality of domination and are constituted by indigenous groups as diverse as the Indians of the Americas, the Innuits and Samis of the Arctic north, the Maori of New Zealand, the Koori of Australia, the Karins and Katchins of Burma, the Kurds of Persia, the Bedouins of the African/Middle Eastern desert, many African tribal peoples, and even the Basques and Gaels of contemporary Europe.
>
> (Semali and Kincheloe 1999: 16)

In my analysis of current 'indigenous' approaches to time, visions for the future, knowledge and educational visions, I remain at the level of the global. That is, I will investigate discursive formation of 'indigenous' knowledge and education as *written* in the emerging *global* language (English). I investigate the role of futures discourse in the formation of educational visions that are explicitly and publicly stated. I do not intend to assume the position of independent and objective knower, nor to speak for indigenous peoples. I will, however, analyse *the discourse* on indigenous knowledge, pedagogy and education in general, mostly within the global context of the recovery of 'indigeneity' as expressed in numerous crucial texts. And although such analysis is indeed fraught by the already mentioned, and many other, dangers (for a more detailed discussion on this, see Milojević 2002b: 272–281), overall, as Semali and Kincheloe conclude, 'the benefits of the study of indigenous knowledge [are] sufficiently powerful to merit the risk' (1999: 3).

Approaches to time and the vision for the future

While prior to colonization some indigenous languages may not have had a word for time or future, indigenous peoples who today write in English are clearly accustomed to the terms. But, as could be expected, the timeline implicit in the teaching of alternative history differs from the western one. As argued earlier, western thought can be characterized by a division of history in accordance with certain technological and economic developments. Depending on what tools and weapons are used, societies are divided along a hunter-gatherer, agricultural, feudal (manufacture), industrial (Fordist) and postindustrial continuum. The divisions, such as between 'pre-modern, modern and postmodern', or 'pre-historic, industrial and information', or 'traditional, nation state-based and globalized' eras, are variations on the same theme. The feminist timeline, on the other hand, divides history as consisting of matrilinear past, patriarchal past and present and (hopefully) gender partnership future (or, alternatively, continuation of patriarchy). Not surprisingly, the timeline proposed by indigenous peoples takes the experience of colonization as the main demarcation point. The timeline here consists of three main phases: traditional societies prior to colonization; colonization – massacres and assimilation; and recovery of indigenous traditions. For example, Moody (1993) in his edited volume on *The Indigenous Voice: Visions and Realities* divides the text into the following parts: 'the species of origin', 'dispossession', 'present struggles', 'conscientization and the recovery of origins', 'dialectics of liberation' and 'in our own ways'. The first phase, 'recovery of origins', describes indigenous ways of knowing and living prior to invasion. Moody (ibid.: 3) argues that these portrayals of 'original' existence are largely drawn from the records of sympathetic nineteenth-century white observers that now seem over-idealized. He also argues that accounts written by indigenous spokespeople can seem over-pessimistic, overly influenced by the need to counter alien influences, expressed in a maxim that 'We are what we are', yet 'We can never be the same again' (ibid.). For him, this is problematic because it can become 'a recipe for hopelessness and the abandonment of origins' (ibid.). The next two parts, on Dispossession and Present Struggles, include a description of the experience and analysis of massacres, invasions and genocide, assimilation, militarization, racism, sterilization, imprisonment and tourism. It also focuses on indigenous peoples' experiences with the nuclear state, with mining and multinational corporations, with missionaries and in schools, within working environments as well as with government policies and actions in respect to dams, forests, pollution and land rights. These two parts could be located within the colonization phase of the three-phase timeline. The last two parts are aspects of the recovery of indigenous traditions. They deal with issues such as self-determination, relationships between 'outsiders' and 'insiders', building independ-ence, schooling for survival and building international links and strategies.

Another important text, *Reclaiming Indigenous Voice and Vision* edited by Battiste (2000), is also indicative of the previously described approach to time. Battiste's classification is based on the Medicine Wheel that symbolically illustrates that 'all things are interconnected and related, spiritual, complex and powerful' (ibid.: xxii). Battiste begins with the Western Door, 'the autumn' of trad-itional Indian education, which focuses on 'mapping colonialism'. The Northern Door is 'the home of winter', it 'evokes feelings of struggle and cold' – survival is challenged but 'from experiences endurance and wisdom are learnt' (ibid.: xxiii). The north is cold and dark and there is just a hint of light that makes it possible to hope and dream – this is the section that 'diagnoses colonialism'. The Eastern Door is the direction of spring, of the sun rising – and it is about healing colonized indigenous peoples (ibid.). The Southern Door is 'the direction of summer', 'the home of the sun and the time of fullest growth' (ibid.: xxiv). It offers the foundation for reclaiming 'ourselves and our voice, as *we vision the Indigenous renaissance* based on Indigenous knowledge and heritage' (ibid.). To paraphrase her classification within western terminology and epistemology, she begins with history, the facts and experiences of colonization, and then moves towards healing and visioning, towards the renaissance – the preferred future.

While both Moody and Battiste identify more than the three phases mentioned above, a three-phase timeline – precolonized societies, colonization, recovery – is implicit in their work. This is similar to the work of Laenui (2000) who, 'based on his individual Hawai'i experience', identifies two main processes in this respect. The first set of processes is aspects of colonization, such as 'denial and with-drawal', 'destruction/eradication', 'denigration/belittlement/insult', 'surface accommodation/tokenisms' and 'transformation/exploitation'. The other set of processes is processes of decolonization, and they include 'rediscovery and recovery', 'mourning', 'dreaming' and 'commitment and action'. According to Laenui, dreaming is 'the most crucial' phase for decolonization:

> Here is where the full panorama of possibilities is expressed, considered through debate, consultation, and building dreams on further dreams, which eventually become the flooring for the creation of a new social order. It is during this phase that colonized people are able to explore their own cultures, experience their own aspirations for their future, and consider their own structures of government and social order to encompass and express their hopes.
>
> (Laenui 2000: 155)

Tuhiwai Smith (1999: 152) also argues that envisioning is also one of the important strategies that indigenous peoples have employed effectively to bind people together politically. This strategy '...asks that people imagine a future, that they rise above present day situations which are generally depressing, dream a new dream and set a new vision' (ibid.). She also gives examples of envisioning by the Maori that has resulted in positive social change, such as negotiating a settlement with the Crown, working to revitalize language, build a new economic base and renegotiate other arrangements with governments (ibid.).

The view of the future as expressed in the work of Moody, Battiste, Laenui and Tuhiwai Smith is in shark contrast to the view that the recovery of indigenous traditions is entirely about the return to the mythical past. As Burke argues:

> Aboriginal people know that the clock cannot be turned back. No one is demanding that the impossible be done. But they are demanding that all that is possible to redress inequity...be explored and implemented. The possible includes the Land Fund legislation being made sacrosanct; guaranteed continued landrights on a National scale; and much more than lip service to self-determination.
>
> (Burke 1997: 27)

The connection between alternative history and the future is again summarized in the following paragraph:

Aborigines are seeking equity. To seek equity is to seek justice. If justice is to become a reality in the present and be a part of the future, we cannot pretend that the past did not exist.

(Smallwood 1995: 11)

To deny the past and to refuse to recognize its implications is to distort the present; to distort the present is to take risks with the future that are blatantly irresponsible.

(Indian Tribes of Manitoba, quoted in Abele,
Dittburner and Graham 2000: 3)

Of course, as argued earlier, *all* visions for the future are informed by particular cultural traditions. In addition, in my literature review of indigenous perspectives, not one text was discovered that argues for the destruction of the built environment and the expulsion of all non-indigenous peoples from colonized lands. As well, given the present marginalized status of most indigenous peoples, there is a desire to reverse this and create a better future. This implies a rejection of the status quo, the way our societies have been structured. In fact, one of the main characteristics of the recovery of indigenous traditions is the focus and the commitment to change.

To conclude, alternative histories play an important part in the development of preferable alternative futures. As argued by Moody (1993), these alternative histories portray indigenous societies prior to colonization as more advanced and healthier than the present society in general, and the present situation of indigenous peoples in particular. For example:

Historical evidence tells us that prior to the settlement of Europeans in this country Aboriginal people led a well-ordered existence, rich in culture, kinship and the essentials of life. In good seasons they made free and wide use of their traditional lands, ate well, enjoyed family and ceremonial life and engaged with neighbouring peoples either in friendship or hostility depending on the current circumstances. In seasons when the weather was not in their favour they lived more frugally, restricted family growth and traveled more widely and in smaller groups. Aboriginal people took the wealth that the land offered where to do so would not irreparably alter or destroy its nature. As with people the world over, their health was better when food was plentiful and the weather not reaching extremes. Indeed, they had a distinct advantage over people in many other parts of the world in that they carried few endemic diseases and then not ones that were catastrophic.

(Parry 1997: 1–2)

However, the guiding image of the future is only partly based on alternative histories that draw on the previously described, almost utopian, image of traditional societies. There are other elements of indigenous futures visioning that predominantly draw on current problems and issues faced by indigenous peoples. The discourse of the future is used to address the most pressing needs of indigenous communities, such as the right to self-determination. While there is certainly a tendency for most colonized societies to glorify their pre-colonized histories, this needs to be viewed in the context of cultural and group survival, and also in the context of strategic essentialism, as described earlier.

Land rights, self-determination and survival

In Australia, the issue of land rights comes as perhaps one of the strongest preferred visions for the futures of indigenous peoples. In the following paragraph, Bayles summarizes this:

We must now have a permanent solution, a temporary solution is not good enough. Tokenism is totally unacceptable. The permanent solution is access to and control of our own land. With our own land we can create our own jobs, control our own economy and solve our own problems, instead of waiting on Government bureaucrats to solve our problems for us. With our own land we can set up our own farms and businesses and various other enterprises. We can establish our own Government and become an independent race of people, an independent nation. We grow the food to feed our people, we raise the cattle and sheep to use the hide, leather and wool to clothe our people. We build the houses from the natural resources from the land to house our people. This is the total solution.

(Bayles 1989: 7)

The issue of land rights is strongly connected to the issues of self-determination, self-management and self-government, as well as economic independence and self-sufficiency. As argued by Coombs and Bayles, '[t]he promotion of Indigenous autonomy [is] part of a larger project of Indigenous identity-building linked to central issues of land rights and self-determination' (Coombs, in McConaghy 2000: 206).

> Land Rights mean: creating racial harmony, no more handout mentality, creating our own community projects, fewer home-less Koories, fewer Koories in gaol, fewer Koories on the dole queues, self-management, self-determination, self-sufficiency, fewer alcoholics and drug addicts, economic independence, self government, this is our right not a privilege.
>
> (Bayles 1989: 13)

In Australia, another issue that is raised as a priority for the future is reconciliation (e.g. Craven 1999, 2000). As stated by Sally Morgan:

> We have to find a way of living together in this country, and that will only come when our hearts and minds and wills are set towards Reconciliation. It will only come when thousands of stories have been spoken and listened to with understanding.
>
> (in Craven 1999: 1)

But most of all, one of the most important visions for the future, in Australia and elsewhere, is connected to the issue of physical and cultural survival. As argued by Tuhiwai Smith (1999: 107), for 'most of the past 500 years the indigenous people's project has had one major priority: *survival*'. While since Second World War and particularly since the 1960s indigenous peoples' projects were indeed reformulated around 'a much wider platform of concerns', survival 'at a basic human level' still remains the priority concern for many indigenous peoples across the world (ibid.).

New hegemonic discourses for the future, such as the globalized and the WebNet visions, are not seen by most authors as 'liberating' for indigenous peoples. As argued earlier, they are seen as part of a continuing process of 'dis-indigenization'. Linda Tuhiwai Smith (1999), for example, argues that while the language of imperialism may have changed, imperialism still exists. New hegemonic futures continue the process of imperialism. They do so through the following means: the patenting, stealing and copying of genealogy and identity (stem cell-lines); the farming of the umbilical cord blood of aborted babies; scientific and political reconstruction of a previously extinct people (Human Genome Diversity Project); and creating virtual culture as authentic culture (ibid.: 100–103). Part of globalization is also 'feeding consumption of indigenous (and other) peoples' which numbs people into believing that they are 'autonomous "choosers" in a culturally neutral marketplace' (ibid.: 103). But, in fact, indigenous peoples are denied global citizenship and their hard-won battles within nation states are everywhere under threat (ibid.).

To conclude, the predominant approach to time within the indigenous alternative has now become linear, divided into a three-phase – pre-colonization, colonization and recovery/indigenous enlightenment – timeline. This timeline exists even among authors who argue that indigenous people still have 'very much a "time is now", immediate gratification approach to life' (Hughes 1987: 7). The vision for the future partially draws on the image of traditional indigenous societies, in particular, to the 'holistic way of living'.

Interestingly, these alternative histories are now on the verge of turning 'mainstream'. The 'growing interest in indigenous knowledge' is 'perhaps directly related to growing concerns about the degradation of the environment' (George 1999: 79). This may explain why an increasing number of people in the west are now willing to listen to alternative histories proposed by indigenous peoples. However, it should also be recognized that the change is directly connected to theoretical arguments and activism developed by indigenous peoples over many decades. The popularity of indigenous alternatives among certain groups of non-indigenous peoples is today mostly related to this desire for holistic and socially, ecologically and economically sustainable societies. It is also related to the rejection of materialistic culture and the need to return to the broader view of what it means to be human. The discourse on indigenous alternatives is a good example of the use of the futures discourses (ecological forecasts, increase in individual and social alienation) to reinforce a particular group's politics.

Another set of defining issues can best be described in terms of 'social justice' and fairness, based on a vision of a society where there is equality between indigenous and non-indigenous peoples. The 'story of the next 150 years' is one in which 'increasing colonization and subjugation [are] being met by resistance, regrouping, and a cultural renaissance' (Rameka and Law 1998: 203) of indigenous peoples. This vision is of an endless struggle for 'social justice, equality and self-determination', whereby indigenous and non-indigenous peoples can 'live as coequals' (Walker, quoted in Rameka and Law 1998: 203). Other elements of this vision are the physical and cultural survival of indigenous peoples and land rights – ownership of land, self-determination, self-management, self-government, self-sufficiency and economic independence. There is a conspicuous absence of issues such as 'the revolution' in new ICTs or the emergence of a new 'globalized' era.

Modern society is not rejected, but social, cultural and environmental issues take precedence. The recovery of indigenous traditions is indeed a global phenomenon, but globalization itself is not theorized along utopian lines. Rather, both new information technologies and globalization are viewed in the light of their potential threats to indigenous societies and potential further colonization of indigenous peoples (e.g. Tuhiwai Smith 1999). Gender rarely plays a prominent role. Furthermore, feminist alternatives are made problematic because they are often based on the experiences of white, middle-class academics (e.g. Huggins 1994; Lucashenko 1994; Moreton-Robinson 2000). Huggins explicitly states that 'Aboriginal women's traditional social, political and spiritual roles gave them a far better position than white women could ever imagine' (1994: 74). She therefore rejects any outside intervention with regard to certain gender issues (e.g. domestic violence) in indigenous communities. This is because, while colonizers have indeed imposed their patriarchal values on indigenous peoples, sexism is seen to be a secondary issue in indigenous communities. In addition, the focus on gender issues is sometimes seen as part of the continuous effort by the colonizer to further divide indigenous communities and justify state intervention. Addressing racism and colonization still form the most pressing issues among indigenous communities.

But gender partnership is implicit within a future based on recovery of indigenous traditions. This vision of the future is based on the 'web of life' argument, where each individual/living being has a place within the broader system, a place that needs to be respected. Given that each part is necessary for the functioning of the whole, differences are not conceptualized in terms of hierarchies that promote inequality. As argued by Henderson:

> The Aboriginal worldview asserts that all life is sacred and that all life forms are connected. Humans are neither above nor below others in the circle of life. Everything that exists in the circle is one unity, of one heart.
>
> (Henderson 2000: 259)

The following section investigates educational visions as they are expressed within indigenous alternatives. In common with feminist alternatives, a large part of indigenous visions is based on a critique of mainstream knowledge and education. Interestingly, the main points of critique are somewhat similar to the critique within the two other alternatives analysed in this chapter – the feminist and the spiritual. However, as is the case with feminist and spiritual alternatives, there is also a set of issues that make indigenous alternatives unique. The following section explores this distinction in more detail.

Educational visions

> Our intention is to challenge the academy and its 'normal science' with the questions indigenous knowledges raise about the nature of our existence, our consciousness, our knowledge production, and the 'globalized' future.
>
> (Semali and Kincheloe 1999: 15)

As discussed in Part I, education has been part of 'the industry' that has aimed at the assimilation and disappearance of indigenous peoples. Willmot (1986: 15) suggests that the education of Aboriginal people in Australia was even a part of an 'Australian Holocaust'. *Development* and *literacy* still represent 'superior truths' that attempt to 'materialize the myth of progress among the "developing" countries in the years since the end of World War II' and serve as a potentially powerful remedy for 'underdevelopment', argues Maurial (1999: 61). It is not surprising then that one of the main tenets within the recovery of indigenous traditions represents a critique of western knowledge and education. This critique is depicted in terms of binary oppositions; that is, everything of indigenous education and knowledge is, and of western education and knowledge is not, and vice versa. This is very similar to feminist alternatives that also critique western patriarchal knowledge in terms of binary oppositions. From these critiques, both indigenous peoples and feminists draw inspiration to establish new ways of teaching and learning. As discussed in the previous chapter, feminists have established Women's Studies to counter hegemonic masculinist epistemologies and education. These feminist alternatives are mainly aimed at post-secondary school levels and tertiary education. At the primary and secondary levels, there are of course no feminist schools *per se*; however, over the last four decades there have been many significant attempts to transform curriculum and pedagogy at mainstream schools to make them more gender-balanced. Indigenous alternatives, however, are intended at every level of education, from the development of primary community schools to the development of higher-education Indigenous and Aboriginal Studies. Alternatives at the primary- and secondary-school level include Band-operated schools in Canada, Charter schools in the USA, Native and 'Tomorrow schools' in New Zealand and Community and 'Two Way' schools in Australia. Alternatives developed at the higher-education level are usually attached to already existing universities and other institutions of higher education, as with Women's Studies.

It is important to stress that, like feminist alternatives, indigenous educational visions are not monolithic. Even while becoming more and more global – and thus, to some extent, shared – there is a considerable debate about the existence of 'indigenous' (e.g. Native American, Maori, Aboriginal) pedagogy amongst indigenous educators. For example, 'Maori practitioners have wrestled with this concept [of Maori pedagogy] and some are constantly redefining their teaching style to address the issue' (Tapine and Waiti 1997: 24). In Australia, Willmot (1986) argues, indigenous educators are divided into three ideological camps. He describes them as 'separatists' ('independent education, separate systems, and separate tertiary institutions' (ibid.: 24)), 'integrationists' (successful integration into the mainstream education systems) and 'evolutionists' (that support strategic separatism).

In addition to diversity in regard to particular educational schools of thought, indigenous alternatives differ according to local complexities. That is, educational strategies are developed with respect to practical needs and main issues faced by local and national indigenous communities. The recognition of these differences is crucial. As argued by Semali (1999: 114), '[c]urriculum designers must be cognizant that there is not one indigenous culture that needs to be incorporated into education. Models of education borrowed from other African cultures can be as oppressive as the Euro-American models'.

Indigenous knowledge

However, as is the case with feminist alternatives, there is a common core that separates indigenous alternatives from other educational visions. The following summary is provided to help identify a common core of what constitutes indigenous knowledge and how that is compared to western knowledge. While written in the present tense, the following features actually represent recommendations for the future. They form the basis of the re-introduction of indigenous traditions for schools with a large indigenous community and for indigenous students. At the same time, they form the basis of preferred visions for educational futures, for the education of both indigenous and non-indigenous students. The characteristics of indigenous knowledge from which educational practices should draw an inspiration are as follows:

- *Indigenous knowledge is holistic*   This means that ideas and practices are one, that all aspects of one's self (intellectual, emotional, physical, creative, moral and spiritual) are integrated and that there is no division among 'disciplines of knowledge'. What western thinking calls 'religion', 'law', 'economics', 'arts' and so forth are united within a unitary worldview (Maurial 1999: 63–64). The holistic basis of indigenous knowledge means that the knowledge is produced and reproduced within human relationships as well as in their relationship with nature (ibid.).
- *Indigenous knowledge is oral*   This is because it is through oral interaction that holistic culture is transmitted and relational aspects of knowledge reaffirmed. To counter the destruction of traditional knowledge systems, strategies that are most often suggested by westerners include ex-situ storage, that is, isolation, documentation and storage in international, regional and national archives, argues Agrawal (1995). However, this is similar to arguing that the creation of libraries is sufficient to stimulate the production of literary works (ibid.). On the other hand, indigenous peoples often argue that if westerners are truly interested in the possible contributions of indigenous knowledge systems, they should support the continuation of indigenous cultures rather than the recording and documenting of existing knowledge (Viergever 1999: 339). Indigenous knowledge needs to be kept alive. This can be done only by supporting existing indigenous communities, so that knowledge can continue to be transmitted as it always was. As Viergever (ibid.) points out, the issue of the conservation of indigenous knowledge is therefore linked to land rights and self-determination (ibid.). As knowledge is not seen to be a commodity, but rather a collective good and intergenerational, it is elders rather than experts who are its legitimate carriers.
- *Indigenous knowledge is alive*   'Indigenous knowledge abounds in many communities, particularly in rural communities, and students growing up in such communities interface with this knowledge on a daily basis' (George 1999: 90). This knowledge

is about what 'local people know and do, and what they have known and done for generations – practices that developed through trial and error and proved flexible enough to cope with change' (Semali 1999: 95). Indigenous knowledge has not only survived colonization, it has managed to continuously regenerate itself, following patterns tens of thousands of years old. Rather than being destroyed by the 'modern invaders', indigenous peoples learned to 'accommodate and adjust themselves to these realities in ways that help indigenous systems not only survive but to regenerate themselves' (Prakash 1999: 168). As argued by Mwadime (1999: 257), new knowledge is continuously generated in line with today's reality and systems.

- *Indigenous knowledge cautiously engages with change* Traditional, indigenous societies are often perceived as being resilient to change. This has been looked upon by mainstream society as a factor that has contributed to the downfall of traditional societies. But authors such as Rodney Reynar argue that cautious engagement with change is one of the main strengths of indigenous knowledge systems. He argues that:

> contrary to what the modern scientific paradigm suggests, the resistance of indigenous knowledge to change is, rather, one of its most enduring strengths, and this [is] for several reasons. Although modern culture has elevated progress or change to a virtue, indigenous cultures have, on the other hand, established their ways of life in balance with a living and dynamic ecology, by cautiously engaging in change. Change is not undertaken for change's sake, as is the case, all too often, in modern cultures.
>
> (Reynar 1999: 298)

- *Indigenous knowledge and education engage in a dialogue with nature* The ecological basis of indigenous education means that indigenous knowledge is learned in a dialogical relationship with nature (Maurial 1999: 66). This means that children learn that nature is alive. To the indigenous child, and from an indigenous education perspective, the plant has a meaning only as a living organism – 'in a garden, in the forest, on the lake, on the mountain fed by water and sun, alive' (ibid.). A plant has no meaning in 'a black-metal microscope' (ibid.):

> In the child's world, she or he will touch the plant, will see it growing up, will be worried if it does not rain, and will ask

gods or goddesses to save it. In the microscope, the plant loses its relationship with the world, the society of plants, animals, and human society.

(Maurial 1999: 66)

All this also means that land is the basis of indigenous knowledge, spiritual and cultural traditions – 'Integral indigenous territoriality is a prerequisite for enabling the creative and inventive genius of each indigenous people to flourish' (ibid.). It is through relationship with the land that people develop a sense of belonging which also requires development of an 'emotional library' – the connection cannot be only understood on an intellectual level, but has to be felt at an emotional level as well (Buxton and d'Arbon 1999: 78).

* *Indigenous knowledge is based on spirituality*   As argued by Mosha (1999: 220), 'according to experience of indigenous peoples everywhere, and the experience of this author, spirituality is the foundation of all human endeavor. It is the foundation of good families, of thriving communities, of enduring cultures and civilizations'. Bayles (1989: 12) also argued that a very important aspect of Aboriginality is spirituality. It is with access to land that indigenous people develop culturally and spiritually as a people, otherwise they do not fully develop as individuals (ibid.). Concepts of spirituality which 'Christianity attempted to destroy, then to appropriate, and then to claim' are critical sites of resistance for indigenous peoples, argues Tuhiwai Smith (1999: 74). She also argues that it is also the most difficult aspect of indigenous cultures for westerners to accept:

> The arguments of different indigenous peoples based on spiritual relationships to the universe, to the landscape and to stones, rocks, insects and other things, seen and unseen, have been difficult arguments for Western systems of knowledge to deal with or accept. These arguments give a partial indication of the different worldviews and alternative ways of coming to know, and of being, which still endure within the indigenous world. The values, attitudes, concepts and language embedded in beliefs about spirituality represent, in many cases, the clearest contrast and mark of difference between indigenous peoples and the West. It is one of the few parts of ourselves which the West cannot decipher, cannot understand and cannot control... yet.

(Tuhiwai Smith 1999: 74)

The reconceptualization of education

These points – that indigenous knowledge is holistic, oral, alive, cautiously engages with change, engages in dialogue with nature and is based on spirituality – form the bases for the indigenous approach to education. Thus, the 'reconceptualization of education' is to be done through 'the conceptualization of indigenous knowledge', argues Maurial (1999: 59). The main attempt should be both to validate indigenous knowledge and 'to widen a perspective that reduces education to "schooling"' (ibid.). Indigenous knowledge differs from school knowledge in several ways, argues George (1999). For example:

> Indigenous knowledge is not normally generated by planned procedures and rules. Instead, it is generated as lay people seek to find solutions to problems in their day-to-day lives by drawing on existing societal wisdom and other local resources that may be available, and by using a fair amount of intuition and creativity. Typically, the knowledge generated is passed on from one generation to the next in the oral mode, although, within recent times, there have been concerted efforts to document and store such knowledge. With few exceptions, indigenous knowledge is not to be found on the school curriculum. That is a position reserved for academic knowledge that has been sanctioned by communities of scholars over the years.
>
> (George 1999: 80)

She also argues that indigenous knowledge may also be embedded in indigenous technologies that have evolved in the community over time:

> Sometimes, the indigenous knowledge is expressed in special prose, poetry, and drama; for example, as stories, calypsos, proverbs, jokes and chants. In these latter forms, the indigenous knowledge is often used for entertainment, but a careful analysis would reveal that these forms are rich sources of national and regional history, social analysis and criticism.
>
> (George 1999: 83)

Goduka (2001) argues that it is through methods such as:

> experiential learning – by doing and seeing; oral tradition – by listening and imagining; ritual/ceremony – through following

and imitating; dreaming – through unconscious imagery and artistic creation – through creative synthesis...[that] the integration of outer and inner realities of educators and learners are fully honored, and the educational needs and aspirations of learners are fully realized.

(Goduka 2001: final par.)

Oral transmission of education seems to be indispensable, even in the information-based 'cyber' era. This is because it is through the oral tradition that indigenous peoples 'transmit their holistic culture; in this way human beings foster relationships among them and between them and nature' (Maurial 1999: 63–64).

Inclusion is the utopian promise of the indigenous educator. However, this promise lies not only in the physical and cultural survival of indigenous peoples, but in humanity as a whole. Indigenous knowledge is not only 'useful', argues Viergever (1999: 332); rather, it is of 'critical importance to the survival of indigenous communities' (ibid.). Abdullah and Stringer (1999: 151) similarly assert that a context is needed to ensure that the primacy of Aboriginal systems of knowledge is based on Aboriginal Studies being 'directed to the survival, continued growth and enrichment of Aboriginal people and their heritage' (ibid.). Semali and Kincheloe (1999: 16) summarize the perspective of 'some indigenous educators and philosophers' who put it 'succinctly' that they want to use indigenous knowledge in order '...to counter Western science's destruction of the earth. Indigenous knowledge can facilitate this ambitious twenty-first century project because of its tendency to focus on relationships of human beings to both one another and to their ecosystem' (ibid.).

Most educational visions expressed within the indigenous alternatives require radical transformation rather than piecemeal strategies within education. For example:

My vision for the future, is an educational system where cultural diversity is cherished and respected, where social justice is a central theme, where indigenous perspectives are incorporated throughout the curriculum, where a true and accurate account of history is taught and respected, where adequately funded proactive programs are established to redress the 207 years that Aboriginal and Torres Strait Islander peoples were systematically excluded or placed on the fringes of society and the educational system. When this occurs, education will be equitable for all.

(Smallwood 1995: 16)

A vision: Somewhere there is a school. Before you have even entered the school grounds you know it is a Maori school. The layout, the architecture, and the people will let you know. What you hear will let you know. The way you are received will let you know. The arrangement of subjects and much of the curriculum will be recognisable. The study of the language will be robust as that currently expected of English. The students will know why they are at school, as will the parents. They will be confident, inquisitive, and engaging. The staff will be in no doubt as to the importance of the education they need to provide and encourage. Let's hope this is not one of those annoying stories that children write, which start so well but end 'and then I suddenly woke up and realized it was just a dream'.

(Uenuku Fairhall, in Tapine and Waiti 1997: 42)

What is the vision? An education that values...the unique identity of the individual and group, the dignity and mana of Maori people...that enables Maori to learn yesterday's knowledge... and today's knowledge, skills, and values...to prepare them for tomorrow...that enables Maori people to communicate and interact as equals with people from other countries and cultures...that empowers Maori people to participate and determine what is appropriate education for Maori people.

(Te Ururoa Flavell, in Tapine and Waiti 1997: 44)

These educational visions correspond to the previously discussed general vision for the future of local and global society. This is because the main issues raised here are also related to physical and cultural survival, self-determination, justice, holistic and socially and ecologically sustainable societies. On one hand, these visions are about 'survival education as cultural possibility' (Reignier 1995: 79). On the other, the incorporation of indigenous perspectives is seen as crucial, not only for redressing previous injustices but also for the benefit of both indigenous and non-indigenous peoples. The incorporation of indigenous perspectives can then help 'liberate' education currently confined to 'a narrow scientific view of the world that threatens the global future' (Battiste 2000: 194). Semali and Kincheloe (1999) argue that there are numerous benefits to be derived from the inclusion of indigenous knowledge in the academy. Indigenous knowledge and perspectives need not be confined in an academic ghetto. This is because indigenous knowledge is 'intellectually evocative' and 'useful for a variety of purposes in a plethora of contexts' (ibid.: 3). For example, the 'transformative power' of indigenous knowledge means that such knowledge can be used to foster empowerment and justice, '[a]s Paolo Freire and Antonio Faundez (1989) argue, indigenous knowledge is a rich social resource for any justice-related attempt to bring about social change' (ibid.: 15).

Indigenous knowledge and education draw their utopian promise for being 'holistic', for addressing ecological issues and social injustices and for fulfilling the spiritual void. In addition, there is no need to invent new solutions, because these alternatives have been proved to 'work' over a period of thousands of years. They are still available because, as argued earlier, one of the main characteristics of indigenous knowledge is that it is still *alive*:

> The essence of indigenous knowledge is that it is alive in indigenous peoples' culture. Different from Western knowledge, it is neither in archives, nor in laboratories. It is not separated from practical life. Thus, indigenous peoples are the actors of their knowledge and not passive repositories of a knowledge separated from everyday peoples' life. However, there are also non-local or non-indigenous factors that influence the recreation of – local – indigenous knowledge. These factors include such phenomena as indigenous responses to technological, market, and state innovations.
>
> (Maurial 1999: 63)

To summarize, because of current ecological and social problems – alienation, the crisis in meaning, the existence of perpetually conflict-ridden societies, global warfare – western ways need to be abandoned. While western technological achievements are to be kept, the general framework within which technological development occurs needs to be fundamentally changed. Knowledge taught in schools should be holistic, produced and reproduced within human relationships as well as in humans' relationship with nature (ibid.). It should be more contextualized (Thomas 1991: 18); an integral part of the physical and social environment of communities. What is considered to be empirical evidence needs to be broadened; empirical data should include experiences of dreams, visions and environmental signs. Multi-literacies should be promoted, including giving higher preference to the oral transmission of knowledge. There should be higher participation by local indigenous elders who will promote this important oral transmission. Learning should be organized as a communal and collaborative exercise, rather than being individual and competitive. Knowledge should be seen as a collective good, and not as something that can be commodified and measured by the economic utility it provides. The vocational aspect of education is important, but morality and spirituality are also crucial.

Summary: analysis of indigenous alternatives

Indigenous alternatives present a viable alternative for the future – for both indigenous and non-indigenous peoples. Indigenous alternatives in education are firmly connected to a preferred vision for the future – that of an equitable, just and fair society (Table 9.1).

This vision for the future is reflected in the preferred educational model. Education is envisioned as more communal, wherein elders are more respected. Multi-literacies and multi-temporalities ensure that indigenous culture keeps its historical connection with ancestors, as well as creating the necessary links with future generations. Relationships among people and between people and nature are seen to be crucial. The biggest change between 'traditional' indigenous education and the recovery of indigenous traditions is the movement from local and nation state level towards global indigenous issues.

Table 9.1 Indigenous renaissance – social futures

Approach to time	Vision for the future	Utopian promise	Dystopian dangers	Social eutopia
Linear (as in creating more just future)	Indigenous renaissance	Saving the earth	[Missing]	Survival and advancement of indigenous peoples
Long-term future (as in seven generations – Native American)	Equitable and just societies	Survival of human species and other living beings		
		Universe kept in balance and harmony		

The traditional view of time has also changed, moving towards a linear western approach. Societies are seen to be able to be improved upon, and justice and equity are seen as achievable human goals. Technologies are not rejected, but they are seen in terms of the need for 'two way' education. Numerous strategies are developed to facilitate the success of indigenous children in 'new (electronic) times' (e.g. Castellano, Davis and Lahache 2000; Kapitzke *et al.* 2001). However, the writings on electronic literacy are not accompanied by utopian imaging; rather, it is part of a broader focus on cultural survival. As argued by Battiste (2000: 202), 'Aboriginal languages and education can be the means to opening the paradigmatic doors of contemporary public education. Creating a balance between two worldviews is the great challenge facing modern educators'.

The suggested/needed transformation of mainstream education corresponds to this vision of the future. In concrete terms it is proposed that education needs to become more holistic, nature-oriented and incorporate moral and spiritual learning. The most pressing issues are seen to be:

- The revision of history and inclusion of indigenous perspectives (such as in the 'settlement' vs 'invasion' debate). In Australia, this would consist of contrasting the myth of 'terra nullius' with historical facts.
- Education to promote respect between various cultures.
- Education that teaches different worldviews and ways of being and acknowledges cultural differences.
- Indigenous peoples to become the subject and not the objects of education. There should be higher involvement of indigenous peoples within educational systems. Schools to work with local indigenous communities.
- Education is no longer to be an instrument of assimilation, but an instrument that promotes the survival and well-being of indigenous communities.

Tables 9.2, 9.3, 9.4 and 9.5 suggest, as argued earlier, that the indigenous alternative is dramatically different from the hegemonic globalized and cyber vision for the future of education. While indigenous authors consider it important to engage with mainstream society and its technologies, the technological is not at the core of their epistemology and vision of the future. The core is consistent with the needs and desires of indigenous peoples, as argued by indigenous theorists and writers. It is their physical, cultural and

Table 9.2 Indigenous educational visions

Underlying vision for the future	Utopian promise	Dystopian dangers	Educational eutopia
Indigenous renaissance	Holistic learning	Missing out on achievements within mainstream society	Learning from indigenous peoples about local history and environment
Equitable and just societies	Improved relationships between peoples, with nature; Education more life-relevant		

Worldview and approach to knowledge	Epistemology	Educated Subject
Holistic, relationship-based, spiritual, nature-oriented and contextual	The dreaming, medicine wheel, web of life	One who continues indigenous culture for future generations

Educational visions/futures

Content	Process	Structure
Land, genealogy and spirituality; Broadens the empirical	Elders, legitimate carriers of knowledge; Oral, multi-literacies and multi-temporalities	Communal learning; Integrated into physical and social environment

Table 9.3 Indigenous futures and educational visions – key words

Change	Future	Society	Education	Other key words
Metaphors of nature	Relationships between ancestors and future generations	Colonized Decolonized	Incorporation of indigenous perspectives Genealogy Equitable education for all	Justice Environmental protection

Table 9.4 Indigenous futures and educational visions – causal layered analysis

Litany	Social cause	Discourse/worldview	Myth/metaphor	Education bottom line
Indigenous people are colonized	Imperialism	Indigenous	Web of life Trauma from colonization	Education for cultural, human and nature survival

Table 9.5 Indigenous futures and educational visions – deconstruction

Who gets to speak	Who and what is silenced	What is missing from a discourse	Continuity	Discontinuity
Indigenous peoples	Non-indigenous peoples	Growth Development	Tens of thousands of years old indigenous civilization/ indigenous cultures	Colonization 1960s social movements in the west

environmental survival, and as well the planet's survival, that is paramount. Gender is not seen as crucial here; racism and imperialism are far more important. External factors are seen as the causes behind the litany of colonization. Utopia is to be found in pre-colonization periods. It is from this reality/history/tradition that directions for the future are inspired and derived. However, this does not mean a return to the past, as social conditions have changed. The technological is incorporated into a vision for the future that values relationships, land and community.

10 Visions V: spiritual alternatives

Spiritual education: introductory remarks

> The spiritualistic educational movement is probably one of the oldest on the planet. Like the tide, it always returns.
>
> (Bertrand 1995: 9)

> Spirituality is not a road on which humans are free to travel or not to travel. They must choose to travel on it in order to be human.
>
> (Mosha 1999: 220)

In the past 25 years, there has been a very strong resurgence of various spiritualistic movements in the west. According to Bertrand this is because:

> Industrialized civilization has failed to fulfill a fundamental human need to understand our presence on Earth...People have always wondered: 'Does life have a meaning?' Hence the proliferation of spiritualistic movements that answer positively: 'Yes, there is another world, an unnameable world with a thousand names that we must experience.' The goal of spiritualistic education is to familiarize the individual with this spiritual reality – also called mystical or metaphysical.
>
> (Bertrand 1995: 9)

As could be expected, proponents of spiritual approaches take issue with the materialistic, mechanistic and secular orientation of modern education. They also take issue with current hegemonic visions for the future, arguing that these are leading humanity towards an undesirable, dangerous terrain, most obviously in relation to the possible environmental, social and spiritual costs of these visions. As was the case with all previous futures visions, the spiritual orientation in education also stems from particular traditions/histories. As summarized in Yves Bertrand's words above, the spiritual[1] education movement is arguably one of the oldest approaches in education. It is also one of the most widely found – throughout history and human societies. According to Bertrand, the idea of a spiritual vision of/for the world stems from 'Platonism and Neo-Platonism, from Hinduism and the Oriental religious philosophies such as Taoism and Zen' (1995: 11). The main sources that the recent spiritual renewal draws upon are, according to him, religions, metaphysics, eastern philosophies, mysticism, Taoism, Buddhism, perennial philosophy and the concept of cosmic consciousness (ibid.: 223). But there is, of course, an indigenous approach to spirituality which I have previously discussed only briefly. As explained by Craven (Craven *et al.* 1999: 240), this topic should be 'out of bounds' for non-indigenous researchers and educators. There is also feminist spirituality (e.g. Plaskow and Christ 1989), including spiritual eco-feminism, most prominently articulated in the work of Starhawk, Charlene Spretnak and Carol Christ, but also implicit in the work of several women futurists. Spirituality has been described only briefly in this book in the section on feminist visions. This is because spirituality is part of some of the strands within feminism but not of others and, therefore, is not a fundamental part of the feminist 'core', of what feminism is mostly about.

In addition to these approaches to spirituality, each of the three major monotheistic religions – Judaism, Christianity and Islam – also includes a 'softer', mystical and spiritual orientation (e.g. Green 1989; McGinn and Meyendorff 1989; Nasr 1989; Pourrat 1922–1927). There is even the 'postmodern' *Quantum Spirituality* (Sweet 1991). Also, more recently, some authors have started using terms such as 'secular' (Miller and Nakagawa 2002: v), 'relational' (Hart 2003: 68) or 'critical' (Bussey 2000a) spirituality.

The analysis here is limited to several influential theorists, and to texts that best demonstrate what kinds of society and education this new resurgence of spiritual issues and concerns envisions. I also limit my analysis to educational alternatives that are developed from the Indian episteme or have basic similarities to this perspective. I broaden the concept of utopia and the predominantly western focus on external social change. Thus, I more closely investigate the concept of eupsychia and the ways it has impacted upon spiritual educational alternatives. The classics and contemporary theorists on spiritual education analysed here include Sri Aurobindo and Mira Alfassa Richard ('The Mother'), Mohandas Gandhi, Jiddu Krishnamurti, Maharishi Mahesh Yogi, Sri Sathya Sai Baba, Prabhat Rainjan Sarkar and Rabindranath Tagore. These authors not only have produced volumes of scholarship, but have influenced many contemporary educators on the Indian sub-continent and Asia, and all over the western world. As well, most have developed/inspired educational alternatives in praxis, from primary- and high-school educational institutions (in the 'independent sector') to various research institutes and communities.[2] Also included are contemporary western writers whose work follows this spiritual paradigm, albeit from different traditions, for example, Palmer, Miller, O'Sullivan and others.

In addition to the above-mentioned authors, a more thorough reading of the classics on spiritual education would also include analysis of the work of both Rudolf Steiner and Maria Montessori. And, it would also include a study of more general literature. For example, Bertrand (1995: 223) identifies the following authors as relevant to spiritualistic theories and practice in education: Richard Bucke, Fritjof Capra, Mircea Eliade, Ralph Waldo Emerson, Marilyn Ferguson, Constantin Fotinas, Willis Harman, Hazel Henderson, Carl Jung, Lao-Tzu, George Leonard, Abraham Maslow, Daisetz Teitaro Suzuki and Henry David Thoreau. Miller's (2000: par. 4) list of 'general holistic literature'[3] includes works by Theodore Roszak, Fritjof Capra, Charlene Spretnak and Ken Wilber. Miller and Nakagawa's (2002) *Nurturing Our Wholeness: Perspectives on Spirituality in Education* includes Tibetan Buddhism, Taoist, Tantric as well as Spiritual Christian Education. In addition to Aurobindo, Krishnamurti, Tagore, Emerson, Thoreau, Montessori and Steiner, they also include authors such as Martin Buber, Aldous Huxley, Thomas Merton, Bronson Alcott and J. G. Bennett. Glazer's (1999) *The Heart of Learning: Spirituality in Education* also includes articles on Buddhist and western spiritual traditions in education. Nakagawa's (2000) *Education for Awakening* discusses, among others, authors such as Kitaro Nishida, Shin'ichi Hisamatsu and Toshihiko Izutsu. His compilation also includes work by Palmer, who has recently become an influential author on spiritual education in his own right (e.g. Palmer 1980, 1993, 1998, 1999a). Analysis of work by most of these authors would be beyond the scope of this book. I therefore analyse twentieth-century classics and the work of contemporary authors who engage more directly with the Indian episteme, have published in English and have discussed and/or developed/inspired educational alternatives in praxis. This group includes an analysis of the main approaches to human society and social change developed within the New Age[4] movement – most of it inspired by Indian philosophy (of Tantric, Vedic and Buddhist varieties).

The influence of the current resurgence of spirituality in the west can best be 'measured' by dystopian readings, to a degree that neither indigenous nor feminist alternatives seem to have. This dystopian reading of the New Age movement, as well as of spiritual alternatives in general, is mostly provided by the Christian Right. The threat of the New Age movement in the USA alone has prompted incredibly detailed texts that 'expose' every approach, movement and philosophy associated with it (e.g. Ankerberg and Weldon 1996).

Religion and spirituality

It is important to note here the distinction between spiritual and religious approaches to education, as well as between the more recent spiritual revival and the traditional spiritual movements. As argued by Laukhuf and Werner (1998), religion is the service and adoration of God expressed in forms of worship; it refers to an external formalized system of beliefs, values, codes of conduct and rituals – it is a codified set of morals. Spirituality, on the other hand, is a very personal and individual value system involving the way that people approach life, varying from person to person, and changing throughout a person's life (ibid.). While religion is 'a specific way of exercising that spirituality and usually requires an institutional affiliation', spirituality does not require an institutional connection (Noddings 1999). According to Palmer (1999b), it is about:

> the ancient and abiding human quest for connectedness with something larger and more trustworthy than our egos – with our own souls, with one another, with the worlds of history and nature, with the invisible winds of the spirit, with the mystery of being alive.
>
> (Palmer 1999b: 6)

Religion does not only attempt to institutionalize spirituality; in many instances this is done 'for the perpetuation of the institution rather than for the explicit welfare of the individual' (O'Sullivan 1999: 260). Unfortunately, spirituality has, in our times, been seriously compromised by its identification with institutional religions, argues O'Sullivan (ibid.: 259). This is problematic, because spirituality is neither religion nor is it in the sole province of religion (ibid.: 260). As Krishnamurti (1995: 25) also argues, spirituality 'does not belong to any cult, to any group, to any religion, to any organized church'. The spiritual mind:

> Is not the Hindu mind, the Christian mind, the Buddhist mind, or the Muslim mind ... [it] does not belong to any group which calls itself religious ... [it] is not the mind that goes to churches, temples, mosque ... nor ... to certain forms of beliefs, dogmas ... It is a mind that has seen through the falsity of churches, dogmas, beliefs, traditions. Not being nationalistic, not being conditioned by its environment, such a mind has no horizons, no limits.
>
> (Krishnamurti 1995: 25)[5]

The mystic notion of God may be replaced 'by the more philosophical notion of truth and still the discovery will remain essentially the same' (The Mother 1965: 23). From a spiritual perspective, religions are problematic because, 'as they are taught and practiced today [they] lead to conflict rather than unity' (Gandhi, in Cenkner 1976: 113). Because of fractionism brought by religions, Tagore, Aurobindo and others argue that religions should best not be officially taught, but that 'the truths' common to all religions could and should be taught to all children (ibid.). According to Palmer (1999b), however, spirituality is less about teaching truths than about helping with articulating and thinking about particular questions. He argues that people rarely raise spiritual issues, partly because of 'the embarrassed silence that may greet us if we ask our real questions aloud' (ibid.: 8). Further, another, perhaps even more significant, reason that people do not ask these questions is because someone will try to give them 'The Answer' (ibid.). Spirituality is not about answers but about questions such as:

> 'Does my life have meaning and purpose?' 'Do I have gifts that the world wants and needs?' 'Whom and what can I trust?' 'How can I rise above my fears?' 'How do I deal with suffering, my own and that of my family and friends?' 'How does one maintain hope?' 'What about death?' ... ' How shall I live today knowing that someday I will die?'
>
> (Palmer 1999b: 6–8, 10)

But it is important to remember that spiritual questions do not have answers 'in the way math problems do', but rather are deeply personal (ibid.). People do not want to be saved, but simply heard; they are not looking for fixes or formulae, but for compassion and companionship. Questions, therefore, are not there to be answered, but to be loved and lived (Rilke, in Palmer 1999b).

Hence, spirituality is primarily concerned with 'a personal interpretation of life and the inner resource of people' (Laukhuf and Werner 1998). In its 'broadest sense, spirituality is the manifestation of the spirit, just as physiology is one manifestation of the body and emotions are a manifestation of the mind' (ibid.). It is 'at the core of the individual's existence, integrity', transcending 'the physical, emotional, intellectual, and social dimension' (Landrum and associates, quoted in Laukhuf and Werner 1998).

Spirituality could then, in fact, be conceived of as 'the umbrella concept under which religion and the needs of the human spirit are found' (ibid.). While it can include, be related to, or expressed through more formal religions, it is, in essence, a much broader notion than the notions of the religious. This is because spirituality is predominantly about 'a personal quest to find meaning and purpose in life and relationship to the mystery/God and the rest of the universe' (ibid.). This 'new God' is markedly different from the God often imagined within the Judeo-Christian–Islamic tradition. That is, the word has come to signify 'a nonathropomorphized, genderless entity, equivalent to the sum total of matter or energy in the universe' (Torgovnick 1997: 175). Similarly, Trenoweth writes:

> As often as not, our God today is androgynous and increasingly our God sides more solidly with the oppressed than the oppressor. Our God is a shape-shifter. When we envisage God, she is as likely to be the colour of chocolate as the colour of snow and might sit high on a cloud or lie curled beneath the earth, birthing the forests, the animals, the mountains, the oceans and, over and again, the human generations. Or perhaps, as the Dalai Lama would have it, we envisage no God at all, for the one true reality lies in blissful emptiness, perfect place.
>
> (Trenoweth 1995: ix)

Another important difference is between the more recent spiritual revival and traditional spirituality. Traditional spiritualists often removed themselves from society, predominantly engaging with meditative and contemplative processes that could bring enlightenment. More recent spiritual revival considers such removal from society, as well as any form of theology or institutionalized religion, as an escape from life (Bertrand 1995: 9). The works of Krishnamurti, Sarkar, Aurobindo and others represent a radical break from the Hindu tradition – which considered the world as mere *maya*, an illusion. Some eastern philosophies have 'distorted spirituality to such an extent that they regard the world as an illusion', argues Sarkar (1998: 145). The traditional approach is seen as problematic, because all attempts to try and develop the material world are therefore seen to be futile (ibid.). This has, according to Sarkar (p. 250), resulted in 'fabricated religious injunctions [that] have been a repeated cause of exploitation'. Especially in the case of women, some of the proclamations of the traditional scriptures (to live the life of a virgin is a vice; polygamy and widow's suttee are accepted and encouraged) resulted in incredibly cruel practices (ibid.).

Krishnamurti also argues that the traditional approach is problematic, mostly because 'you cannot withdraw from life' (1974: 122), but have to live in this (though 'monstrous') society. Krishnamurti's (ibid.: 94) argument is based on the belief that such an (traditional) approach cannot help bring in the 'new man' and the new society but merely reproduces age-old problems:

> And there are also those who are concerned only with the inner world. They emphasize the so-called inner world, and become more and more isolated, more and more self-centered, more and more vague, pursuing their own beliefs, dogmas and visions.
>
> (Krishnamurti 1974: 94)

For Aurobindo, the world is, rather, 'an inseparable power of the divine through which the latter manifests itself' (Cenkner 1976: 148). Sai Baba (1988: 9, 43) also argues that, '[b]orn in society, one has the duty to work for the welfare and progress of society... Man cannot live in isolation like a drop of oil on water. He is a product of society. He has to live in it, grow with it and work for it'.

The goal of contemporary approaches to spirituality is thus not to isolate oneself from the world but rather to find a centre, to balance inner and outer, to somehow find an approach which does not divide, and to be able to function in both worlds equally (Krishnamurti 1974; Sarkar 1998; Sri Aurobindo 1965). And both this inner and outer development are critical in the visions of the future that follow.

Approaches to time and the vision for the future

Spiritual education alternatives do not deny the linearity of time, but this linearity exists within a broader context: within both cyclical movements of time and within 'timeless' time. This alternative view of time leads to a different interpretation of human history and different views on future directions for humanity.

The concept of timeless time is based on a conviction of the existence of a Transcendental Reality that is beyond time and space. This Reality cannot be intellectually understood, theorized or analysed. It is the non-negotiable foundation of the episteme. It can only be felt, experienced. The one, and possibly only, avenue which can enable access to this Reality is spiritual practice.

Although humans exist within the boundaries of time, space and person, these limitations can and should be transcended. Mind, which is of time and space, needs to enter the non-spatial, timeless state because it is only in that state that there is creation, argues Krishnamurti (1974: 173). Unless the mind is emptied of all previous conditioning, unless the mind is free and totally new, no real change is possible. It is in that state that one is finally free of fear, and it is that state that enables feeling of all time '...not today, tomorrow, the day after day, but the feeling of all time. To think in terms of man, the world, the universe is an extraordinary feeling' (ibid.: 135–136).

There is no other alternative but to break free from the bondages of these limitations and 'merge with the Infinite', argues Sarkar (1998: 166). When one merges with the Infinite, one becomes omniscient. By knowing one, a person can know all (ibid.: 329). Once this omniscience is achieved, it is possible to see all three ages – past, present and future (ibid.: 269). Of course, for Sarkar, Krishnamurti and others, while endeavouring to go beyond, one should also remain within the scope of time, space and person. That is, one needs to live in both worlds, inner and outer. Once this balance is achieved – between time of the clock, psychological time and timeless time (Krishnamurti 1974) – the path towards 'realization' is open.

The time of the clock can also be termed 'objective time' (Miller 2000: 24). Miller argues that this objective time corresponds to the ego. It is the ego that sees objects as separate, focusing on controlling reality. The soul, on the other hand, exists in a space that enables it to see multiplicity and unity at the same time. It exists within subjective time and focuses on love (ibid.). Miller makes a further distinction between ego, soul and spirit. It is spirit that sees unity and connection and exists outside time. It is therefore neither ego nor soul but rather spirit – 'this divine essence within' – that is the part of us which exists beyond time and space (ibid.). It is through spirit (variously called *Atman*, *paratman*, Buddha nature or the Self) that humans experience unity with the divine (e.g. *Brahman*, God, Tao) (ibid.). For Sri Aurobindo and The Mother, an important distinction between spiritual and psychic life needs to be made. The former is 'a return to the unmanifest, beyond time and space', while the latter is about 'higher realization in time and space' (The Mother 1965: 27):

> the psychic life is the life immortal, endless time, limitless space, every progressive change, unbroken continuity in the world of forms. The spiritual consciousness, on the other hand, means to live the infinite and eternal, to throw oneself outside all creation, beyond time and space. To become fully aware of your psychic being and to live a psychic life you must abolish in you all self-ishness; but to live a spiritual life you must be selfless.
>
> (The Mother 1965: 27)

Timeless time can only be approached through spiritual practice. Spiritual education thus remains one of the most important, if not *the* most important, social institution and practice.

Of course, the 'timeless time' approach immediately assumes a long-term (eternal) vision. It is timeless time that contains within it all other times: the time of the clock, personal and social cycles and one-way directional movements through time. Both linear and cyclical approaches to social change are therefore theorized at the macro level: they last from anywhere between a few thousand years and eternity.

Human evolution revisited

Judith's (1993) interpretation of human history and social change is reflective of the dominant worldview that exists within the New Age movement. It is also a good example of a completely different timeline to the dominant, technologically oriented one. Most familiar to the wider audience is the notion of astrological time. The present era is seen as a transition to the so-called 'Age of Aquarius' (Ferguson 1980), the spiritual rebirth of humanity. According to Judith, who summarizes the New Age interpretation of history well, human evolution is analogous to the rise of the *Kundalini* (activating energy force that connects *chakras*) up through the main *chakras* (energy centres) that exist within the human body. Human evolution follows a pattern that can best be described as a growth towards higher consciousness: as a species we are 'destined' to 'rise' towards 'true' progress and the development of higher levels of 'sophistication' (Judith 1987: 435). The summary of this view of history, social change and trends towards the future is presented in Table 10.1.

Typically, the greatest attention is given to the transformation of the current phase, based on the age of the third *chakra*, towards 'The Age of Aquarius'. The transformation is seen to be following a linear pattern, and is 'destined' as the 'world of man is being irresistibly forced to form one single whole ... converging upon itself' (Teilhard de Chardin 1970: 53). Each new phase brings humanity towards 'greater freedom and understanding', but the coming New Age is first to be 'fully expected and anticipated' (Judith 1993: 439). In the words of Marx Hubbard (1998), the 'new story of creation' (ibid.: 2) is about 'the awakening of humanity' (ibid.: 7), conscious evolution by choice, which now marks a dawn of 'co-creative society' (ibid.: 3).

Although this view of history and social change is represented in very firm deterministic terms, and it is reminiscent of the dominant timeline described in Part II (in that it is applicable to 'all' societies, Age of Nomads is less 'sophisticated'), it is also often stressed that this change is not inevitable. Rather, it is up to humans to decide whether the upcoming change will be 'a graceful, natural, or violent birth to the next stage of evolution' (ibid.: 27). While the seeds of change are here, if humans do not act positively, they may not be able to bypass the nuclear age and bring forth the new one (Judith 1993; Eisler 1987, 1997, 2000). Still, the main problem with the previous classification is its determinism. Another problem lies in its organicism – the patterning of social change according to 'energy centres' that reside within the human body. The major problem with this scheme is that it does not allow for differentiation between various social, cultural, national and civilizational patterns of social change. In common with the mainstream linear approach to history, all stages and all phases are to be experienced by all societies simultaneously. Still, it is a good example of a different way to see history, the present and the future. That is, it is an example of yet another effort to challenge the hegemony – naturalization – of one particular interpretation of time, history and the future.

This view of history and social change, while popular within the New Age movement, is not universally shared by all who have focused on the development of spiritual alternatives. For example, Krishnamurti's (1974: 64–65, 1985, 1995) 'three stages or hierarchies'

Table 10.1 Chakras as an evolutionary system

Chakra	Location	Element	Associated with
One	Base of the spine	Earth	Survival
Two	Sacral plexus	Water	Emotions and sexuality
Three	Solar plexus	Fire	Personal power and metabolic energy
Four	Sternum	Air	Love
Five	Throat	Sound	Communication and creativity
Six	Centre of the forehead – 'Third Eye'	Light	Clairvoyance, intuition and imagination
Seven	Top of the head – head crown	Thought	Knowledge and understanding

Chakra	Phase in history	Technology	Age of
One	Early stone age	Made of natural materials (stone, wood and bone)	Nomads, lives short and dangerous
Two	From 8500 BCE to 1500 BCE	Control of water, development of agriculture, beginning of ship building	First agricultural communities
Three	Iron age From about 1500 BCE to about CE 2000	Tools forged in the fire, including weapons	Aggression, power and technology
Four	From CE 2000 to CE 3750	New information technologies	Balance (between spirit and matter, sexes, peoples of all races and creeds)
Five	From CE 3750 to CE 4625	Technologies that promote communication	Space travel
Six	From CE 4625 to CE 5062	Psychic powers, travel at the speed of light	Seeking and developing visions
Seven	From CE 5062 to CE 5280	Development of awareness and body of knowledge	Harmony with the universe

Adapted from Judith (1993).

and Sarkar's (1998, Inayatullah 1997) description of social change in terms of the movement between four classes/castes differ from the previous timeline. While all three are cyclical, the length of each cycle and the actual number of phases differ. But, although these approaches differ in their interpretation of human history, they are quite similar in their conviction about desired directions for the future; about where humanity *should* be going. This 'conscious evolution by choice' needs to bring 'the new man' and 'the new society' (Krishnamurti), a new type of leader who is spiritual, universal in outlook and ready to take on the burden of human suffering (Sarkar's *sadvipra*, Buddhist *bodhisatva*). Eupsychia – the development of the self – has to go hand in hand with eutopia – the development of the good society.

So, whether the New Age perspective is that of Judith, Krishnamurti or Sarkar, the emergence of the new 'total' human being is a consistent theme, cutting across the diversity amongst various authors on spiritual education. There are also several other similarities. First, change is constant. Second, change is theorized from an evolutionary macro perspective. Third, behind visible change there is also an entity that exists beyond the scope of time, place and person. Such an entity is the only eternal, undecaying, imperishable, immutable entity (Sarkar 1998: 319). And fourth, we are in the midst of radical transformation. This transformation is about the possible (but urgently needed) emergence of a 'new human'[6] and a new society.

The coming of a spiritual age and the awakening of the self

This new bright future is part of a greater evolution, and can best be labelled using Sri Aurobindo's (1962: 353) 'the coming of a Spiritual Age'. As Sri Aurobindo wrote:

> the coming of a spiritual age must be preceded by the appearance of an increasing number of individuals who are no longer satisfied with the normal intellectual, vital and physical existence of man, but perceive that a greater evolution is the real goal of humanity and attempt to effect it in themselves, to lead others to it, and to make it the recognized goal of the race.
>
> (Sri Aurobindo 1962: 353)

But the highest utopian promise lies in personal liberation. As described by The Mother:

an inner door will open suddenly and you will come out into a dazzling splendour that will bring to you the certitude of immortality, the concrete experience that you have lived always and always shall live, that the external forms alone perish and that these forms are, in relation to what you are in reality, like clothes that are thrown away when worn out... And yet this release from all slavery to the flesh, this liberation from all personal attachment is not the supreme fulfilment. There are other steps to take before you reach the summit. And even these steps can and should be followed by others which will open the gates of the future. It is these later steps that will be the subject-matter of what I call spiritual education.

(The Mother 1965: 27)

The final goal of authors within the spiritual tradition – Aurobindo, Krishnamurti, Gandhi, Tagore, Sarkar, Sai Baba and Maharishi – is transformation, the awakening of humans as spiritual beings. Of course, societies should change as well; however, this cannot be achieved by external change alone. As argued by Krishnamurti, 'You have to change society, but not by killing people. Society is you and I. You and I create the society in which we live. So you have to change' (1974: 15).

The first step in bringing total transformation in all spheres of life is to 'transform ourselves' (Anandamitra 1987a: 210). One can become a Marxist by reading books about Marxism or listening to lectures on Marxist ideology, argues Anandamitra (ibid.), but one cannot awaken as a spiritual being unless 'the vision of oneness of all creation... [is] experienced in the core of one's being... [becoming] an undeniable part of one's reality'. People must purify their own personalities of all narrowness and tendencies to harm others, as well as develop the powerful discernment and force necessary for the struggle against tyranny in all its forms:

We must become *embodiments* of the vision of New-Humanism [Sarkar's social and educational vision], not just spokespeople for it – for no great idea can prevail unless it is embodied in individuals whose *lives* are the message. When we have transformed ourselves, we can transform the world.

(Anandamitra 1987a: 213)

To summarize, the central concepts within spiritual alternatives are: the concept of inner transformation; the movement towards enlightenment, *Brahma*; and perfection of one's self towards 'true' nature and reality. The main approach towards change could be encapsulated in the phrase, 'be the change you want to see'. The main vision for the future is, therefore, one where society is constituted by self-actualized individuals. It is also about accessing 'cosmic' time, where the individual is liberated through access to 'infinite time', entrance to 'spacelessness' and a 'timeless' state. This access is only possible through silence, withdrawal within one's self, going beyond words and 'therefore out of time' (Krishnamurti 1974: 173). As Krishnamurti argues, 'the word is time' (p. 173), and therefore one needs to go beyond words, beyond fixed thoughts, beyond intellect and into a space free of any preconceptions, with a mind 'that is astonishingly quiet, still' (p. 175). Only then can the mind create something new; otherwise the person remains a specialist, technician, repeating and adding onto the old. To achieve this, spiritual practice is necessary. And it is education that is crucial, both in the learning of spirituality and in the creation of a new human and a new society.

Educational visions

> *Sa vidya ya vimuktaye* – Education is that which liberates.
>
> (Sarkar 1998: 111)

Before discussing the preferred educational vision, I briefly summarize the main critique of current education from within the spiritual perspective. This critique is based on a conviction that the modern system of education is universally flawed. What is seen to be lacking is a focus on full human development. The accumulation of information and knowledge does not lead to 'intelligence', goodness, nor 'flowering', argues Krishnamurti (1995). Actually, mere acquisition of knowledge without a moral and spiritual approach is outright dangerous: 'If you have no intelligence, no sensitivity, then knowledge can become very dangerous. It can be used for destructive purposes' (Krishnamurti 1974: 30).

To make education 'fit into' current mainstream society is a mistake, because current society is riddled with problems, conflicts and misery, argues Krishnamurti (1974, 1995). Mainstream society is 'compulsively authoritarian...brutal and tyrannical, not only in the immediate relationships but in social relationships' (Krishnamurti 1974: 101). Further, humans have created a society which 'demands all their time, all their energies, all their life', argues Krishnamurti

(1995: 77). As there is no leisure to learn, life becomes 'mechanical, almost meaningless' (ibid.).

Today there is little talk of 'pleasure or ecstasy, or even joy in the world of educational discourse', argues Kesson (2002: 31). Because in the current educational system spiritual elements have no place, it cannot be said that such a system represents 'true education' (Sai Baba 1988: 9). Today's education is only 'yielding a harvest of pride and envy' (ibid.: 29). Our present educational institutions are in line with, and are feeding into, 'industrialism, nationalism, competitive transnationalism, individualism and patriarchy', argues O'Sullivan (1999: 7). The most familiar words in education are 'assessment, standards, zero tolerance, and accountability', which are 'the words of the corporate boardroom, not the human potential movement' (Kesson 2002: 30). Emerging hegemonic futures visions are also problematic because they rely on competition, fear, insecurity and materialism. It is fear that is essentially involved in competition – 'to be afraid of being nobody, of not arriving, of not succeeding' (Krishnamurti 1974: 53). But when there is fear, 'you cease to learn' (ibid.). The primary economic emphasis in education means that 'education' has become a series of tests and hurdles rather than focusing on learning (Miller 2000: 4). Education has, therefore, become an institution whose purpose in the modern world is '…not to make culture, not to serve the living cosmos, but to harness humankind to the dead forces of materialism. Education as we know it, from preschool through graduate school, damages the soul' (Sardello 1992: 50).

Not only is the soul damaged, it is almost murdered and is definitely seriously ill, argues O'Sullivan:

> 'globalization' is becoming a religion. [But] it is not a religion that cultivates the human spirit; in fact, it warps the human spirit by its egregious emphasis on material goods. What is happening in our time under the guise of 'globalization' is nothing less than soul murder. It is pervasive and appears to move at the speed of an aggressive cancer. The movement into 'globalization' of the world economy is most certainly a cancer of the human spirit.
>
> (O'Sullivan 1999: 260)

Kushner (1999) goes even further, arguing that not enabling children to nourish their souls (through a sense of ritual and a sense of magic) should be considered 'a form of child abuse' (p. 21). They need to be enabled to understand and experience that there is 'a reality beyond the reality of everyday life and that there is something wonderful about this', because it is that realization that nourishes the soul (ibid.).

Current education violates 'the deepest needs of the human soul' with some regularity, argues Palmer (1999b: 6). Because the system of education is so fearful of things spiritual, it fails to address the real issues of our lives, it dispenses facts at the expense of meaning, and information at the expense of wisdom (ibid.). The price paid is:

> a school system that alienates and dulls us, that graduates young people who have had no mentoring in the questions that both enliven and vex the human spirit... When we fail to honor the deepest question of our lives, education remains mired in technical triviality, cultural banality, and worse: It continues to be dragged down by a great sadness. I mean the sadness one feels in too many schools where teachers and students alike spend their days on things unworthy of the human heart – a grief that may mask itself as boredom, sullenness, or anger, but that is, at bottom, a cry for meaning.
>
> (Palmer 1999b: 6, 8)

While the WebNet vision of the world assumes technology as our saviour, this perspective is seen as undesirable. Neither markets nor technology can produce balanced individuals and develop holistic societies. Technology cannot help achieve 'a perfect or a good society', argues Krishnamurti. That is:

> It may produce a great society, where there is no poverty, where there is material equality and so on. A great society is not necessarily a good society. A good society implies order. Order does not mean trains running on time, mail delivered regularly. It means something else. For a human being, order means order within himself. And such order will inevitably bring about a good society.
>
> (Krishnamurti 1974: 93)

So what remains is to 'write an obituary for the great god Progress' (Keen 1994: 13–14). This is because we are living in the last days of 'the myth of unlimited growth and technoutopia, and the religion of the Mall' (ibid.).

Changing priorities, transforming education

Spiritual educational visions are, therefore, based on the radical transformation of modern education, and on a change in the perception of current emerging 'future realities' (cyber and globalized education).

As is the case with feminist and indigenous alternatives, spiritual educational visions also require radical transformations rather than piecemeal strategies within education. The main change is thus epistemological and paradigmatic. While ideally, spiritual education is conducted within a setting that facilitates spiritual growth (e.g. small classes, natural surroundings), the change could as well be implemented in 'industrial type' inner-city classrooms. The issue of implementation is seen as secondary when compared with the paradigmatic change that needs to occur:

> Why do you [not] give time to dance, to music? Why not give time to this as you give to mathematics? You are not interested in it. If you saw that it was also necessary you would devote time to it. If you saw that it [spiritual education] was as essential as mathematics, you would do something.
>
> (Krishnamurti 1974: 177)

At heart, Sarkar, Krishnamurti, Sai Baba and Aurobindo offer a vision of transformation. They write:

> You must try your best to reshape the system... Every village school is to be transformed into a *gurukula* (the forest schools of the past in which sages taught spiritual practices along with other subjects) and every teacher into a *rishi* or sage, who will lead the children along material, moral, ethical and spiritual paths, until they become ideal citizens.
>
> (Sai Baba 1988: 49–50)

> We will establish the *Gurukul*. We will dye each and every bud with the light of knowledge. No one will stay away. We will bind everybody with the thread of love and create a garland of incomparable beauty. No one will stay behind, none will be thrown at the bottom. All will exist with kith and kin with their minds full of sweetness and tenderness for all.
>
> (Sarkar 1998: 11)

> thousands of kindergarten and primary schools must be started with this new system of education [neo-humanism], to create a spiritual urge amongst children throughout the entire world.
>
> (Sarkar 1998: 182)

> There should be somewhere upon earth a place that no nation could claim as its sole property, a place where all human beings

of goodwill, sincere in their aspiration, could live freely as citizens of the world, obeying one single authority, that of the supreme Truth; a place of peace, concord, harmony, where all the fighting instincts of man would be used exclusively to conquer the causes of his suffering and misery, to surmount his weakness and ignorance, to triumph over his limitations and incapacities; a place where the needs of the spirit and the care for progress would get precedence over the satisfaction of desires and passions, the seeking for pleasures and material enjoyments. In this place, children would be able to grow and develop integrally without losing contact with their soul.

(*Auroville Charter* 2002: vision statement)

The essence of spiritual education is summarized below. The summary of a 'core' that follows is more concerned with the epistemic and paradigmatic change than with the issue of pedagogy. It only briefly focuses on pedagogy, the 'how' of teaching. Concrete suggestions on how to approach spirituality in education are developed in detail in articles and books by, for example, Ananda Rama (2000), Anandamitra (1987a,b), Bussey (1998, 2000a,b), Dermond (2001a,b, 2002), Daleo (1996), Palmer (1980, 1993, 1998, 1999a), Miller (2000), Kessler (2000) and Myers (1997). Many articles in Miller and Nakagawa (2002), Glazer (1999) and in a special issue of *Educational Leadership* (Vol. 56, No. 4, December 1998/January 1999) also deal with spirituality and educational pedagogy. As well, all of the twentieth-century educational 'classics' that developed educational alternatives from within the Indian episteme contain extensive writings on issues of spirituality and educational pedagogy. The following summary is not complete; rather, it focuses on the main elements of educational visions as expressed by the most influential and best-known authors on spiritual education. It should be seen as a point of departure.

• *The focus is on human and cosmic unity* Knowledge and education should facilitate bringing humans to a consciousness of unity. The goal is to achieve harmony with the universe, which means unification of both spiritual and social life with the Supreme. Contrary to the dominant western view of education, which constitutes the individual as 'fundamentally alone in the universe and in competition with others for resources and status' (Kesson 2002: 41), humanity is envisioned as 'intimately linked with the fabric of the universe' (Bussey 2000b: 10). The individual is seen as 'a soul, a portion of the Divinity enwrapped in mind and body, a conscious manifestation in Nature of the universal self and spirit' (Sri Aurobindo 1965: 4). Therefore, educational practices ought to include the 'examination and contemplation of the awe, wonder, and mystery of the universe' (Purpel 1989: 113). Education is the realization of an inner quality of man that places human life in harmony with all existence (Tagore, in Cenkner 1976). The focus on unity also means that education should be about going beyond anthropocentrism. As all life is seen to be sacred, this general understanding of unity results in the development of respect for all forms of life, animate and inanimate. The spiritual unity of humans should be realized through both nature and neighbour, argues Krishnamurti. So education is to be about building relationships. Life in itself is 'a movement in relationship. If we do not understand what is implied in relationship, we inevitably not only isolate ourselves, but create a society in which human beings are divided, not only nationally, religiously, but also in themselves and therefore they project what they are into the outer world' (Krishnamurti 1995: 34). Relationship with another human being is, therefore, one of the most important things in life. Hence, 'every person in the primary school must feel a sense of kinship with everyone' (Sai Baba 1988: 64). Students should cultivate a spirit of mutual regard and harmony (ibid.: 96). The highest mission of education is 'to help us realize the inner principle of unity of all knowledge and all the activities of our social and spiritual being' (Tagore, in Cenkner 1976: 45).

- *Spirituality can be known and should be taught* The aim of education is to facilitate spiritual growth (Tagore, in Cenkner 1976). The only 'true' education is that which makes one central objective, the growth of the soul and its powers and possibilities (Sri Aurobindo 1965: 5). Without knowledge of the Absolute, and without the practice of meditation to unfold the mental facul-ties, education is incomplete (Maharishi 1988). This is important as it helps centre individuals, and helps them live in the midst of all relative values of the world and forms and phenomena (ibid.: 212). Education should facilitate movement towards greater wholeness, towards the infinite, towards the Supreme Consciousness. It should facilitate the growth of the human soul, the self, the mind, in all its powers and potentialities (The Mother 1965). As argued by Krishnamurti (1995: 67), 'this is our intent and why these schools have come into being; not to turn out mere careerists but to bring about the excellence of spirit'. To develop the spirit means building character and enabling 'one to work towards a knowledge of God and self-realization' (Gandhi, in Cenkner 1976: 81). Moral, ethical and spiritual knowledge and experience are the best foundation for education (Sai Baba 1988: 51). Of course, within the individual there is 'a mental, an intellectual, an ethical, dynamic and practical, an aesthetic and hedonistic, a vital and physical being, but all these have been seen as powers of a soul that manifests through them and grows with their growth' (Sri Aurobindo 1965: 4). And yet, all these aspects of a being are not all the soul, because 'at the summit of its ascent it arises to something greater than them all, into a spiritual being' (ibid.).

- *Education is that which liberates*   Enlightenment is possible. The path towards 'bliss' (*ananda*) is through education, discipline and spiritual practice. Education should help achieve *moksha/*liberation. The highest aspiration is the realization of the relationship between the deepest self (*atman*) and the Absolute (*Brahman*). As humans are encouraged to go 'beyond the self', this freedom also includes freedom from the bondage of ego (Sarkar, Krishnamurti, Aurobindo, Tagore, Gandhi). Spiritual education also liberates the individual from 'the misconception that they are alone' (ibid.). Spiritual education liberates the self and society from all bondage (Bussey 2000b: 10).
- *Education should promote cardinal human values*   Education should therefore promote compassion, love, bliss, sympathy and joy (Tagore, in Cenkner 1976). Everyone should practice 'Truth, Right Conduct, Peace, Love and Non-Violence' (Sai Baba 1988: 19). Children should learn how to practice compassion and understanding rather than blame, forgiveness rather than retaliation, active calm rather than anger or passive victim-consciousness (Dermond 2001b). Education should be about teaching 'harmony, mindfulness, service, self-reliance, community, history, compassion, beauty, balance and joy' (Daleo 1996). Sarkar's neo-humanist education is to promote values such as *ahimsa* (non-harming), *satya* (truthfulness), *asteya* (non-stealing), *aparigraha* (minimizing one's needs), *bramacarya* (seeing everyone as an expression of the Divine), *shaoca* (cultivation of a strong healthy body) *santoca* (contentment), *tapah* (serving others), *svadhyaya* (going beyond dogma and ritualism) and *ishvara pranidhana* (mental effort, through meditation, towards union with cosmic

consciousness) (Kesson 2002: 38). True human values are based on service to others, compassion and humility. Education should also promote service to others, the Gandhian *sarvodaya* – the uplift of all. The knowledge that is gathered in schools and colleges should be 'capable of being used for service to society and helping to improve the conditions of one's fellow men' (Sai Baba 1988: 10). This includes 'the cultivation, nourishment, and development of attitudes of outrage and responsibility in the face of injustice and oppression' (Purpel 1989: 118). Real education should enable one to 'utilise the knowledge one has acquired to meet the challenges of life and to make all human beings happy as far as possible' (Sai Baba 1988: 9). Most of all, it is love that should be promoted. Without love, 'you are a dead human being' (Krishnamurti 1974: 85). Everyone should find out what is it to 'love people, to love dogs, the sky, the blue hills and the river' (ibid.). Learning love is getting accustomed to the feeling that there is 'gentleness, quietness, tenderness, consideration...beauty' (ibid.: 82). And, it is in love that 'there is no ambition, there is no jealousy' (ibid.). Love is 'at the origin of the world and Love is its Goal' (The Mother 1965: 37). There is 'only one religion, the religion of love. There is only one language, the language of the heart' (Sai Baba 1988: 7). This is why real education 'leads to a pervasive sense of love and compassion for all creation' (Sarkar 1998: 111).

• *Education comes from within*   It is about unfolding the full potential that already exists within an individual. In that sense, 'nothing can be taught' (Krishnamurti, Tagore, Sri Aurobindo). That nothing can be taught is 'the first principle of true teaching' (Sri Aurobindo 1965: 6). The teacher is 'not an instructor or taskmaster, he is a helper and a guide' (ibid.). The second principle of true teaching is that 'the mind has to be consulted in its own growth' (ibid.). Educational centres should help the student and the education to 'flower naturally' (Krishnamurti 1995: 59). The flowering incorporates constant change, not a finished outcome. Education is the constant change of 'the inner man' (Krishnamurti 1974: 65).

• *The outcome of education should be total, whole, integrated, free, happy, joyful, blissful and peaceful human being*   For Krishnamurti (1995: ii), the only concern should be to 'set man absolutely, unconditionally free'. For Gandhi, the goal is development of *satyagrahi*, a non-violent personality. For Sai Baba (1988: 99), education is 'merely an opportunity' to become an exemplary human being. For Moore (2000: vii), the educated person is one who is 'free of paranoia and narcissism...has sufficient tranquility of heart to be compassionate and can make a real contribution to the community'.

- *Pedagogy and curriculum are to cultivate inner peace, harmony and balance* The 'curriculum for the inner life' is composed of specific education processes and techniques that include meditation, visualization, dreamwork and autobiography (Miller 2000: 10). Techniques could also include experiences in nature (Tagore, Krishnamurti), through art (Tagore) or craft (Gandhi). The main principle is that 'the thirst for knowledge should be awakened' (ibid.: 293). School should be a place where students (and teachers) are helped to find out for themselves 'through discussion, through listening, through silence, to find out, right through your life, what you really love to do' (Krishnamurti 1974: 76). People can only learn where there are both attention and silence; these are prerequisites for learning (ibid.). The role of silence is seen to be crucial. This is because 'the inner self needs silence and solitude to develop' (Dermond 2002). In order to have any time at all for 'her own thoughts, to get in touch with her own feelings, to imagine, to create, a child needs to have quiet times' (ibid.). It is considered that when information is taken in without regular breaks, very little is retained. Time is needed for information to become knowledge. While this challenges the predominant trend of mainstream society, it is an integral part of spiritual education. It is in stillness and beauty that 'the answers to your dreams' lie (http://www.visionsof-heaven.com/). Or, it is 'in silence more than in argument [that] our mind-made world falls away and we are opened to the truth that seeks us' (Palmer 1993: 80). A school should therefore also be 'a place of leisure' because 'to learn the art of living one must have leisure' (Krishnamurti 1995: 77). Freedom of learning is also connected with discipline and responsibility. But responsibility has different meaning than when imposed from outside. As Krishnamurti (1995: 74) argues, 'if one grasps the full significance that one is psychologically the world, then responsibility becomes overpowering love' (ibid.). Through such attitudes, schools should promote our responsibility to the earth, to nature and to each other. Fear is considered to be the worst incentive for education. It is seen as 'the surest way of attracting what is feared' (The Mother 1965: 32). Children should feel both free and safe to learn; fear is directly opposite to this. Fear prevents 'the flowering of the mind, the flowering of goodness' (Krishnamurti 1974: 52).

- *The separation between the spiritual (sacred) and the secular is false*   Education should be about integration, harmonization and balancing of the material and spiritual aspects of one's life. It needs to balance inner and outer, the rational and the intuitive, the qualitative and the quantitative (Miller 2000: 9). Education therefore has a dual meaning. First, it refers to 'worldly education', which teaches skill and discipline and imparts information useful for earning one's livelihood and for attaining and maintaining a decent standard of living (Sai Baba 1988: 55). Secondly, it is moral and spiritual education which imparts 'equanimity, tolerance, sense-control, gratitude, devotion to God and dedication to the realization of the Reality' (ibid.). In fact, the real meaning of education is trilateral development – 'simultaneous development in the physical, mental and spiritual realms of human existence' (Sarkar 1998: 111). A proper and all round development of the mind can therefore take place only 'when it proceeds *pari passu* with the education of the physical and spiritual faculties of the child' (Gandhi 1980: 189). Raising the standard of living, therefore, must also mean raising ethical, moral and spiritual standards (Sai Baba 1988: 38). It is only then that education can lead to 'progress in human values and harmony in social life' (ibid.).

- *Science and technology are invaluable but even here human values should be emphasized*   There should be no dichotomy between science and spirituality (Sai Baba 1988: 42). In fact, eternal truth/absolute knowledge is based on 'spiritual science' – invented about 7000 years ago by Lord Shiva (Sarkar 1998: 331). While this spiritual science also describes certain physical laws that exist within the universe, it fundamentally differs from and is broader than western science. For example, one of the universal laws is that '...matter is false and impotent unless it becomes the manifestation of the Spirit' (The Mother 1965: iii). Alternatively, matter is seen to be 'the crudified form of the universal mind' (Sarkar 1998: 324). And, since 'All human energy has a physical basis' (Sri Aurobindo 1965: 18), it is important to live in accordance with the laws of nature. Experiential learning remains crucial and so does physical education. As well, children should be equipped 'with the most excellent technological proficiency' so that they may function with 'clarity and efficiency in the modern world' (Krishnamurti 1974: 89). But technology 'must be dedicated to the promotion of high ideals' (Sai Baba 1988: 17). Rejection of science leads to inertia and dogmatism, therefore 'cultivation of science must go forward' (Sarkar 1998: 102). But there are limits to science. This is because 'science can never change a person's *samskaras* [reactive moments of the mind]' (ibid.). So, while scientific development should be encouraged, at the same time, for the development of personalities there is 'no alternative for human beings other than spiritual practice or *Sadhana*' (ibid.).

- *Respect for teachers*   Respect for teachers, even devotion to teachers (*guru-bhakti*), needs to be cultivated. Teaching is one of the most important occupations. Every teacher should feel secure in the sense of being at home, cared for and without financial worries, argues Krishnamurti (1995). If the teacher does not feel secure and happy, it is the students that suffer, and ultimately all society. So the first thing teachers should do in order to be able to educate the child is to educate themselves (The Mother 1965: 31). It is only those that can love that can (should) teach (Tagore, in Cenkner 1976: 58). To be able to do that, to nurture and develop a student's soul, the teacher should bring their authentic presence to the classroom each day, attune themselves empathetically to their students; in short, the whole process must begin with the teacher's soul (Miller 2000: 121).

- *The aims of education should be at one with the aims of life*   The aims of good education are always one with the aims of life – integral education is possible only when both the knowledge of things and the knowledge of the self are achieved. On the other hand, when one or the other is lost educational decay occurs (Gandhi, Tagore, Sri Aurobindo). The school is 'a place where one learns not only the knowledge required for daily life but also the art of living with all its complexities and subtleties' (Krishnamurti 1995: 104). As argued by The Mother (1965: 36), 'to know is good, to live is better, to be, that is perfect'. The subjects taught should be such that they bring home to the students the full scope of life (Maharishi 1988: 209). Education should be 'for life, not for a living' (Sai Baba 1988: 14). That the aims of education should be one with the aims of life also means that education is a lifelong process – continuity should be more fully ingrained in the process of education (A contributor, in Sri Aurobindo 1965: 71).

- *Education should be free, especially spiritual education*   There should be 'no link between money and education' (Sai Baba

1988: 6). Education should be 'free at all levels' (Sarkar 1998: 113). Both 'mundane knowledge' and 'spiritual knowledge' must be 'as free as light and air; and like the unhindered flow of a fountain, they must keep society in a dynamic state and be a continuous source of inspiration to one and all' (ibid.: 200).

Summary: analysis of spiritual education

The following tables summarize spiritual society and educational visions. Table 10.2 presents a summary of key features of the spiritual vision of society. This vision differs dramatically from the western utopian tradition in that, instead of the perfect society, it is the perfect self – eupsychia – that is paramount. Instead of the hyper time of globalization, timeless time and 'cosmic flow' are central. The main goal of spiritual society is to achieve a balance between self and society.

The dystopian danger, however, lies in verticality, male bias and essentialism. For example, given the vertical nature of the *chakra* model of evolution, what of children who find themselves on the lower rungs? Is not the *karma* theory of causality a determinism similar to the gene theory of causality? Will not a spiritual view of education lead to the blaming of the victim – that it is their bad *karma* that they failed an exam or had an accident? What of children who are not able to meditate or experience the spiritual? While all spiritual writers call for compassion towards the Other, and state that everyone is by definition a spiritual being, the vertical nature of spiritual education may still over time create structures that judge the spiritual-less, even if individual teachers and students exhibit compassion. As well, there is an issue of gender. Spiritual authors tend to be male, and use male categories of the spiritual, referring to the transcendental as Him. In addition, the private and public spheres challenged by feminism tend to be reinscribed by spiritual education. This is partly because the vision of the spiritual emerges from classical epistemes, where patriarchy was not contested. It is also a result of the translation of Sanskrit and Bengali texts into English. Still, the discourse is gendered in ways that do not lead to women's inclusion. Although spiritual society is intended to be all-inclusive, it is clear that without engagement with feminism (women's movements) patriarchy may not be challenged. And the third potential dystopian danger is the essentialist nature of spirituality. The spiritual is not open to negotiation; it must be experienced. Thus, it can be exclusionary for those who reject the spiritual either

Table 10.2 Spiritual society – social futures

Approach to time	Vision for the future	Utopian promise	Dystopian dangers	Social eutopia
Timeless time	The coming of spiritual society	Eupsychia – perfection and liberation of self	Occultism, pantheism, etc. (Christian right)	Balance – between self and society
Cosmic flow	New Age	Ananda – bliss	Essentialist	Integrated society
Cyclical	Age of Aquarius	Merger with the Infinite – achieving omniscience	Verticality	Counterbalancing excesses in materialism
Spiral		Planetary civilization in peace	Exclusion of the less spiritual	Sadvipra society (Sarkar)
Spiritual evolution		Living in truth	Male-biased	Service to society

for *a priori* reasons or because they have no such experiences. Thinkers who espouse spiritual education do not take a strategic essentialist position, as was the case with some feminist and indigenous theorists. Spirituality is not strategic, but the ground of being. This can result in unresolvable ontological debates with no possibility for pedagogical improvement or transformation.

From the perspective of the Christian Right, the most vocal critics of the emerging spiritual movement in the west, the main problem with spiritual alternatives is in ideas such as occultism, pantheism/animism, reincarnation, lack of a God creator and so on. Spiritual alternatives are 'foreign' and in stark contrast to a 'biblical Christian way of seeing' (Ankerberg and Weldon 1996: ix).

Table 10.3 presents the vision of spiritual education. Educational utopia and eutopia lie in liberation and the integration of body, mind and spirit. Educational dystopia, on the other hand, lies in the danger of reproducing religious dogma – as devotion and faith in the spiritual can become paramount, this can encourage closing the doors to inquiry.

Tables 10.4, 10.5 and 10.6 suggest, as argued earlier, that spiritual education is challenging and foundationally different from the hegemonic globalized and cyber vision for the future of education. The former is focused on transcendence and the perfected realized self, and the latter two focus on pan-capitalism and the satisfaction of material needs, and increased/enhanced information and the freedom to create new selves. However, there are points of similarity with the indigenous (respect for elders and gurus, for example), and with the feminist (giving birth as similar to re-birth and the focus on transformation). Still, the educational eutopia does differ. For the spiritual system it is 'education that integrates body, mind and spirit', while for the indigenous it is 'learning from indigenous people about history and environment', and for the feminist it is the 'removal of gender bias and prejudice in education'. In terms of content, for the spiritual it is a focus on 'human and cosmic unity', for the indigenous it is 'land, genealogy and spirituality', and for the feminist it is 'interdisciplinary, holistic and experience-based'. For the spiritual system, the educational bottom line is 'education for spiritual realization' and 'students and teachers living their bliss', while for the indigenous it is 'education for cultural, human and nature survival', and for the feminist it is 'education for social transformation' and 'education for the creation of more gender balanced societies'.

Table 10.3 Spiritual education – educational futures

Underlying vision for the future	Utopian promise	Dystopian dangers	Educational eutopia
Spiritual society	Education that liberates Education that nourishes the soul	Education that reproduces religious dogma	Integration of body, mind and spirit

Worldview and approach to knowledge	Epistemology		Educated subject
Indian episteme – Tantric, Vedic and Buddhist	Intuition Devotion		Unconditioned (Krishnamurti) Self-aware, centred
Universe is causal and there is a purpose to life	Direct experience of reality Unified		Total, whole, integrated, free, happy, joyful, blissful and peaceful human being

Educational visions/futures	Process		Structure
Content			
Focus on human and cosmic unity	Education comes from within		Free education
Spirituality explored and thought	Cultivates inner peace, harmony and balance		Society values and rewards teachers
Promotes cardinal human values	Respect for teacher – guru		Gurukul
Aims of education one with the aims of life			

Table 10.4 Spiritual society and education – key words

Change	Future	Society	Education	Other key words
Be the change you want to see	Bright	Transformed	Liberating	Spiritual practice
Rebirth	Blissful	Balanced	Intelligence	Karma
Transcendence		Unified	'True' education	Dharma
		Integrated		Mind, spirit
				Intuition
				Fear, conditioning
				Love, compassion
				Realization

Table 10.5 Spiritual society and education – causal layered analysis

Litany	Social causes	Discourse/worldview	Myth/metaphor	Education bottom line
Marginalization of spiritual within materialistic societies	Materialistic society Expansion of the secular west and reductionist science	Purpose of life is spiritual realization and evolution	Kundalini rising Karma and dharma	Education for spiritual realization of the individual and spiritual advancement of the human species Students and teachers living their bliss

Table 10.6 Spiritual society and education – deconstruction

Who gets to speak	Who and what is silenced	What is missing from discourse	Continuity	Discontinuity
All – everybody included	Perspectives based on materialism Belief in randomness and purposelessness	'Accidents' Gender-balanced language	Indian episteme	Nineteenth-century transcendental movement 1960s west

However, the deeper similarity that does come across is the commitment to holism and integration. As well, all three seek to contest the modernist educational paradigm and challenge the global and cyber view of the future and of education; at the very least, to see it as one possible future, not the only future, and certainly not the future that defines the core of education.

Part IV
Towards educational eutopias and heterotopias

> Most difficult decisions require making a choice between alternative futures.
>
> (Hicks and Holden 1995: 14)

11 Postmodern visions, costs and multi-temporalities

Educational futures discourses

> Those who control the past, control the future; Those who control the future, control the present; Those who control the present, control the past.
>
> (George Orwell 1949)

In the earlier parts of this book, I made the following arguments: (1) modern education is under increasing pressure to change; (2) this pressure comes from across the political, cultural, civilizational and gender spectrum; (3) the pressure is strongest when it comes to pushing modern education towards a globalized and technologized version of the future; (4) this globalized and technologized vision takes a particular form which is in accordance with the neo-liberal, western and patriarchal vision for the future; and (5) there are numerous alternatives to both modern education and these hegemonic visions of the future.

I also argued that all educational visions are based on particular approaches to time, social change, history and the future. To be able to create another future, social groups recreate, reinvent and reconstruct foundational givens of mainstream interpretations of past and history. While mainstream interpretations of the future focus on the technological, alternative positions focus on social or other empirical realities. For example, feminists interpret history in terms of gender relationships, creating a two-phase history, the movement from matrilocal/partnership towards patriarchal/dominator societies. Even if the classification remains the same, it is interpreted in a different light. For example, as Miles argues, historical periods of great progress (for men) have often involved losses and setbacks for women:

If there is any truth in Lenin's claim that the emancipation of its women offers a fair measurement of the general level of the civilization of any society, then received notions of 'progressive' developments like the classical Athenian cultures, the Renaissance, and the French Revolution, in all of which women suffered several reversals, have to undergo a radical revaluation: for, as the American historian Joan Kelly dryly observes, 'there was no Renaissance for women – at least in the Renaissance'.

(Miles 1993: 13)

The discovery of 'hidden histories' played 'a critical role in the emergence of many of the most important social movements of our time – feminist, anti-colonial and anti-racist' (Hall 1997: 52). Where we desire our societies to go is often connected with views of where we have been, how have we got here and which parts of our remembered history are to be seen in a positive and which in a negative light.

The discovery of 'hidden histories' is part of the overall redefinition of time. 'Time is power', writes Levine (1997: 118). There is 'no greater symbol of domination, since time is the only possession which can in no sense be replaced once it is gone' (ibid.). Indeed, Jeremy Rifkin believes that the politics of time will increasingly dominate the politics of the future, to the extent that we may witness *Time Wars*, 'A battle is brewing over the politics of time...Its outcome could determine the future course of politics around the world in the coming century' (1987: 10).

Conflict over the pace of life 'has been the center of power struggles on many levels', both personal and on the level of nations and cultures (Levine 1997: 77–78). While people react very strongly to intrusions on their understanding of time (ibid.: 76), this has not prevented an imposition of industrial, clock time and attempts to standardize, to unify, global temporal diversity. Education has always been instrumental in the teaching of time – this has always been its hidden curricula – and it continues, now moving from teaching industrial time towards the imposition and teaching of 'compressed' instantaneous time, as in the 'time of computers' which will 'hammer the final nails into the coffin of natural time' (ibid.: 75):

The events in the computer world exist in a time realm that we will never be able to experience. The new 'computime' represents the final abstraction of time and its complete separation from human experience and rhythms of nature.

(Rifkin 1987: 15)

Globalization helps this process, as it tends to 'shift the ontology of time from a link with distance to a connection with speed' (Scholte 2000: 196). The result is the general acceleration of life, allowing 'ever more activity to crowd into a person's time' (ibid.: 196–197):

> A day becomes a deluge of telephone calls, e-mails, channel hopping between radio and television transmissions, electronic money transactions, etc. In a word, life becomes far more 'busy'. The combination of faster and fuller time in a highly globalized life can present substantial coping challenges. In this regard it is probably no accident that stress and supraterritoriality have grown concurrently in contemporary history. Indeed, like notions of 'globalization', the concept of 'stress' has in recent decades spread to countless languages across the world.
>
> (Scholte 2000: 196)

The need to continuously increase the speed is inherent in modern capitalism, argues Richard Swift. 'The most revolutionary' of social systems, dynamic, aggressive and technologically innovative, capitalism always thrusts into the future (Swift 2002: 10):

> The faster capital is turned over, the faster it can realize a profit. The faster that profit can be reinvested, the faster it can expand in its turn. This quick turnover of capital is of course connected with volume – more widgets produced, more energy used, more money in circulation, more infrastructure needed. The key to the process is to speed everything up, whether in production, transport, the circulation of money or – nowadays particularly – consumption.
>
> (Swift 2002: 10)

The current hegemonic approach to time can be described as western, Christian, linear, abstract, clock-dominated, work-oriented, coercive, capitalist, masculine and anti-natural, argues Griffiths (2002: 14). But there is also revolt: 'The challenge to Hegemonic Time has come from the radiant variety of times understood by indigenous peoples; from self-conscious political protest, from children's dogged insistence on living in a stretchy eternity; from women's blood and from carnival' (ibid.: 14–15).

Religious authorities, colonizers, capitalists and revolutionaries alike have all tried to take control of the calendar 'as a way of asserting and legitimizing their power', argue Levine (1997: 78) and Griffiths

(2002). These individuals and groups have also always attempted to create educational systems that reflect their own worldview and utopian vision for the future. Taking control of time and taking control of education go hand in hand. For any *educational reform* to break away from and transform the dominant system of education, a *different approach to time* and a *different vision for the future* are necessary. The educational alternatives that I explored earlier, hegemonic and alternative alike, attempt the transformation of the current dominant approach to time – industrial, commodified and linear. They aim to transform the modernist desire for 'progress' and 'development', at the very least defining these categories differently. But while claiming to disturb the modernist project, hegemonic visions of a globalized cyber world, in fact, help maintain, and further cement at the global level, western and patriarchal domination. They do not fundamentally disturb western linear time, they accelerate it; they do not fundamentally disturb the western and patriarchal future, they just name it differently. In this future, differences are coopted – 'the Other' continues to be controlled.

Feminist alternatives, on the other hand, are informed by a different history, that of women's subordination within patriarchy, as well as women's strengths in pre-patriarchal and non-patriarchal spaces. They argue for a different, 'women's' understanding of time and for different priorities in creating the future. Indigenous alternatives remember the traditional approach to time while explicitly engaging with western time – as defined within the modernist 'project of time and history'. They use categories developed from the Enlightenment to argue for social justice, fairness and the incorporation of diversity. The traditional approach to time is implicit in the discourse of 'indigenous knowledge'. To deal with the problem of the west, to challenge being constituted as 'undeveloped', 'primitive' and 'idle', as was the case during early colonization, indigenous peoples have engaged with western categories of time and the future. While western revolutionaries increasingly look towards indigenous time for 'salvation', indigenous peoples seem to have recently encased their needs and priorities within a framework understood by mainstream society. Spiritual alternatives, on the other hand, continue advocating for 'timeless time', for silences and for reflection. They too envision different futures.

As Tables 11.1 and 11.2 show, different understandings and views of time and the future are implicit in the creation of different goals and aims for education.

Table 11.1 Hegemonic and alternative futures visions comparison – approaches to time

Futures visions	Approach to time	Historical phases
Globalized world and education	Linear/compressed, instantaneous Time as product	Pre-industrial – industrial – postindustrial
WebNet vision of the world, cyber education	Linear/compressed Time replacing distance	Technological theory of evolution, from simple to complex, BC–AC (before computers and after computers)
Feminist alternatives	Linear (as in progress) Cyclical (women's biological rhythms) Eternal (as during labour) Long-term future (glacial, intergenerational) Time as lived, made and generated	Matriarchy – patriarchy – gender egalitarianism Partnership – dominator – partnership or dominator societies
Recovery of indigenous traditions	Linear (as in creating a more just future) Long-term future (as in intergenerational)	Traditional societies – colonization – further colonization or indigenous renaissance
Spiritual alternatives	Timeless time Spiritual evolution	Simple to more complex forms – deeper, intuitive – of consciousness

Table 11.2 Hegemonic and alternative futures visions comparison – vision of the future and of education

Futures visions	Vision of the future	Vision of education
Globalized world and education	Global pan-capitalism Global age	Education as human capital formation, investment in economy, about providing vocational skills in order to achieve and compete
WebNet vision of the world, cyber education	Post-information society Digital age	Education about increased access of information

Table 11.2 (Continued)

Futures visions	Vision of the future	Vision of education
Feminist alternatives	Gender-balanced, inclusive, partnership, gentle society	Education for social transformation and for creation of more gender-balanced societies
Recovery of indigenous traditions	Indigenous renaissance Equitable and just societies	Education for cultural, human and nature survival
Spiritual alternatives	Spiritual society	Education for spiritual realization of the individual and spiritual advancement of the human species

As Toffler (1974: 19) argues, 'all education springs from some image of the future'. While the image of the future is, in general, informed by a broad civilizational approach to time, there are other co-existing discourses. In hierarchical societies, the broad civilizational approach to time does not necessarily inform the education of all the members of society. That is, while a particular 'hegemonic' futures image is used to inform the education of *everybody*, it is also followed by specialized entries – specialized futures images that inform the education of marginalized social groups.

Postmodernism and alternative futures

The question I now ask is why and how have certain futures visions become hegemonic? Numerous authors, particularly those informed by neo-Marxism and postmodernism, suggest that the push towards current hegemonic visions is dominated by the neo-liberal agenda. This domination has partly been successful because they have managed to change the discourse about the future, for example, how globalization is defined and perceived. Globalization defined in economic terms, coupled with new information technologies, is increasingly seen 'as the solution' for the future, even part of our 'salvation'. Critical social and educational thinkers, meanwhile, have been too busy critiquing and decon-structing – and even outrightly refusing to offer – futures visions. This is because futures visioning is in itself seen as prescriptive, as part of a meta-narrative formation. What has resulted, however, is not a rejection of desired futures and old meta-narratives on progress and development; rather, we have seen the emergence of a new meta-narrative – globalization – as 'the mother of all meta-narratives' (Luke and Luke 2000: 278). The decision by the Left to abandon meta-narratives has turned out to be costly. Neo-liberal educational governance and the new globalized political economy of education have colluded with leftist scepticism towards grand narratives, argues Luke:

> Taken together, these two ostensibly opposite forces can set the practical and administrative conditions for a fragmentation of the educational work of teaching and learning. This fragmentation is achieved both through the narrow instrumental technicism of a test or package-driven classroom, and through an overly developed epistemological sensitivity to the local, the 'cultural' and the diasporic that eschews grand constructions of discipline, field and discourse and thereby effectively narrows the curriculum to parochial concerns.
>
> (Luke 2002: 2)

Similar arguments are developed by McLaren:

> The Leftist agenda now rests almost entirely on an understanding of asymmetrical gender and ethnic relations... The educational Left is finding itself without a revolutionary agenda for challenging inside and outside the classrooms of the nation the effects and consequences of the new capitalism...
>
> (McLaren 1998: 435, 439)

In the face of the 'the current lack of Utopian and the postmodern assault on the unified subject of the Enlightenment tradition' (ibid.: 444), what has resulted is a 'political paralysis', at least at the Left end of the political spectrum. Modernity, stemming from the Enlightenment tradition, has not been 'destroyed by alternative visions, but by the collapse of all visions; everything goes, but nothing much counts' (Giddens 1992: 21). To fill that vacuum, a 'new alliance' and a 'new power block' has formed (Apple 2000: 226) – in the USA in particular and in developed western countries in general. This new power bloc:

> combines multiple fractions of capital that are committed to neoliberal marketized solution to educational problems,

neoconservative intellectuals who want a 'return' to higher standards and a 'common culture', authoritarian, populist, religious fundamentalists who are deeply worried about secularity and the preservation of their own traditions, and particular fractions of the professionally oriented new middle class who are committed to the ideology and techniques of accountability, measurement, and 'management'.

(Apple 2000: 226)

Most importantly, this new power block has utilized a particular image of the romantic past (see Figure 8) to fill the vacuum created by the disintegration of the old and the lack of articulation of new futures narratives. As argued by Apple, 'Its [the new alliance's] overall aims are in providing the educational conditions believed necessary both for increasing international competitiveness, profit, and discipline and for returning us to *a romanticized past* [italics added] of the "ideal" home, family, and school' (ibid.).

But, at the same time, we have also witnessed the emergence of numerous alternatives, developed outside and on the margins of the western/patriarchal world. As argued by Polak (1973), it is always marginalized social groups that lose the most from the abandonment of utopia. Therefore, we can see that the three alternatives analysed in more detail here – feminist, indigenous and spiritual – still make claims for a particular 'truth' that can be discovered and recovered. This truth is 'the truth' about the suppression of their own worldviews and priorities, as well as 'the truth' that societies and education could, indeed, be better, be improved. There is still 'truth' in certain 'universal laws', as described within indigenous and spiritual science. These traditions are, therefore, 'true' in themselves, and it is this truth that alternatives for the future build upon.

Paradoxically, postmodernists, while critical of essentialism, by destabilizing earlier hegemonic meta-narratives, have enabled the opening of new discursive spaces – of differently imagined futures and histories – hegemonic and alternative visions. While this has always been the case (i.e. desire as contested by different social groups), postmodernism has destabilized the hegemonic present by contextualizing it as a western and patriarchal project. While postmodernists have, in general, stopped short of articulating futures visions, they have helped open some 'spaces of enclosure'.

Ever since Foucault (1977) reconceptualized schools as institutions of surveillance, discipline and control, and aligned them with factories, armies and prisons, postmodernist scholars have questioned

Figure 8 Learning from the Fifties. © www.photolibrary.com[1]

education's role in continuing and enhancing the modernist project. Most importantly, postmodernism has abandoned a positivistic search for 'facts' as constitutive of knowledge, and has challenged the modernist belief that knowledge is, in itself, inherently emancipating and liberating. Rather, knowledge is seen as 'constructed' rather than 'discovered', and is also seen as a method of surveillance and discipline. For Foucault, truth is not 'the reward of free spirits, the child of protracted solitude, nor the privilege of those who have succeeded in liberating themselves' (Rabinow 1984: 72). Truth is never outside of power or lacking in power. Instead, it is 'a thing of this world' (ibid.). Therefore, each society has its own 'regimes of truth', its general 'politics of truth', which in effect are a type of 'discourse which it accepts and makes function as true' (ibid.: 73). What counts as knowledge, to be included in the curriculum, is not so much the result of 'objective evidence' but of negotiations between various social groups.

Some of these groups have more power than others to 'negotiate' the curriculum, and what is accepted as knowledge usually serves their own group interests. Foucault (1977) has argued strongly that knowledge and power cannot be separated, and that knowledge embodies the values of those groups that have enough power to create it, legitimate it and distribute it. Important for the arguments in this book are the questions that such a view of truth, reality and knowledge raises: What is considered legitimate knowledge? And, what is 'disqualified as inadequate...[and]...located low down on the hierarchy'? (ibid.: 82). What regimes of truth are subjugated? How is education itself situated in various discourses? How is education constructed in alternative futures? What are the current struggles for hegemony and the production of meaning between and among various groups and individuals based upon? Whose values, production and interpretation of meaning have become dominant?

The work of postmodern thinkers, and particularly Foucault (1972, 1977, 1980, 1986; Rabinow 1984), thus enabled a major challenge to the conventional framing of how the future is given and understood. By uncovering and giving voice to multiple histories, postmodernism has opened up the possibility of understanding the future differently. In particular, it has promoted a shift from *predicting the future* to *deconstructing the future* (which discourses are privileged, for example), and offering *genealogies of the future discourses* which show that none of these 'futures' are inherently inevitable. Any particular future is the consequence of a multitude of factors – many of which are constantly being 'negotiated'. So, instead of attempting to predict the future – as with most corporatist, educational and state-planning ventures – or leaving the future to 'utopian' studies (i.e. as not important to the construction of the present), postmodernism enables analysis of the ways in which the notion of the future circulates in contemporary discourse. From a postmodernist perspective, the future becomes one more meta-narrative that needs to be made problematic – a contested arena. For example, Baudrillard (1994) explored how the year 2000 has functioned in modernist discourses. He deconstructs its pre-eminence by arguing that '[e]veryone remains aware of the arbitrariness, the artificial character of time and history' (ibid.: 8).

The costs of postmodern futures

But, as is the case with all systems of thought, this approach to the future also has costs. As argued by Luke, McLaren and Apple earlier, the most obvious cost is in the future being defined by those 'still daring to dream', conservatives and radicals alike. Dissent, of course, is more important for historical 'others' who have not yet reached 'the end of history'. In common with numerous feminist theorists, we should ask, 'Who is to benefit from the deconstruction of the term "Woman"? Whose interests are served within postmodern theory?' (Schwartz 2001, par. 5). As Fox-Genovese argues:

> Surely it is no coincidence that the Western white male elite proclaimed the death of the subject at precisely the moment at which it might have had to share that status with the women and peoples of other races and classes who were beginning to challenge its supremacy.
>
> (Fox-Genovese 1986: 134)

A similar point is made by Brodribb (1992), who argued that 'postmodernism is the cultural capital of late patriarchy' (pp. 7–8). This position is also summarized by Nancy Hartsock, who then raises crucial questions:

> Somehow it seems highly suspicious that it is at the precise moment when so many groups have been engaged in nationalisms which involve redefinitions of the marginalized Others that suspicions emerge about the nature of the subject, about the possibilities for a general theory which can describe the world, about historical progress. Why is it that just at the moment when so many of us who have been silenced begin to demand the right to name ourselves, to act as subjects rather than objects of history, that just then the concept of subjecthood becomes problematic? Just when we are forming our own theories about the world, uncertainty emerges about whether the world can be theorized. Just when we are talking about the changes we want, ideas of progress and the possibility of systematically and rationally organizing human society become dubious and suspect?
>
> (Hartsock, quoted in Moon 2001, par. 57)

And, more importantly, how can we motivate for political action if there was no 'firm' identity from which to launch both the critique and the alternatives? How could women mobilize against patriarchy if there was no such thing as 'woman's experience' of patriarchy? If the sites of resistance are always local, how can we mobilize against the global system which patriarchy clearly is? If categories such as 'woman' or 'black' or 'Asian' are dissolved, on which grounds can we develop dissent to androcentric and Eurocentric visions for the future? And, how can we even talk about 'women's' or 'non-western' visions of the future; how are they intelligible?

Postmodernism, even though it is highly useful as a theoretical framework in deconstructing hegemony, also has civilizational costs. The impact of postmodernism has been devastating for the futures of the non-west, argues Sardar (1998). For him, post-modernism 'kills everything that gives meaning and depth to the life of non-western individuals and societies' (p. 14). In a world without 'Truth' or 'Reason' – or any other grand narrative such as 'Morality', 'God', 'Tradition' and 'History' – there is nothing that 'can remotely provide us with meaning, [and] with a sense of direction' (ibid.: 10). He further argues that postmodernism is firmly rooted in both colonialism and modernism and is about 'appropriating the history and identity of non-western cultures as an integral facet of itself, colonising their future and occupying their being' (p. 13). While postmodernism is often seen as promoting pluralism and giving representation to the marginalized, Sardar argues that it is even more successful than modernism in 'silencing the Other':

> Alterity (along with other euphemisms signifying the Other or the non-west) is a key postmodern term. Postmodern relativism embraces the Other, making alterity far more than just the repre-sentation of all non-western cultures and societies. Alterity is the condition of difference in any binary pair of differences; there is even alterity within the self. Thus postmodernism avoids, by glossing over, the politics of non-western marginalization in history by suddenly discovering Otherness everywhere, and arguing that everything has its own kind of Otherness by which it defines itself. While this proves the triumph of the postmodern thesis that everything is relative, it is incapable of suggesting that anything is in some distinctive way itself, with its own history. The postmodern prominence of the Other becomes a classic irony. Instead of finally doing justice to the marginalized and

demeaned, it vaunts the category to prove how unimportant, and ultimately meaningless, is any real identity it could contain.

(Sardar 1998)

Of course, as is the case with all systems of thought, postmodernism itself is not monolithic. That is, it is possible to distinguish between 'deconstructive' (Hicks 1998: 227), 'postmodernism of reaction' (Lather 1991a: 160), 'constructive', 'revisionary' (Hicks 1998: 227) and 'postmodernism of resistance' (Lather 1991a: 160).[2] As well, even deconstructive postmodernism can be liberating and enabling for suppressed social groups. As argued by hooks:

The critique of essentialism encouraged by postmodern thought is useful for African-Americans concerned with reformulating outmoded notions of identity. We have too long had imposed upon us from both the outside and the inside a narrow constricting notion of blackness. Postmodern critiques of essentialism which challenge notions of universality and static over determined identity within mass culture and mass consciousness can open up new possibilities for the construction of self and the assertion of agency.

(hooks 2001: par. 10)

Still, even though postmodernism is not monolithic, most postmodernists 'in the tradition of Foucault...generally refuse to offer a vision of the future', argues Fendler (1999: 185). This increases the likelihood of the above-mentioned dangers and costs. Unlike modernists, postmodernists believe that offering *a vision* 'such as providing a solution, ideal or utopian hope...would set limits on possibilities for the future' (ibid.). In addition, they believe that offering a vision of the future means 'to assume a position of political authority (intellectual as center)', which is a position that is generally declined on 'ethical grounds' (ibid.). This has led Frederic Jameson to assert that 'postmodern culture no longer has the capacity to imagine the future' (Wolmark 1999: 232). Such 'incapacity to imagine the future...the atrophy in our time of what Marcuse has called the *utopian imagination*' is '...not owing to any individual failure of imagination but...[is]...the result of the systemic, cultural, and ideological closure of which we are all in one way or another prisoners' (Jameson 1982: 153).

According to Baudrillard (1991), 'the end of metaphysics, the end of fantasy, the end of SF [science fiction]' has happened because 'the era of hyper-reality has begun' (ibid.: 311):

It is no longer possible to manufacture the unreal from the real, to create the imaginary from the data of reality. The process will be rather the reverse... to reinvent the real as fiction, precisely because the real has disappeared from our lives.

(Baudrillard 1991: 311)

Postmodernism, therefore, seems to be, in essence, 'a nihilistic cluster of philosophical perspectives which are built upon a sense of finality rather than of beginnings' (Hughes 1994: 8). Postmodernism cannot account for, or help us:

transcend through analysis, the concrete inequities which fundamentally structure our society, our ways of thinking about this, and our visions of ways to make things better... the epistemology and political theory of postmodernism involves the surrendering of any hopes of analysing the structural causes of oppression or even understanding them... These processes [of marginalization and oppression] can place a closure on our imaginations, or visions of a more equal future, and our respect for viewpoints or analyses which are not supportive of the *status quo*.

(Hughes 1994: 7–8)

Authors engaged in postmodern inquiry are often aware of these limitations. For example, Gore concludes her *The Struggle for Pedagogies* by writing:

Some readers will be disappointed with this concluding chapter because of its lack of prescriptive guidance. The changes I suggest for my own teacher education practice are small in magnitude, and I am aware of the possibility that they too are dangerous.

(Gore 1993: 155–156)

However, Gore (ibid.: 156) believes that her analysis does open new spaces of freedom and does not mandate rejecting visions of different societies, but instead, 'proposes that they get worked out locally' (ibid.). While this insight is invaluable, it has become increasingly difficult to be realized, given the globalizing tendencies of neo-liberal, capitalist visioning of the future, as discussed in the previous parts. The approach suggested by those coming from the discipline of futures studies, such as Boulding, Eisler and Henderson, addresses this limitation. Henderson (e.g. 1999) has repeatedly argued that intervention is needed at all levels – including the development of alternatives at both local and global levels. While Henderson focuses her analysis on the reshaping of the global economy, her template is important for the development of alternatives in other areas as well, including education. Paraphrasing Henderson's (1999) work, development of educational alternatives is, then, necessary at many levels: the family–individual, civic society, provincial and local systems, corporate system, the nation state, the international system and the global system.

Postmodern utopianism

It is also important to note here that the view of postmodernism – as at its core a nihilistic philosophy – is arguable. Some authors (e.g. Doll 1995; Siebers 1994) claim that postmodernism has indeed developed a vision for the future. According to these authors, the postmodern vision is mostly characterized by its focus on heterogeneity, multiplicity, difference and equality (not of samenesses, but of differences). Differences include sexual differences – which are why utopian desire and postmodernism are often defined 'in some connection to sexual happiness and the human body' (Siebers 1994: 10). Siebers actually furthers his argument by claiming that postmodernism is in essence a utopian philosophy:

> What postmodernism wants is what has been lacking, which is to say that postmodernism is a utopian philosophy. Utopianism demonstrates both a relentless dissatisfaction with the here and now as well as bewilderment about the possibility of thinking beyond the here and now. Utopianism is not about being 'no where'; it is about desiring to be elsewhere. Postmodernists, then, are utopian not because they do not know what they want. They are utopian because they know that they want something else. They want to desire differently.
>
> (Siebers 1994: 2c3)

Similarly, Bill Doll argues that the postmodern utopian vision takes on a new frame which can be called 'post-liberal' as it refers to its 'move beyond individualism' and focuses on the 'ecological, communal, [and] dialogical' (Doll 1995: 96). The postmodern vision is born from 'our own collective, creative imaginations', rather than from a 'firmly set, a priori ideology' (p. 89). It is a vision built on doubt and irony, a vision that recognizes its own limits and the centrality of the dialogic process and dialogic community (pp. 89–101). It seems that even when consciously abandoned, utopia keeps on coming back.

Postmodernism has opened up spaces for 'desiring differently', and has challenged traditional views of knowledge, education and the future, including the desired, utopian ones. The very idea of pluralistic, alternative futures as opposed to 'the future' (i.e. always singular) is, indeed, postmodern. But while postmodern theory is effective in offering critical analysis of futures discourses, it cannot replace other theoretical perspectives and approaches, particularly those that do not refuse to offer directions, 'solutions', 'ideals' and 'utopian hope'. At the same time, postmodernism has also influenced a transition from a singular 'utopia' to more contested categories such as 'heterotopia' and 'eutopia'. The Foucauldian notion, that everything is 'dangerous' and that we cannot create knowledge that is not influenced by power relationships, demands the development of alternatives that are made of clay rather than cement. It also demands that we stay ever vigilant, as today's utopias often become tomorrow's nightmares (Nandy 1987). This position advocates resistance as 'a way of life rather than a one-off event' (McPhail 1997: par. 65), and leads 'not to apathy but to a hyper-activism' (Foucault, quoted in McPhail 1997: par. 65). Deconstruction of mainstream future educational discourse and investigation of alternative discourses is important, but so is the ethical evaluation of such futures visions.

In this respect, it is crucial, as argued by Gunew (1990), Grosz (1990) and Hughes (1994), to pose, outline and articulate the alternatives, even while aware of their limitations and dangers. As well, while it is important to contextualize the inquiry and question grand theories, it is also important:

> to retain some form of large-scale theorising in order to under-
> stand the systematicity as well as the diversity of women's [and
> other groups'] oppression...Both large- and small-scale narratives
> are required as one will counteract the distorting tendencies of
> the other.
>
> (Fawcett and Featherstone 2000: 13)

Such a balance between large- and small-scale narratives addresses the tendency of large-scale theorizing to transform into '...quasi meta-narratives, while larger contextualising accounts help prevent local narratives from devolving into simple demonstrations of "difference"' (Fraser 1995: 62).

Dominant systems of thought and alternative futures

Still, while postmodernists may indeed be 'guilty' of weakening the western Left, to give them sole responsibility for the emergence of new hegemonic images of the future is to give them, in a way, *too much* agency. That is, hegemonic futures visions have emerged for other reasons as well. As I have repeatedly argued throughout this book, hegemonic futures visions of a globalized and technologized world and education have also emerged because they 'make the most sense'. They are seen as the best option for the future – are easily recognizable and intelligible – within mainstream views of time, history and the future.

The hegemonic future convinces of its inevitability because it 'fits' within the already existing 'imaginaire'. As seen from Villemard's (1910) utopian image of the school in the year 2000 (see Figure 3 in Part I), the 'new' 'techno-literate' citizen of the twenty-first century has a long history. This techno-literate subject has been imagined, discussed and portrayed in detail for many decades, if not the whole century (also see Figure 5 in Part II). Villemard's school of the future, for example, has teachers wiring directly students to a 'book feeding machine'. The image on the further education billboard (Figure 5) describes high-tech as 'leading the way' in higher education. The 2001 brochure by the University of Southern Queensland asserts that 'the future begins with e'. Another brochure by the same university portrays a mechanical approach to nature and instantaneous digital time of the 'three minute culture'. These representations are 'signs of our times' – we've got an 'e-university in an e-World'. It is precisely this imaging that creates demands to 'put a computer in every classroom' (1980s) and 'have every classroom wired' (1990s) (Luke 2001b: 426); that is, demands for future literacies to be defined within technological terms.

Hegemonic futures also fit well with the mainstream interpretation of human history, the way our experience of time is interpreted and how social change is seen to occur. That is, history is seen as a linear progression from simpler, pre-modern and primitive towards more complex, modern/postmodern and advanced societies. In addition, history is seen to be created by technological change. Therefore, the measure of complexity, progress and development is through the accumulation of material goods and services, through technological advances. As this worldview is based on the linear view of time, it is a perspective that sees technology as the solution for most, if not all, problems and the purpose of life as the accumulation of material goods. The desired future is thus about the continuation of the present but with more technology and more goods: the magnified present.

Emergent hegemonic futures remain so because they fit into the worldview that legitimates. This worldview also has an 'inevitability' to it; the trajectory of the future is predicated on past and present trends and developments. It also presents what reality is, and is going to be. I have, however, repeatedly argued throughout this book that the discourse about 'globalized and cyber education' is only partly about 'the push' towards the future. That is, rather than being only an attempt to 'objectively' and 'impartially' describe 'the way things are/going to be', these discourses are also about what is desired, hoped for, or alternatively, about what is feared. They are also discussions about future directions. Most significantly, their description of inevitable futures is itself embedded in politics.

I have argued against the claims of objectivity of globalized and cyber education. I have shown that these are historical processes based on particular worldviews – western, technological, instrumental rationalism, consumerism – and supported by myths, such as the Land of Cockaygne, the Global Brain, Network, 'New World', and the myth of the 'free market'. I have also argued that, historically, the 'globalization hypothesis' coincided with the coming of the Christian second millennium, emerging in the 1980s and increasing in influence during the last decade of the twentieth century. It has coincided with a period in western history that can be characterized by a certain void in socio-economic futures visions. It has become a useful replacement for the old and tired narrative of 'progress' and 'development'. However, I have also argued that globalization – as process and theory – does not fundamentally disturb the patriarchal and western historical project. Rather, it fortifies it.

The important part of the process to assert hegemony is the ability to control discourse. Changes in discourse are often followed by changes in politics, and vice versa. For example, the 'globalization hypothesis' has been hijacked from supporting earlier demands for multiculturalism, inclusiveness and ecological sustainability to mean irreversible, unstoppable economic forces that demand competition between individuals, corporations and nation states. Globalized visions *for* the (desired, inclusive, cooperative) future became a vision *of* the (feared, exclusive, competitive) future. Visions of the future, like visions about the future, do nothing but 'prepare students actively for a tomorrow that will be very different from today. It merely tells them what might happen' (Hicks and Holden 1995: 10). Furthermore, such visions imply passivity. Education for the future, on the other hand, Hicks and Holden argue, '... requires exploration of [our] own and others' hopes and fears for the future and the action required to create a more just and ecologically sustainable future. It empowers children to feel that they can work towards their chosen future' (ibid.).

The ways out?

But this hegemonic process is never complete. There are always alternatives that resist some of the previously described changes and help to further advance their own and (other than economic and technological) global human needs and interests. These alternatives are also an attempt to control and transform the discourse. In that regard, some have been more and some less successful. Feminism has, in general, seen the appropriation of the 'liberation discourse' to mean the empowerment of individual women and girls *within* the patriarchal dystopian future. The new language feminists have tried to create has often been appropriated to mean something else (as in, e.g. 'Ms' becoming a signifier of a divorcee). But there have been some successes for those wishing to change education and coming from alternative paradigms, such as the feminist, indigenous and spiritual. The reason why proponents of spiritual education have been so successful in the USA, argue Ankerberg and Weldon (1996), is that they have managed to effectively neutralize and depoliticize their own 'religious jargon'. That is, 'occult, metaphysical and New Age terminology is removed' and replaced with neutral concepts and techniques, making it acceptable to the general public (ibid.: 432). For example, '[t]he Hindu practice of transcendental meditation may be termed the "Science of Creative Intelligence"; the religious practice of yoga may be called "psychophysiological exercise", and meditation may be called "centering" and "visualizing"' (ibid.: 431).

Insights gained from 'the upsurge of interest in meditation, bio-feedback, martial arts, Eastern thought, and altered states of consciousness' have therefore managed to find 'their ways into the classroom' (Gay Hendricks and James Fadiman, quoted in Ankerberg and Weldon 1996: 431). From the perspective of the Christian Right, this is, of course, a disastrous development. But for those wishing to introduce change into mainstream education – even though from a position of marginality – this is a sign of hope. It is *not only dominant social groups that can*, therefore, *control the discourse*. Rather, discourse can be manipulated, changed and transformed to serve the interests of marginalized social groups and marginalized worldviews as well.

Still, an important part of the hegemony of the new emerging dominant futures visions is to deny other alternatives. As argued by Postman (1993: 48), they do so not by making them illegal, immoral or unpopular, but by making them invisible and therefore irrelevant. Global dominant knowledge 'destroys the very conditions for [local] alternatives to exist, very much like the introduction of monocultures that destroy the very conditions for diverse species to exist', argues Shiva (1993: 12). In other words, 'local knowledge is made to disappear' when the dominant system negates 'its very existence', or when it erases or destroys the reality which the local knowledge attempts to represent (ibid.: 9, 12). The erasure of localized regimes of educational truths has been central to the colonialist project. While colonialism and imperialism could never erase various experiences of time, this being integral to human existence, these processes did, however, erase or marginalize the way different cultures and historical periods perceived and conceptualized that experience. Erasure of localized regimes of truths about time has thus also been central to the colonialist project. As a consequence, the tendency of the new emerging hegemonic future is to bring about one (standardized) education as well as one (standardized) approach to time and vision for the future. The seeds necessary for the expansion and colonization of nature and lands were already sown in the western worldview, its approach to time and the vision for the future. The use of particular technological innovations has only helped manifest western Dreaming. The forward projection of the west's own linear view of time is an essential part of the west's ontology, focused as it is on progress, development, expansion and change. It is foundationally related to the western conviction of the superiority of western culture and western educational models. That they are to be, must be, exported worldwide is part of the same equation.

But the intervention of marginalized social groups has recently also moved to the global level. That is, marginalized discourses on feminist, indigenous and spiritual alternatives assert that their alternatives are not only good for themselves but are also the solution for all. Arguments can be made that the alternatives that have become the most popular also satisfy the particular needs of 'the centre' (west, patriarchy). For example, ecological education and the Gaian paradigm may become 'new grand narrative' (Myerson 2001) because they help address the ecological crisis in the west, as well as globally. As well, the recent upsurge in spirituality may not only be related to efforts made by those who object to the creation of materialistic technologized futures. The need for spirituality may also come from people, particularly those in First World nations as they become more uncertain of 'their identities, rights, privileges and very existence' (Tuhiwai Smith 1999: 102). Spirituality could also be commodified to become 'a profitable experience' (ibid.). Alternatives are always in danger of being coopted. This is especially the case when alternatives develop within the context of the dominant continued growth worldview. What this suggests is that while material changes are crucial, changes in the episteme/worldview/paradigm are equally, if not more, important.

The challenge to hegemonic futures

I have thus examined alternatives that come from significantly different epistemological positions; they fundamentally challenge hegemonic visions of the future. Feminist education challenges the patriarchal assumptions of globalization and the WebNet vision of the future. It also challenges the view of time and the dominant mode of rationality that underlies these two visions. The indigenous vision of the future, while linear, challenges the fundamental epistemological assumptions of the nature of society – the role of the individual, who teaches, the purpose of education, the role of nature. It disturbs the essential globalist and technopolist nature of the determined future. The final vision disturbing the hegemonic future offered in this book was the spiritual. By definition, it challenges the materialistic nature of the current models of the world and the futures of education. These alternatives were also selected as they are derived from civilizations outside the emporium of the west.

The alternatives that were discussed were each seen as a possible future. They have the capacity to dramatically transform education – who learns, how we learn, the structure of teaching and what is taught. While awareness of the hegemonic tendency of globalized and cyber education is important, it is even more important to argue that these dominant images do not need to remain so. Furthermore, they will not be able to remain so, as change is the only constant. However, change is also always created in the context of the 'weight of history'. Hegemonic futures visions are thus about both 'discontinuity' and a certain 'continuity'. Being part of 'continuity' they may help maintain and expand the worldwide western and patriarchal domination for quite some time to come. Education can both help adapt and adjust to these futures and help to create transformative, alternative ones. Such transformative, alternative futures would then be based on their 'continuity' or alternative histories, defined in their own terms.

Alternatives are not only possible, but they also always parallel hegemonic visions. Still, hegemonic futures visions are described, imagined and theorized in much more detail than are the alternatives. This also explains why there is a paucity of images of alternatives. Hegemonic futures are better known, in terms of both their promise and their potential downfall. A higher presence of dystopia signifies engagement by those who disagree with the particular visions. In general, dystopia is not as well developed in the alternatives that I have explored. Except for some critique by the Christian Right of spiritual education and the critique of feminism from within and by the 'what-about-the-boys' backlash, the dystopian element is barely evident. While I have added some dystopian elements to both feminist and spiritual alternatives, I have not done so for the indigenous alternative. This is because, as a non-indigenous person, I am not in an epistemological position to do so. Table 11.3 compares utopian and dystopian aspects of each vision.

Table 11.3 Hegemonic and alternative futures visions comparison – social utopias and dystopias

Futures visions	Social utopia	Social dystopia
Globalized world and education	Material benefits, satisfaction of material needs More consumer and employment choices Pushing towards international democracy globally	Widening gap between rich and poor, rampant poverty Increase in gender inequality Single culture and society dominating the planet Environmental degradation Hierarchical, unequal and insecure social environment
WebNet vision of the world, cyber education	Cyber democracy and world harmony Environmental crisis resolved Freedom from repetitive boring tasks as well as from the limitations of time, geography, class, disability, race, gender Freedom to create new virtual identities and communities	Digital divide, formation of cyberghettos Electronic surveillance, lack of privacy Adcult and infoglut, ubiquitous advertising and information overload Temporal and cultural impoverishment

Feminist alternatives	Everyone able to fulfil potential irrespective of their gender, race, ethnicity, religion, ability, culture, sexual preference	Dystopia developed as a method to critique patriarchy
	Survival of the human race	Critique internal-sympathetic
		External critique that would bring the vision towards the dystopian edge missing
Recovery of indigenous traditions	Saving the earth	[Missing]
	Survival of human species and other living beings	
	Universe kept in balance and harmony	
Spiritual alternatives	Ananda – bliss	Occultism
	Planetary civilization in peace	Essentialist
	Living in truth	Verticality
		Exclusion of the less spiritual
		Male-biased

The important question to be asked here is: Is it the presence of both utopian and dystopian perspectives that makes a particular vision seem 'realistic'? As argued by Boulding (1995: 100), is it because we now take it as axiomatic that fears are somehow realistic and hopes not? Or, is it that only alleged 'realistic' futures are critiqued if we disagree with them, and not the ones seen as 'impossible' and irrelevant? Or, is it because hegemonic futures visions are indeed 'more dangerous'? In any case, both textual and visual images of a future technologized world are incredibly easy to find. This can be compared with the general difficulty in finding images, particularly visual ones, that disturb this hegemony. The same is true of education in general. For example, it is much more difficult to find visual representations of futures of education than to find visual representations of the futures of war, transportation, communication and so on. Education thus remains either invisible or mediated through the technological. How are created futures, then, going to be different? If a transformed and improved educational system is absent from mainstream consciousness of the future, what then?

What is the consequence of replaying the images that do exist? As argued by Hicks (2001), most educators thus 'make things worse' by communicating what is assumed about the future. What is assumed as real is often, for both adults and children, dominated by popular imaging, as in science fiction. This popular imaging is now also dystopian, following the general change in how the utopian has been constituted in the second half of the twentieth century. Children's images of the future, in particular, are likely to be 'stereotyped and critically unreflective' (Hicks and Holden 1995: 12):

> In the same way that children have preconceptions and stereo-types about other countries, so they also make a range of assumptions about the future. In large part these come from portrayals of the future in popular films, advertisements, television, books, comics, computer games and toys...Children are not blank tables, nor does schooling take place in a cultural vacuum.
>
> (Hicks and Holden 1995: 12)

To counteract such a situation, the detailed expression, articulation and envisioning of alternatives is necessary (see Table 11.3). The alternative futures need to be explicit or they remain taken for granted, tied to the hegemonic future. While the future is 'often a missing dimension within the curriculum' (Hicks 2002: 11), both critical futures and utopian thinking is crucial if the hegemonic, patriarchal and western future is to be destabilized. For example, recent reflections on the major research study titled *Images of the World in the Year* by Galtung (2000) discovered that what 'people' desired most was a peaceful future, community, environment and safety, but what they received was more and more technology. This is largely because such a future has been pushed by the dominant elite groups because it serves their interests and fits within their worldview. They have historically benefited from this future, and would resist alternatives. But it is also because critique, usually continuously replayed by those who disagree with a particular present or future, also somewhat reaffirms the very present or future it critiques. Critique without envisioning, without proposing dissenting alternatives, remains futile, incapable of transforming what it opposes. Images of the future, on the other hand, thus become 'an agent of social change' (Boulding 1995: 95), a place to begin 'practical journeys of hope' (Hutchinson 1996: 210).

12 Epistemic change and the transformation of education

Towards educational eutopia

> The world is now far too dangerous for anything except Utopia.
> (Buckminster Fuller, quoted in Anandamitra 1987a: 168)

Tables 12.1 and 12.2 compare hegemonic and alternative visions so as to clarify the choices. This is done for both educational utopias and dystopias, as well as for social and educational eutopias. They provide the concluding map of the questions raised in this book. Clearly, while each vision promises a bright future, each vision also comes with a dystopian possibility.

This book has presented several alternative visions for the transformation of education that desire to play an important role in creating more balanced societies of tomorrow. It also critiqued the foreclosing of the future, which occurs when some visions are privileged and seen as the only 'real' possibilities. The question now becomes: What can be done today to create some of these desirable futures? If the continuation of the present is desired, or if the realization of hegemonic futures visions is desired, not much effort is needed. The continuation of what the majority is already doing would suffice. On the other hand, if the disruption of hegemonic futures and of the continuation of present trends is desired, much more fundamental and difficult work is required. This is because there is a need to rebuild on the 'faulty foundations', and to sustain that effort through the generations and not expect 'solutions' to occur either immediately or in our lifetimes. Utopias take a long time to materialize – the best measurement of this achievement is when they are no longer recognized as such.

Table 12.1 Hegemonic and alternative futures visions comparison – educational utopias and dystopias

Futures visions	Educational utopia	Educational dystopia
Globalized world and education	Dynamic synergy of teachers and students collaborating globally	Education a product to be bought and sold, commercialization and corporatization of education
	Transnational and transcultural dialogues and learning	Sacrifice of individual styles and idiosyncratic enthusiasm to satisfy global criteria, increase in bureaucratic rigidities
	Expansion of knowledge	Smothering of all forms of creativity, creation of docile, hard-working conformist students
	Student-centred education	Further westernization
		In non-OECD countries decrease in both quantity and quality
WebNet vision of the world, cyber education	Improved access and quality, education less costly and more flexible	Linguistic colonization
	Student-centred lifelong learning	Suppression of other forms of learning (e.g. oral)
	Self-directed, collaborative learning	Too much stress on individualized learning and personal autonomy leads to competition
	Learning by doing	Education teaches about progress without limits, rights without responsibilities and technology without cost
	Increase in students independence, curiosity and autonomy	
	Faster acquisition of skills than ever before	
	The era of 'pedagogical plenty'	
	Equitable sharing of classroom authority – authority of the teaher decentred	
	Knowledge available 24 hours a day, 365 days of the year	

Feminist alternatives	Truly holistic education Education bringing about positive social change Positive effects on personal lives and relationships	Neglect of boys' and men's issues Feminist education ideological, anti-intellectual, intolerant, dogmatic Circular classroom arrangement replicates panopticon – students visible to an all-seeing eye, self-surveillance of each other also promoted
Recovery of indigenous traditions	Holistic learning Improved relationships between peoples, with nature Education more life-relevant	Missing out on achievements within mainstream society
Spiritual alternatives	Education that liberates and nourishes the soul	Education that reproduces religious dogma

Table 12.2 Hegemonic and alternative futures visions comparison – social and educational eutopias

Futures visions	Social eutopia	Educational eutopia
Globalized world and education	Potential for global transformation, inter-transnational government and cooperation	Benefits from globalizing student body and globalizing curriculum
	Potential to move from the 'tyranny of the local community'	Improvement of access to educational resources and expertise
WebNet vision of the world, cyber education	Potential environmental benefits	Expansion in approaches to teaching and learning
	Increased efficiency	Powerful method of learning that can meet the needs of some students the best
	Increased possibilities for inter-cultural exchange within the discourse of rationalism	
Feminist alternatives	Improvement in women's lives, more choices and opportunities	Removing of gender bias and prejudice in education
Recovery of indigenous traditions	Survival and advancement of indigenous peoples	Learning from indigenous peoples about local history and environment
Spiritual alternatives	Integrated, balanced and service-oriented society	Integration of body, mind and spirit
	Counterbalancing excesses in materialism	

Beyond crypto-utopia

Throughout this book, I have repeatedly argued that by focusing on utopian, eutopian and dystopian elements in all futures visions, whether hegemonic or marginal, claims about a particular future as external to a worldview are weakened. The future is de-colonized and returned to its true meaning of 'not yet' or 'in times to come'. I have also repeatedly argued that 'utopian' does not lie solely in the jurisdiction of alternatives. Further, it has been seen that, at any given time in history, there are numerous, often competing, utopian and dystopian visions that are constantly being negotiated, both locally and globally. In that process, not all social groups have the opportunity to exercise equal power and contribute towards the 'universalization' of utopian ideals. Thus, certain utopian visions are always privileged, defining what becomes the dominant image of the future. In our present historical moment, it is predominantly cyber-utopia and the utopia of free and open markets that have become the privileged utopian discourse. Of course, discourses on a 'postindustrial', 'information society' and on a 'globalized', 'pan-capitalist' world are rarely termed as 'utopian'. Rather, they are seen to form 'rationalistic' and 'realistic' futures discourse where discussion about the desired is apparently taken out of the equation. As such they represent what could be termed *crypto-utopia*, or utopia that is hidden, disguised, veiled, concealed and covert. While they purport to communicate the 'truth about the future', such 'realistic' futures in fact also subtly promote implicit assumptions about the nature of future society (high-tech, globalized), and impose these views on other futures discourses. All other discourses about the future are made to adjust to and negotiate with these, arguably, most-likely futures. But hegemonic futures visions also address certain hopes and desires – they too portray imaginary good or perfect places and prescribe improved imagined states of collective and individual being. That is, both utopian and dystopian narratives underlie hegemonic futures visions.

Despite postmodern efforts to destabilize all meta-narratives, including futures and utopian visions, we have witnessed the emergence of both new meta-narratives and new utopias. This is the case for both hegemonic and alternative discourses, although the former is disguised as 'the truth' about the future. I have also argued that visions of globalized and cyber education exist in the context of the western patriarchal tradition. However, as part of the continuous human endeavour to survive and improve living conditions, they also in some ways satisfy the needs and desires of the 'universal' human (i.e. health and happiness). However, the alleged linear progression towards this end is far from clear. There is, of course, a great imbalance in the redistribution of these goods and services, as most beneficiaries are (still) those located in advanced capitalist economies, as well as men (ILO 2004). The cost of this particular future is also incredibly high, threatening the conditions necessary for basic human survival. The proponents of the globalized/cyber future believe that the issue of such costs will be resolved through the very (technological) means that have seen western civilization flourish. For example, it is also through the technological solution that the problem of the Other will be magically resolved, through media such as Cyberspace, the Internet and so forth, which 'equalize' everybody. Others believe that much more work is needed if we are to create (or recreate) egalitarian societies, and that current problems cannot be solved with the means that helped to create them in the first place. Thus, alternatives developed outside the western civilizational and patriarchal framework are sought. In either case, there are certain *underlying myths and metaphors* that *make the story function as true*. The underlying worldview determines what the litany is, whether there is the 'reality' of globalization or the 'reality' of impending ecological crisis. Both base their claims on particular empirical evidence focusing on some data but not on other data. The position I take is closer to the one less concerned with technological salvation and more concerned with social and ecological 'resolutions'. That is, since the costs of globalized cyber futures are much higher, it is these visions that are much more 'dangerous'. There are, thus, foundational problems in the western project of expansion and technologism. Saving our futures, creating more peaceful, gender-balanced, sustainable and planetary futures requires conversion and conversation, as well as entry into other visions of the future, other models of education. Not entering these doors certainly puts humanity at risk. Postmodernism may see this risk as yet another discourse; however, the possible pain of the future makes this risk far more foundational.

Dismantling hegemonic panopticon time

As argued by Swift, we are currently in the midst of a 'rush to nowhere':

> We drive fast cars. We are expected to 'multitask' and some people have even come to enjoy it. Children are rushed to grow up. We are under ever-increasing pressure to work faster and

faster. Some people work themselves to death...We gobble fast food...We sleep less than we used to...There is a macho ethos of speed that goes with it all. It's like the Mike Douglas character in the Oliver Stone movie *Wall Street* says: 'Lunch? Lunch is for wimps'.

(Swift 2002: 9)

The main need has now become to find liberation from the globalized, computer-generated compressed time that threatens life itself (Griffiths 2002: 15). In doing so, modern 'time liberators' can learn from women and cultures that have different ideas of time – both essentially opposed to linear time (ibid.). As argued throughout this book, this is a crucial prerequisite for any substantial social or educational reform:

We need to take back control of our time, not only so we can spend it with our children, but so we can work on rebuilding and re-cementing the social bonds that will allow them to grow up in real communities and have contact with a variety of interested, caring adults.

(McDonnell 2002: 23)

The challenge of liberation from hegemonic time, in society and in schools, is akin to saving childhood itself:

One of the most tenacious conceptual threats to work, and to Captain Clock's hegemonic Time, is childhood itself. Children have a dogged, delicious disrespect for worktime, punctuality, efficiency and for schooled uniform time. Their time is *an eternal present* [italics added]. They live (given half the chance) pre-industrially, in tutti-frutti time, roundabout time, playtime; staunch defenders of the ludic revolution, their hours are stretchy, ribboned, enchanted and wild: which is why adults want to tame their time so ferociously, making them clock-trained, teaching them time-measurement as if they were concrete fact. The school clock is pointed to as the ultimate authority which even the Head obeys.

(Griffiths 2002: 15)

This liberation is crucial, as hegemonic time represents 'a temporary disciplining of the body in the everyday social practices of the classroom' (Jenks 2001: 68):

children's bodies – seen as aged bodies in terms of years lived through – have been used as the primary ordering principle through which the social organization of the school is achieved.

(Jenks 2001: 76)

This is evident within organizational principles of chronological age as well as of 'levels' and 'stages':

Within the national structuring of educational provision, levels of achievement take precedence over age specifically in relation to the core curriculum subjects of maths and English, which are viewed as fundamental to all other learning. By contrast, in those other subjects that more apparently focus on the techniques and abilities of the body (skills such as manual dexterity, artistic ability, physical agility, even musicality) children find themselves, once more, regrouped according to the chronological age of their bodies.

(Jenks 2001: 78)

The disciplining of the body is achieved through these and numerous other practices – all consisting of hegemonic time and indeed, 'the modernist project writ small!' – maintains Jenks (ibid.: 75). For example, hegemonic time is reinforced:

- in understanding of the child as an unfolding project, a natural trajectory, a staged becoming and an inevitably incremental progress into adulthood (e.g. the theories of Piaget and others) (ibid.: 75);
- through the judgement of children's social competence and intellectual 'maturity' by their ability to manage their time 'effectively' (ibid.: 76);
- by the existence of age hierarchy in the school, wherein 'silly' children may be degraded publicly through rituals such as placement of a loud/misbehaving ten- or eleven-year-old child in front of the four- and five-year-olds' line during the assembly time (ibid.: 82);
- by the very public reward of past (good) behaviour in the present (ibid.: 82);
- in the distinction between 'curriculum time' (time controlled by teachers) and 'play time' (time seen by children as being under their control) (ibid.: 69);

- through the use of 'shaping one's own future' rhetoric to maintain children in 'their own place' (ibid.: 71) and
- through teaching that time is a scarce resource not to be wasted,
  but indeed to be invested (ibid.: 70).

Furthermore, hegemonic time is a 'panopticon time' (Lesko 2001,
McClintock 1995), used to discipline both colonized peoples (ibid.:
36–42) and many generations of students (Lesko 2001). As was the
case with colonized peoples, youth too were defined as 'always
"becoming", a situation that provoked endless watching, monitoring,
and evaluating' (ibid.: 38). The developing child is closely watched
so that 'its learning proceeds according to its nature, neither too fast
nor too slow' (ibid.: 39):

> I suggest that a dominant aspect of the discourse on adolescence
> is its location within panoptical time, within a time framework
> that compels us – scholars, educators, parents, and teenagers –
> to attend to progress, precocity, arrest, or decline.
>
> (Lesko 2001: 41)

Lesko suggests that some problems of adolescence (i.e. identity crisis,
disorientation and self-estrangement) are related to the way youth
and adults are perceived:

> Adults are people who *are*, adolescents *will be* in the future...
> the end of the adolescence story remains primary...Adults
> know what the correct and happy ending is (increasing maturity
> and responsibility, school achievement, full-time employ-
> ment, marriage and children, property ownership, in that order),
> only deviations or pitfalls along the prescribed plot merit att-
> ention. The panoptical gaze makes youth into cartoonlike, or
> clownish, figures...Thus, the characters in the narrative of
> adolescence may easily lose their humanity and become stereo-
> types.
>
> (Lesko 2001: 57, 59, 60)

But, while such temporal positioning perhaps made sense at the
turn of the twentieth-century west, it no longer serves its original
purpose – helping identify and create 'a vision of the modern
citizen, who would be equipped for the challenges of the new social,
economic, and world arrangements' (ibid.: 61). This is because the
emerging temporal and spatial arrangements – as defined within

globalization narratives – no longer allow for the slow development in time:

> [this] slow development in time...is under pressure exerted by global capitalism and technology...the time and space compression that Harvey describes further erodes support for meeting adolescents' (and children's) needs. The era of child saving in the United States ended with welfare reform in 1997. The resources once committed to education, health, and social welfare programs of panoptically viewed youth and children are now utilized to build prisons, install metal detectors in schools, and criminalize younger children as adults. As children below ten years of age have become erotic, spectacular, and marketable, the teenager's market share has sunk. Slow development in time may no longer be functional, and quick leaps from childhood to adulthood may be called for by virtual workplaces and education provided on-line...The clear boundary between adolescence and adulthood is blurred, as everyone needs to keep becoming.
>
> (Lesko 2001: 62–63)

The best way to de-colonize the system of education is, however, not to replace one hegemonic approach to time with another, but to teach how to critically engage with multi-temporalities. Alternatively, teaching hegemonic time and the future will remain part of the hidden curriculum. Critical engagement with multi-temporalities is important, because it exposes the linear understanding of time that informs current mainstream discourses on education as not necessarily constitutive of objective reality, as is assumed. Rather, it shows the ways in which such an approach to time is a cultural and social phenomenon, created within a particular civilizational framework. This also means that the 'shrinking of time and space' narrative is also a representation. The current push towards new temporal arrangements is thus not an accomplished fact, and as such immutable, universal and inevitable. This matters because a particular approach to time may *create discursive spaces for the creation of some educational futures and not the others*. If it is 'multiplex visions' of the world that are sought, teaching would need to include 'multi-temporal proficiency' and 'time literacy', enhancing one's own temporal repertoire and learning of alternative approaches to time (Levine 1997: 187–191).

But the multiplex vision of the world needs to be coupled with the debate on 'normative visions about what education can and should be' (Luke 2002: 8). Critical educational theory, coupled with critical futures and utopian thinking, can help promote the educational rationale behind each educational change. Education needs not be seen as a passive recipient of current social trends. Critical educational theory is to remain 'hybrid and polyvocal', both articulating 'visions of social and cultural utopias and heterotopias while blending this with a continued skepticism towards totalization' (ibid.: 1). It is through these critical traditions (critical educational and futures thinking, as well as *strategic utopianism*) that those who oppose hegemonic futures visions can, perhaps, '...develop a political project that is both local yet generalizable, systemic without making Eurocentric, masculinist claims to essential and universal truths about human subjects' (ibid.: vi–vii).

To de-colonize the future, alternative histories are also needed. But alternatives must recognize that knowledge never exists in 'objective, decontextualized forms, but is intimately linked to specific contexts, people and issues' (Abdullah and Stringer 1999: 142). Critical futures thinking here remains paramount. Part of critical futures thinking is critical discourse analysis that can help determine where the discourse is going, how it is dominated by mainstream social groups and how it can be transformed. It can also help unmask what the main issues, priorities, worldviews and myths are that underlie the litany of the future. By searching for particular key words used within each vision, main issues and priorities become more visible.

Educational alternatives

Rather than marginalizing alternative education, Martin (2000) suggests that we may instead consider 'all schools and learning environments to be *educational alternatives*' (final par.). Then, the schools that are chosen are to be based on 'a deeper level of reflection about what you think it means to be human and to live and to grow in a self-sustaining and nurturing community' (ibid.). What needs to be changed is the situation in which:

> Very rarely does school curriculum deal with intercultural worldviews, religion, corporeality, time, space, feelings, emotions, fluidities, liminalities, transformations or relations between people, and other animate beings or their environmental ecologies. Yet these aspects of life are of great concern to us all.
>
> (Marshall 1999: 42)

The continuous articulation of utopias – and critical engagement with them – is important. Stating that utopias are utopian, impossible to achieve, is not a 'scientific' statement but a political statement. Part of the thrust of this book is to take back the power of utopia and use it to create an alternative future. As argued by Giroux and Freire:

> Radical pedagogy needs to be informed by a passionate faith in the necessity of struggling to create a better world. In other words, radical pedagogy needs a vision – one that celebrates not what is but what could be, that looks beyond the immediate to the future and links struggle to new human possibilities. This is a call for a concrete utopianism.
>
> (Giroux 1983: 242)

> When education is no longer utopian, that is, when it no longer embodies the dramatic unity of denunciation and annunciation, it is either because the future has no more meaning for men, or because men are afraid to risk living the future as creative over-coming of the present, which has become old.
>
> (Freire 1998: 492)

Epistemic changes do not just mirror changes within society, but help bring about new resolutions, policies and actions. Bringing many different, excluded, pseudo-included, directly or structurally invisible, groups and perspectives into the future of education discourse and debate will help change not only what is taught in schools but also 'everyday life pedagogies' (Luke 1996b) and, critically, how we imagine and situate 'education' itself.

The transformation of our societies is not possible without the transformation of how we see and imagine our common futures. In this respect, it is crucial to allow for alternative visions of the future to develop. The most important aspect of such visions is that alter-natives to colonized futures conceptualized by patriarchy and the west do exist, and 'that these alternatives can be as "real" as our reality' (Halbert 1994: 29). We can learn from both hegemonic and alternative futures visions; that is, what is utopian, dystopian and eutopian.

What this book has offered is not a prescriptive of what education in the future *should* be like. While I, like anyone else, clearly consider certain visions preferable, this is not the main point. Nor did this book investigate which utopia/eutopia/dystopia is more plausible. Rather, it offers an appeal to engage with multiple educational regimes of truths about the future – both western and non-western, patriarchal and feminist, and secular and spiritual.

Questioning the future, rethinking the present

This book concludes with an invitation for all educators, educational administrators, students, parents and citizens to engage with the following questions:

- What is the range of possible (local and global, social and educational) futures ahead?
- What are the (utopian) promises and the (dystopian) dangers of each one of these visions?
- Which vision(s) is(are) the most popular/dominant, among the majority in our community/society and among children? Why?
- Can we think of the vision(s) that most deeply challenges(challenge) the dominant one(s)?
- Can we think of the vision(s) most likely to challenge current mainstream education and society in the near and distant future?
- What are the perspectives, issues and concerns of the main stakeholders of the future – children, students and young people? What may be the views, issues and concerns of future generations not yet born?
- What is(are) the preferred vision(s) for our school, community and society?
- What is the cost of our preferred vision, what is missing and who is excluded?
- How could these costs best be ameliorated?
- Which groups and worldviews hold the most power in our education, community and society? Who and what do such power relationships advantage? Who and what do they disadvantage?
- How does the most popular/dominant vision translate into everyday life and work practices, in our education, community and society? And how does the most preferable?
- What *can* be done now to encourage such vision materializing in the future?
- How *can* actions we take today and tomorrow *benefit* the others and us in the near and distant future the most? Who are 'we', and who are 'the others'?

It is my belief that only through such engagement – with these questions and with the full diversity of worldviews and 'ways of knowing' – can social and educational eutopias that benefit the greatest number emerge.

Notes

Introduction

1 Utopia means both 'nowhere' or 'no place', and a 'good place', or 'perfect place'. Most commonly, it is understood as an idealistic but unrealistic vision of the future. Eutopia literally translates as a 'good place', and denotes utopias that are 'imperfect', marked by self-doubt, critical evaluation, reflection and questioning.

2 Dystopia denotes 'bad place'. Dystopian visions take two basic forms: being a description of 'a place or condition in which everything is as bad as possible' or taking the form of anti-utopias (Jennings 1996: 211). In the first form, dystopias play the important role of emphasizing 'the serious problems that may result from deliberate policies, indecision and indifference, or simply bad luck in humanity's attempts to manage its affairs' (ibid.). As anti-utopias, dystopias are 'satirical or prophetic warnings against the proposed "improvement" of society by some political faction, class interest, technology, or other artifact' (ibid.). It is in this latter sense that dystopias can 'poison our outlook on the present, or even prompt us to give up trying to do better' (ibid.).

3 Heterotopia, the term partially developed by Foucault (1986) has been further developed by postmodern thinkers to denote imaginary 'places of otherness'. It has also come to denote multiplicity and pluralism of futures visions. Similar to the term eutopia, heterotopia also denotes conceptual components within the broader term of utopia which sanctify self-doubts, openness and dissent.

4 For more detailed discussion on this, see Milojević (2002b, 2003).

Part I   Historical futures discourses in education

1 Today, the single common denominator indicating educational futures is technology. Interestingly, even this image by Villemard would, most likely, be immediately recognized as having something to do with the future, although it is almost 100 years old (1910). Is this denominator – technology – to replace the current dominant image of schooling, of children 'ordered, stiffed, grouped together, with a teacher looking stern and authoritative'?

1 Future, time and education: contexts and connections

1 Such an understanding and concept of time has been present among some indigenous societies, for example, North American and Australian indigenous peoples.

3 Turn of the spiral: alternative histories

1 The word 'Dreamtime' was apparently first used in print in 1896 by anthropologists Spencer and Filler (Morphy 1999). Dreamtime broadly corresponds to a word or set of words that exist in many Aboriginal languages, such as the Yolngu *wangarr*, the Warlpiri *tjukurrpa* and the Arrente (Aranda) *altyerrenge* (ibid.). While this English translation was accepted by many Aboriginal people early on, some felt that 'the connotation of "dream" is inappropriate: [Yolngu] *wangarr* is not a dream, but a reality' (ibid.: 265). So the words 'Dreaming' and 'Dreamtime' should not be understood in their ordinary English sense but rather as time existing independently of the linear time of everyday life and the temporal sequence of historical events (ibid.). In that sense, Dreaming is as much a dimension of reality as a period of time gaining temporality, because it was 'there in the beginning, underlies the present and is a determinant of the future' (ibid.).

Part II Destabilizing dominant narratives

1 The *Cosmic Evolution* image by Robert McCall is an excellent representation of the dominant (western, patriarchal) understanding of time and the future. Time is linear, moving in a sequential manner from the past, to the present, and then to the future. The past is conceived in terms of evolutionary pattern from rudimentary to more evolved forms. Human history is a history of the intellectual elite, only 'important people' feature. Among those, there are only a few women and non-white people and only one person with hands (Pablo Picasso), denoting that it is an intellectual development that is paramount for humans and in creating the future. The foundation of the present is what feminists call the 'cereal package family' – nuclear family with a boy and a girl but boy being taller, older and stronger. It is the man that is under the sun and the whole family is standing in the centre of the painting and *on the top* of the Earth – being of it yet above nature. The future is portrayed solely in technological terms, no nature exists, not even people, let alone relationships, society and culture.

6 Visions II: cyberia; the information age

1 'Leading the way in higher education' is a highway billboard by TAFE (Technical and Further Education), Caboolture, Australia, July 2002. This image corresponds to imaging that often exists in science fiction – education in the future is instantaneous and almost always technologically mediated (e.g. *The Matrix*, *Battlefield Earth*, *Johnny Mnemonic*).

7 Contextualizing global dreams and nightmares

1 'New Look for e-classroom'. But in which ways have computers changed the industrial model of schooling? The image accompanying the article by Cynthia G. Wagner, 'Facing the Electronic Future in Classrooms: Classroom design integrates computers into the learning environment', *The Futurist* (January–February, 2001: 68). Previously, this photo appeared accompanying the article 'The classroom of the 21st century', by Kofi Akumanyi, London Press Service, International Press Unit, FCO, www.londonpress.info.

Part III   Searching for social and educational alternatives

1 Millennium Tree by Josephine Wall represents a different way to think of the time and the future. It portrays time evolving in a more organic manner, not sequentially as in the industrial 'clock' time. The tree trunk – the base of our global human society – embraces many 'ordinary' and not-so-'ordinary' people (not just the 'big names' from the past), the Earth is in the centre (humans are not standing on the top of it as in the *Cosmic Evolution* image), the focus is on human relationships (multicultural, interracial, perhaps even inter-gender ones) and future generations (as in many non-western, eastern and indigenous visions of the future). Peace has as much importance for the future as does technology. And above all, there are the gentle and guiding hands of a larger Entity that supports humans on their quest (physical, social and spiritual evolution?). Wall's image is interesting because it rescues the image of the tree from social evolutionists and scientists focused on race as a crucial explanatory variable. As shown in the work of McClintock (1995), the tree was often used to show human history as 'naturally teleological, an organic process of upward growth, with the European as the apogee of progress' (ibid.: 37):

> Mapped against the tree, the world's discontinuous cultures appear to be marshalled within a single, European Ur-narrative...disobliging historical discontinuities can be ranked, subdued and subordinated into a hierarchical structure of branching time...In the tree of time, racial hierarchy and historical progress became the *fait accomplis* of nature. [the racial Family Tree] was attended by a second, decisive image: the Family of Man...[which] provided scientific racism with a *gendered* image for popularizing and disseminating the idea of *racial* progress...the family Tree [also] represents evolutionary time as a *time without women*. The family image is an image of disavowal, for it contains only men, arranged as a linear frieze of solo males ascending toward the apogee of the individual *Homo sapiens*.
>
> (McClintock 1995: 37–39)

2 For example, in Serbia, the main tension is between the hegemony of the modernist and the contending nationalistic and humanistic.

10 Visions V: spiritual alternatives

1 The term 'spiritualistic' is perhaps an inadequate translation from the original French into English; it is reminiscent of the tradition of spiritualism and spiritism, while spiritual and spirituality are more adequate terms here.

2 More detailed overview in Milojević, 2002b.

3 Spiritual, holistic and eco-centric education have basic similarities in their visions of education, and have sometimes been used as interchangeable terms. What distinguishes spiritual education, though, is its main concern with fulfilling 'a fundamental human need to understand our presence on Earth' (Bertrand 1995: 9). Its focus is on the relationship between humans and the cosmos, universe, *prana* (life force), *noosphere* (Teilhard de Chardin's 'mind sphere'), collective (human, universal) consciousness. With spiritual education, 'we come to the problem of the true motive of life, the reason of our existence upon earth' (The Mother 1965: 23).

4 Some parts of the western New Age movement developed over at least a century, but, as a whole, the New Age movement is quite recent. As Bertrand (1995: 10) explains, while spiritual revival 'so popular nowadays' really took off at the beginning of the twentieth century, it was in the last two decades that the movement was established and the idea of a New Age culture popularized.

The New Age movement is also incredibly broad:

> As the end of the millennium approaches, the New Age seems to be everywhere but continues to elude specific definition. The genealogy of New Age thinking can be traced to the sixties and the Age of Aquarius, and, much earlier, to Positive Thinking, Mind Cure, Christian Science, Theosophy, and spiritualism, and even further back, to Transcendentalism and the influence of Indian religions on American Protestantism. But the New Age cannot be accounted for in terms of a single root influence. It includes phenomena as diverse as Yoga and the Kabbalah, holistic healing and Wicca, veganism and acupuncture, contact with angels and spiritual computer interfaces, wilderness trips and tours of holy places, self-help and Jungian psychology, goddess revivals, and even the mythopoetic men's movement...
>
> (Torgovnick 1997: 172)

The movement is therefore eclectic, drawing upon a variety of cultural and religious traditions, 'past and present, Western and Eastern, modern and primitive, familiar and exotically Other' (ibid.: 173). What seems to be beyond doubt is that it is continuously growing.

5 In this paragraph, Krishnamurti talks about the 'true religious mind', but the way he describes this 'true' religious mind is in opposition to established religions and along the lines of the more recently developed and accepted term 'spiritual'/'spirituality'. I have therefore omitted from the paragraph the words 'religious mind' because that would confuse the true meaning of Krishnamurti's phrase.

6 In the original text, the word 'man' is used. It has here been altered to 'human' in line with more gender-aware language.

11 Postmodern visions, costs and multi-temporalities

1 US elementary school students perform a daily ritual of the 1950s, pledging allegiance to the flag. This illustration appeared on the cover page of *The Wilson Quarterly*, Summer 1995, Vol. XIX, No. 3. It referred to the article by Alan Ehrenhalt, 'Learning from the Fifties'. In this article, Ehrenhalt argued that 'many Americans long for the virtues of the 1950s – community, security, certainty' (e.g. stable relationships, civil classrooms, safe streets, etc.) (ibid.: 1, 8). But these virtues all came with the price, for example, limits on the choices, existence of inflexible rules, obedience to authority, difficulty to divorce even if joint life is extremely difficult and stressful, lack of social and sexual options for women, racism, curriculum of required memorization and classroom drill, tyrannical fathers, headmasters and bosses, lectures on 100 per cent Americanism and the sinfulness of dissent. As well, the 1950s in America were 'not years of stasis but of rapid and bewildering change: nuclear tension, population explosion, the creation of a new world in the suburbs, [and] the sudden emergence of a prosperity and materialism...' (ibid.: 28). And, rather than being a pre-modern, pre-capitalist Eden, the 1950s were also the decade of 'tail fins, mass-produced suburban subdivisions, and the corruption of television quiz shows by greedy sponsors' (ibid.: 22) The golden days of the 1950s were thus not only an illusion but also not 'a happy time for everyone in America. For many, the price of the limited life was an impossibly high one to pay' (ibid.: 23).

2 For example, David Ray Griffin argues for a constructive postmodernism; indeed, calls for a postmodern spirituality. Postmodern spirituality does not seek to return to the pre-modern, but acknowledges the advances of the modern world (Atkisson 1990), and seeks a dialogic spirituality focused on the re-enchantment of the world. Griffin rejects other forms of postmodern, calling them deconstructivist, as they tend towards the nihilistic. He seeks a constructive postmodernism focused on hope and goodness, very much part of the utopian spiritual project (Griffin 1988a,b).

Rosenau (1992) also sees this distinction. She tends to define forms of postmodernism geographically, seeing the deconstructivist as largely European and the constructivist as largely North American. The former is sceptical of the possibility of a new politics of hope, while the latter uses postmodernism to create new social, cultural and spiritual projects.

Bibliography

Abdullah, J. and Stringer, E. (1999) 'Indigenous knowledge, indigenous learning, indigenous research', in L. M. Semali and J. L. Kincheloe (eds) *What is Indigenous Knowledge? Voices from the Academy*, New York: Falmer Press, 143–157.

Abele, F., Dittburner, C. and Graham, K. (2000) 'Towards a shared understanding in the policy discussion about aboriginal education', in M. B. Castellano, L. Davis and L. Lahache (eds) *Aboriginal Education: Fulfilling the Promise*, Vancouver: UBC Press, 3–25.

Aburdene, P. and Naisbitt, J. (1992) *Megatrends for Women*, New York: Villard Books.

Adam, B. (1995) *Timewatch: The Social Analysis of Time*, Cambridge: Polity Press.

—— (1998) *Timescapes of Modernity: The Environment and Invisible Hazards*, London: Routledge.

Afshar, H. and Barrientoes, S. (eds) (1999) *Women, Globalization and Fragmentation in the Developing World*, London: Macmillan.

Agrawal, A. (1995) 'Indigenous and scientific knowledge: some critical comments', *Indigenous Knowledge and Development Monitor*, 3(3): 3–6.

Albrow, M. (1997) *The Global Age: State and Society Beyond Modernity*, Stanford, California: Stanford University Press.

Alcoff, L. (1988) 'Culturalism feminism versus poststructuralism: the identity crisis in feminist theory', *Signs*, 13(3): 405–436.

Altbach, P. (1987) *The Knowledge Context: Comparative Perspectives on the Distribution of Knowledge*, Albany, NY: State University of New York Press.

—— (2003) *The Decline of the Guru: The Academic Profession in Developing and Middle-Income Countries*, New York: Palgrave Macmillan.

Altekar, A. S. (1957) *Education in Ancient India*, Varanasi: N. Kishore.

Amara, R. (1981) 'The futures field: searching for definitions and boundaries', *The Futurist*, 15(1): 25–29.

Anandamitra, A. A. (1987a) *Neo-Humanism: A Vision for a New World/Avadhutika Anandamitra Acarya*, Calcutta, India: Acharya Mantreshvarananda Avadutha, Neo-Humanism Subcommittee.

—— (1987b) *Neo-Humanist Education: Education for a New World*, Tiljala, Calcutta, India: Ananda Marga Women's Welfare Section.

Ananda Rama, A. A. (ed.) (2000) *Neo-Humanist Education*, Mainz, Germany: Ananda Marga Gurukula Publications.

Anderson, B. (1983) *Imagined Communities: Reflections on the Origin and Spread of Nationalism*, London: Verso.

Angus, L. (1993) *Education, Inequality and Social Identity*, London: Falmer Press.

Ankerberg, J. and Weldon, J. (1996) *Encyclopedia of New Age Beliefs*, Eugene, Oregon: Harvest House Publishers.

Annas, P. J. (1978) 'New worlds, new words: androgyny in feminist science fiction', *Science-Fiction Studies*, 5(part 2): 143–156.

Appadurai, A. (1996) *Modernity at Large: Cultural Dimensions of Globalization*, Minneapolis, MN: University of Minnesota Press.

Apple, M. (2000) 'The shock of the real: critical pedagogies and rightist reconstructions', in P. P. Trifonas (ed.) *Revolutionary Pedagogies: Cultural Politics, Instituting Education, and the Discourse of Theory*, New York: RoutledgeFalmer, 225–251.

—— (2001) *Educating the 'Right' Way: Markets, Standards, God and Inequality*, New York: RoutledgeFalmer.

Armstrong, T. (1996) 'Utopian schools' [Originally published in *Mothering*, Summer 1989] http://www.thomasarmstrong.com/articles/utopian_schools.htm (accessed 21 April 2001).

Arnot, M. (1994) 'Male hegemony, social class and women's education', in L. Stone (ed.) *The Education Feminism Reader*, London: Routledge, 84–105.

Atkisson, A. (1990) 'Interview with David Ray Griffin', *In Context*, Winter: 20 http://www.context.org/ICLIB/IC24/Griffin.htm (accessed 9 December 2002).

Auroville Charter (2002) http://www.auroville.org/vision/adream.htm (accessed 24 June 2000).

Bartkowski, F. (1989) *Feminist Utopias*, Lincoln, Nebraska: University of Nebraska Press.

Battiste, M. (ed.) (2000) *Reclaiming Indigenous Voice and Vision*, Vancouver: University of British Columbia Press.

Baudrillard, J. (1991) 'Two essays', *Science-Fiction Studies*, 18(3): 309–320.

—— (1994) *The Illusion of the End*, Stanford, CA: Stanford University Press.

Bayles, T. (1989) *We Live with the Problems, We Know the Solutions*, Armidale: University of New England.

Beare, H. (2001) *Creating the Future School*, London: RoutledgeFalmer.

Beare, H. and Slaughter, R. (1993) *Education for the Twenty-First Century*, London: Routledge.

Belenky, M. F., Clinchy, B. M., Goldberg, N. R. and Tarule, J. M. (1986) *Women's Ways of Knowing*, New York: Basic Books.

Bell, D. (1973) *The Coming of Postindustrial Society: A Venture in Social Forecasting*, New York: Basic Books.

Bell, D. (2000) 'Cybercolonization: introduction', in D. Bell and B. M. Kennedy (eds) *The Cybercultures Reader*, London: Routledge, 697–702.

Bell, W. (1994) An Overview of Futures Studies. Unpublished manuscript. Revised version of a paper first published in Italian, Futuro. *Enciclopedia Delle Scienze Sociali*, 4, Roma, Italia: Marchesi Grafiche Editoriali.

—— (1997) *Foundations of Futures Studies: Human Science for a New Era*, New Brunswick and London: Transaction Publishers.

Bell, G. and Gray, J. N. (1997) 'The revolution yet to happen', in P. J. Denning and R. M. Metcalfe (eds) *Beyond Calculation: The Next Fifty Years of Computing*, New York: Copernicus/Springer-Verlag, 5–32.

Berston, R. and Moont, S. (1996) 'School ain't what it used to be', *Internet.au*, 40–45.

Bertrand, Y. (1995) *Contemporary Theories and Practice in Education*, Madison, WI: Magna Publications.

Bignell, K. C. (1996) 'Building feminist praxis out of feminist pedagogy: the importance of students' perspectives', *Women's Studies International Forum*, 19(3): 315–325.

Birkerts, S. (1994) *The Gutenberg Elegies: The Fate of Reading in an Electronic Age*, New York: Fawcett Columbine.

Blackmore, J. (2000) 'Globalization: a useful concept for feminists rethinking theory and strategies in education', in N. Burbules and C. Torres (eds) *Globalization and Education*, New York: Routledge, 133–157.

Bohen, A. (2001) 'Information nebula', *Social Alternatives*, 20(1): 54–59.

Boulding, E. (1977) *Women in the Twentieth Century World*, New York: Sage.

—— (1990) *Building a Global Civic Culture: Education for an Interdependent World*. New York: Teachers College Press.

—— (1992) *The Underside of History: A View of Women Through Time*, Thousand Oaks: Sage, previously published under same title by Westview Press, Boulder, Colorado, in 1976.

—— (1995) 'Image and action in peace building', in E. Boulding and K. Boulding (eds) *The Future: Images and Processes*, Thousand Oaks, CA: Sage, 93–117.

Boulding, E. and Boulding, K. (1995) *The Future: Images and Processes*, Thousand Oaks, CA: Sage.

Bowers, C. A. (1997) *The Culture of Denial*, Albany: State University of New York Press.

Brabazon, T. (2002) *Digital Hemlock: Internet Education and the Poisoning of Teaching*, Sydney: University of New South Wales Press.

Briggs, J. C. (1996) 'The promise of virtual reality', *The Futurists*, 30(5): 13–18.

Bright, C. (1993) 'Teaching feminist pedagogy: an undergraduate course', *Women's Studies Quarterly*, 21(3–4): 128–132.

Brock, P. (ed.) (1989) *Women's Rites and Sites: Aboriginal Women's Cultural Knowledge*, Sydney: Allen & Unwin.

Brodribb, S. (1992) *Nothing Mat(t)ers: A feminist Critique of Postmodernism*, Melbourne: Spinifex Press.

Brown, J. (1992) 'Theory or practice: what exactly is feminist pedagogy', *The Journal of General Education*, 41: 51–63.

Bruce, B. C. (ed.) (2003) *Literacy in the Information Age: Inquiries into Meaning Making with New Technologies*, Newark, Delaware: International Reading Association.

Bruce, C. and Candy, P. (2000) *Information Literacy Around the World*, Wagga, New South Wales: Centre for Information Studies, Charles Sturt University.

Bunch, C. (1983) 'Not by degrees: feminist theory and education', in C. Bunch and S. Pollack (eds) *Learning Our Way: Essays in Feminist Education*, Trumansburg, New York: The Crossing Press, 248–260.

Bunch, C. and Pollack, S. (eds) (1983) *Learning Our Way: Essays in Feminist Education*, Trumansburg, NY: The Crossing Press.

Burbules, N. and Torres, C. (2000) 'Globalization and education: an introduction', in N. Burbules and C. Torres (eds) *Globalization and Education*, New York: Routledge, 1–27.

Burchill, S. and Linklater, A. (1996) *Theories of International Relations*, New York: St Martin's Press.

Burke, J. M. M. (1997) 'Why feel responsible', in S. Harris and M. Malin (eds) *Indigenous Education: Historical, Moral and Practical Tales*, Darwin: NTU Press, 23–28.

Burniske, R. W. and Monke, L. (2001) *Breaking Down the Digital Walls: Learning to Teach in a Post-modern World*, New York: State University of New York Press.

Bussey, M. (1998) 'Tantra as episteme: a pedagogy of the future', *Futures*, 30(7): 705–717.

—— (2000a) 'Critical spirituality: neo-humanism as method', *Journal of Futures Studies*, 5(2): 21–35.

—— (2000b) 'Sa' vidya' ya' vimuktaye: education is that which liberates', in A. A. Ananda Rama (ed.) *Neo-Humanist Education*, Mainz, Germany: Ananda Marga Gurukula Publications, 10–12.

Buxton, L. and d'Arbon, M. (1999) 'Guyunggu: an aboriginal way of being', in R. Craven (ed.) *Aboriginal Studies: Educating for the Future*, Sydney: University of Western Sydney, 77–81.

Cajete, G. A. (1999) *Igniting the Sparkle: An Indigenous Science Education Model*, Skyand, NC, USA: Kivaki Press.

Case, J. (2001) 'New technologies: culture and education', *Social Alternatives*, 20(1): 29–33.

Castellano, M. B., Davis, L. and Lahache, L. (2000) *Aboriginal Education: Fulfilling the Promise*, Vancouver: UBC Press.

Castells, M. (1996) *The Rise of the Network Society – The Information Age: Economy, Society, and Culture*, Vol. I, Malden, MA: Blackwell Publishers.

—— (1998) *End of Millennium – The Information Age: Economy, Society and Culture*, Vol. III, Malden, MA: Blackwell Publishers.

Castle, E. B. (1961) *Ancient Education and Today*, Harmondsworth: Penguin.

Cenkner, W. (1976) *The Hindu Personality in Education: Tagore, Gandhi, Aurobindo*, Columbia, USA: South Asia Books.

Clark, V., Garner, S. N., Higonnet, M. and Katrak, K. (1995) *Antifeminism in the Academy*, New York: Routledge.

Coffey, A. and Delamont, S. (1990) *Feminism and the Classroom Teacher: Research, Praxis, Pedagogy*, London: Routledge.

—— (2000) *Feminism and the Classroom Teacher: Research, Praxis, Pedagogy*, London: Falmer Press.

Cogburn, D. (2002) 'Globalization, knowledge, education and training in the information age', Unesco www.unesco.org/webworld/infoethics_2/eng/papers/paper_23.htm (accessed 7 February 2002).

Cohee, G. E., Daumer, E., Kemp, T. D., Krebs, P. M., Lafky, S. and Runzio, S. (eds) (1998) *The Feminist Teacher Anthology: Pedagogies and Classroom Strategies*, New York: Teachers College Press.

Cohen, D., Lee, A., Newman, J., Payne, A. M., Scheeres, H., Shoemark, L. and Tiffin, S. (eds) (1998) *Winds of Change: Women and the Culture of Universities*, Vols I and II, Sydney: Equity and Diversity Unit, University of Technology.

Cohen, D., Lee, A., Newman, J., Payne, A. M., Scheerer, H., Shoemark, L. and Tiffin, S. (1999) *Winds of Change: Women and the Culture of Universities*. Proceedings of the Winds of Change Conference, Vols I and II, Sydney: Equity and Diversity Unit, University of Technology.

Commonwealth of Australia (2002) *Getting it Right: Report on the Inquiry into the Education of Boys*, Canberra: House of Representatives Standing Committee on Education and Training.

Connell, W. F. (1980) *A History of Education in the Twentieth Century World*, Canberra: Curriculum Development Centre.

Cornish, E. (1996) 'The cyber future: 92 ways our lives will change by the year 2025', *The Futurist*, 30(1): 27–67.

—— (1999) 'The study of the future', Future Society http://www.wfs.org/studytoc.htm (accessed 7 November 2000).

Council for Aboriginal Reconciliation (1993) *Addressing the Key Issues for Reconciliation*, Canberra: AGPS.

Craven, R. (ed.) (1999) *Teaching Aboriginal Studies*, St Leonards, NSW: Allen & Unwin.

—— (2000) *Aboriginal Studies: Self-Concept for a Nation*, Sydney: University of Western Sydney.

Craven, R., d'Arbon, M. and Wilson-Miller, J. (1999) 'Developing teaching activities', in R. Craven (ed.) *Teaching Aboriginal Studies*, St Leonards, NSW: Allen & Unwin, 231–260.

Cromer, A. H. (1997) *Connected Knowledge: Science, Philosophy, and Education*, New York: Oxford University Press.

Cuban, L. (2001) *Oversold and Underused: Computers in the Classroom*, Cambridge, Massachusetts: Harvard University Press.

Culley, M. and Portuges, C. (eds) (1985) *Gendered Subjects: The Dynamics of Feminist Teaching*, Boston: Routledge & Kegan Paul.

Cunningham, S., Tapsall, S., Ryan, Y., Stedman, L., Bagdon, K. and Flew, T. (1997) *New Media and Borderless Education: A Review of the Convergence between Global Media Networks and Higher Education Provision*, Canberra: Department of Employment, Education, Training and Youth Affairs.

Cvetkovich, A. and Kellner, D. (1997) *Articulating the Global and the Local*, Boulder, Colorado: Westview Press.

Daleo, M. S. (1996) *Curriculum of Love: Cultivating the Spiritual Nature of Children*, Charlottesville, VA: Grace Publishing and Communications.

Daly, M. (1978) *Gyn/Ecology: The Metaethics of Radical Feminism*, Boston: Beacon Press.

Davies, S. and Guppy, N. (1997) 'Globalization and educational reforms in Anglo-American democracies', *Comparative Education Review*, 41(4): 435–460.

Davison, C. (1999) 'Partnerships in education and training: empowering our communities', in R. Craven (ed.) *Aboriginal Studies: Educating for the Future*, Sydney: University of Western Sydney.

Deeds Ermarth, E. (1989) 'The solitude of women and social time', in J. Forman and C. Sowton (eds) *Taking Our Time: Feminist Perspectives on Temporality*, Oxford: Pergamon, 37–47.

De Francisco, V. L. (1996) 'The world of designing women: a narrative account of focus group plans for a women's university', *Communication Education*, 45(4): 330–337.

De Jouvenel, H. (1996) 'The futuribles group', in R. Slaughter (ed.) *The Knowledge Base of Futures Studies*, Vol. 2: *Organisations, Practices, Products*, Hawthorn, Victoria: DDM Media Group and Futures Study Centre, 3–15.

Depaepe, M. (1998) 'Educationalisation: a key concept in understanding the basic processes in the history of western education', *History of Education Review*, 27(1): 16–28.

Dermond, S. (2001a) 'Raising your child in spirit...with nature', *Tikkun*, 16(4): 80.

—— (2001b) 'Peace begins inside', *Tikkun*, 16(5): 80.

—— (2002) 'Raising your child with spirit: eloquence in silence', *Tikkun*, 17(1): 80.

Dicken, P., Peck, J. and Tickell, A. (1997) 'Unpacking the global', in R. Lee and J. Wills (eds) *Geographies of Economies*, London: Arnold, 158–166.

Dimitriades, G. and Kamberelis, G. (1997) 'Shifting terrains: mapping education within a global landscape', *The Annals of the American Academy of Political and Social Science*, 551(14): 137.

Doll, B. (1995) 'Post-modernism's utopian vision', in P. McLaren (ed.) *Postmodernism, Post-Colonialism and Pedagogy*, Albert Park, Australia: James Nicholas Publishers, 89–101.

Drahos, P. (1995) 'Information feudalism in the information society', *The Information Society*, 11(3): 209–222.

Ebo, B. (ed.) (1998) *Cyberghetto or Cybertopia: Race, Class, and Gender on the Internet*, New York: Praeger.

Edwards, R. and Usher, R. (2000) *Globalisation and Pedagogy: Space, Place and Identity*, London: Routledge.

Eisler, R. (1987) *The Chalice and the Blade: Our History, Our Futures*, San Francisco: Harper & Row.

—— (1995) *Sacred Pleasure: Sex, Myth, and the Politics of the Body*, San Francisco: HarperCollins.

—— (1997) 'Riane Eisler: dominator and partnership shifts', in J. Galtung and S. Inayatullah (eds) *Macrohistory and Macrohistorians: Perspectives on Individual, Social, and Civilizational Change*, New York: Praeger, 141–151.

—— (2000) *Tomorrow's Children: A Blueprint for Partnership Education in the 21st Century*, Boulder, CO: Westview Press.

Ellwood, W. (2002) *The No-Nonsense Guide to Globalization*, Oxford: Verso and New Internationalist Publications Ltd.

Ellyard, P. (1998) *Ideas for the New Millenium*, Carlton South, Victoria: Melbourne University Press.

Encyclopedia Britannica (2001) 'History of education', Encyclopedia Britannica www.britannica.com (accessed 4 May 2001).

Erricker, C. and Erricker, J. (2001) *Contemporary Spiritualities: Social and Religious Contexts*, London: Continuum.

Faigley, L. (1992) *Fragments of Rationality: Postmodernity and the Subject of Composition*, Pittsburgh: University of Pittsburgh Press.

Fallows, S. and Bhanot, R. (2002) *Educational Development: Through information and Communications Technology*, London: Kogan Page.

Fawcett, B. and Featherstone, B. (2000) 'Setting the scene – an appraisal of notions of postmodernism, postmodernity and postmodern feminism', in B. Fawcett, B. Featherstone, J. Fook and A. Rossiter (eds) *Practice and Research in Social Work: Postmodern Feminist Perspectives*, London: Routledge, 5–24.

Feffer, J. (2002) *Living in Hope: People Challenging Globalization*, London: Zed Books, vii–viii.

Fendler, L. (1999) 'Making trouble: prediction, agency, and critical intellectuals', in T. S. Popkewitz and L. Fendler (eds) *Critical Theories in Education: Changing Terrains of Knowledge and Politics*, New York: Routledge, 169–189.

Ferguson, K. (1993) *The Man Question: The Visions of Subjectivity in Feminist Theory*, Berkeley: University of California Press.

Ferguson, M. (1980) *The Aquarian Conspiracy: Personal and Social Transformation in the 1980s*, Los Angeles: J. P. Tarcher.

Fien, J. F. (1992) 'Education for the environment: a critical ethnography', PhD thesis, Queensland: Department of Education, University of Queensland.

Fletcher, G. H. (1979) 'Key concepts in the futures perspective', *World Future Society Bulletin*, 13(1): 25–32.

Forbes.Com magazine (2000) 'The virtual classroom vs. the real one', Forbes. http://www.forbes.com/bow/2000/0911/bestofweb_print.html (accessed 18 May 2001).

Forester, T. (1992) 'Megatrends or megamistakes? What ever happened to the information society?', *The Information Society*, 8(3): 133–146.

Forman, J. and Sowton, C. (eds) (1989) *Taking Our Time: Feminist Perspectives on Temporality*, Oxford: Pergamon.

Foucault, M. (1972) *The Archeology of Knowledge*, London: Tavistock Publications.

—— (1973) *The Order of Things: An Archaeology of the Human Sciences*, New York: Vintage Books.

—— (1977) *Discipline and Punish: The Birth of the Prison*, New York: Pantheon.

—— (1980) *Power/Knowledge: Selected Interview and Other Writings*, New York: Pantheon.

—— (1982) 'Afterword: the subject and power', in H. L. Dreyfus and P. Rabinow (eds) *Michel Foucault: Beyond Structuralism and Hermeneutic*, Chicago: University of Chicago Press, 208–226.

—— (1986) 'Of other spaces', *Diacritics*, 16(1): 22–27.

Fox, M. (1989) 'Unreliable allies: subjective and objective time', in J. Forman and C. Sowton (eds) *Taking Our Time: Feminist Perspectives on Temporality*, Oxford: Pergamon, 123–136.

Fox-Genovese, E. (1986) 'The claims of a common culture: gender, race, class and the canon', *Salmagundi*, 72(Fall): 134–151.

Fraser, N. (1995) 'False antitheses', in S. Benhabib, J. Butler, D. Cornell and N. Fraser (eds) *Feminist Contentions: A Philosophical Exchange*, New York: Routledge, 59–75.

Freire, P. (1998) 'The adult literacy process as cultural action for freedom' (reprint) *Harvard Educational Review*, 68(4): 471–521.

Friedman, S. S. (1998) *Mappings: Feminism and the Cultural Geographies of Encounter*, Princeton, NJ: Princeton University Press.

Fukuyama, F. (1992) *The End of History and the Last Man*, London: Penguin.

Galtung, J. (1980) *Peace and World Structure: Essays in Peace Research*, Vol. 4, Copenhagen: Christian Ejlers.

—— (2000) 'Who's got the year 2000 right – the people or the experts?', *Futures Bulletin*, 25(4): 1, 6–9, 24.

Ganderton, P. (1996) 'Concepts of globalisation and their impact upon curriculum policy-making: rhetoric and reality – a study of Australian reform', *International Journal of Educational Development*, 16(4): 393–405.

Gandhi, M. (1980) *All Men are Brothers: Autobiographical Reflections*, New York: Continuum.

Garate, M. (2002) 'Preface', in J. Feffer (ed.) *Living in Hope: People Challenging Globalization*, London: Zed Books, vii–viii.

Gardner, H. (1983) *Frames of Mind: The Theory of Multiple Intelligences*, New York: Basic Books.

—— (1993) *Multiple Intelligences: The Theory in Practice*, New York: Basic Books.

Gates, B. with Myhrvold, N. and Rinearson, P. (1995) *The Road Ahead*, New York: Viking.

George, J. M. (1999) 'Indigenous knowledge as a component of the school curriculum', in L. M. Semali and J. L. Kincheloe (eds) *What is Indigenous Knowledge? Voices from the Academy*, New York: Falmer Press, 79–95.

Giddens, A. (17 January 1992) 'Uprooted signposts at century's end', *The Times Higher Education Supplement*, 21–22.

Gil Calvo, E. (2000) 'Internet, Tocqueville and the genius of the place', MISTICA Virtual Community Archives http://funredes.org/mistica/bdd/attachado.php3/lengua/en/idarchi/16 (accessed 18 May 2001 [Gil Calvo's article is written in Spanish and it can be automatically translated if using Google search engine. This translation does not give full meaning. So in addition, consult: Case, J. (2001) 'New Technologies: culture and education', *Social Alternatives*, 20(1): 29–33]).

Giroux, H. (1983) *Theory and Resistance in Education: A Pedagogy for the Opposition*, London: Heinemann.

—— (1989) *Schooling for Democracy: Critical Pedagogy in the Modern Age*, London: Routledge.

Glazer, S. (ed.) (1999) *The Heart of Learning: Spirituality in Education*, New York: Penguin Putnam.

Glenn, J. (1996) 'Post-information age', in G. Kurian and G. Molitor (eds) *Encyclopedia of the Future*, Vol. 2, New York: Macmillan Library References, 744–746.

Goduka, I. N. (2001) 'San youth and their educational aspirations' http://www.hri.ca/racism/Submitted/Theme/san.htm (accessed 15 May 2001).

Goldstein, T. and Selby, D. (2000) *Weaving Connections: Educating for Peace, Social and Environmental Justice*, Toronto: Sumach Press.

Gore, J. M. (1993) *The Struggle for Pedagogies: Critical and Feminist Discourses as Regimes of Truth*, New York: Routledge.

Gough, N. (1990) 'Futures in Australian education: tacit, token and taken for granted', *Futures*, 22(3): 298–311.

—— (2000) 'Globalization and curriculum inquiry: Locating, representing, and performing a transnational imaginary', in N. Stromquist and K. Monkman (eds) *Education: Integration and Contestation Across Cultures*, Lanham, USA: Rowman & Littlefield Publishers, Inc, 77–99.

Grabe, M. and Grabe, C. (1998) *Learning with Internet Tools: A primer*, Boston: Houghton Mifflin.

Grant, U. E. (1997) 'Holistic approach to teaching and learning', in R. Craven and J. Wilson-Miller (eds) *Aboriginal Studies in the 90s: Sharing Our Stories* [Collected papers of the 7th annual ASA Conference, Powerhouse Museum, Sydney, August, 1997], Sydney: Aboriginal Studies Association, 56–59.

Graves, F. P. (1909) *A History of Education before the Middle Ages*, New York: The Macmillan Company.

Green, A. (ed.) (1989) *Jewish Spirituality: From the Bible through the Middle Ages*, London: SCM.

Greenberg, S. (1982) 'The women's movement: putting educational theory into practice', *Journal of Curriculum Theorizing*, 4(2): 193–198.

Griffin, D. R. (ed.) (1988a) *Spirituality and Science: Postmodern Visions*, Albany: State University of New York Press.

—— (1988b) *The Reenchantment of Science: Postmodern Proposals*, Albany: State University of New York Press.

Griffiths, J. (2002) 'Boo to Captain Clock', *New Internationalist*, 343(March), 14–17.

Grosz, E. (1990) 'Contemporary theories of power and subjectivity', in S. Gunew (ed.) *Feminist Knowledge: Critique and Construct*, London: Routledge, 59–120.

Gunew, S. (ed.) (1990) *Feminist Knowledge: Critique and Construct*, London: Routledge.

Halbert, D. (1994) 'Feminist fabulation: challenging the boundaries of fact and fiction', *The Manoa Journal of Fried and Half-Fried Ideas*, Honolulu: Hawaii Research Center for Futures Studies.

Hall, S. (1997) 'Cultural identity and diaspora', in K. Woodward (ed.) *Identity and Difference*, London: Sage Publications, 51–59.

Harding, S. (1986) *The Science Question in Feminism*, Milton Keynes, England: Open University Press.

Hart, T. (2003) *The Secret Spiritual World of Children*, Maui, Hawaii: Inner Ocean.

Hartsock, N. C. M. (1983) 'The feminist standpoint: developing the ground for a specifically feminist historical materialism', in S. Harding and M. B. Hintikka (eds) *Discovering Reality*, Dodrecht, Holland: D. Reidel Publishing Co, 238–310.

Hawthorne, S. (2002) *Wild Politics: Feminism, Globalisation, Bio/Diversity*, Melbourne: Spinifex.

Haywood, T. (1995) *Info-Rich/Info-Poor: Access and Exchange in the Global Information Society*, London: Bowker/Saur.

Hedley, R. A. (2002) *Running Out of Control: Dilemmas of Globalization*, Bloomfield, Connecticut: Kumarian Press, Inc.

Henderson, H. (1999) *Beyond Globalization: Shaping a Sustainable Global Economy*, West Hartford, Connecticut: Kumarian Press.

Henderson, J. S. Y. (2000) 'Ayukpachi: empowering aboriginal thought', in M. Battiste (ed.) *Reclaiming Indigenous Voice and Vision*, Vancouver: University of British Columbia Press, 248–278.

Hertzler, J. O. (1965) *The History of Utopian Thought*, New York: Cooper Square Publishers.

Heyzer, N., Kapoor, S. and Sandler, J. (eds) (1995) *A Commitment to the World's Women*, New York: UNIFEM.

Hicks, D. (1994) *Preparing for the Future: Notes and Queries for Concerned Educators*, London: Adamantine Press Limited.

—— (1998) 'Identifying sources of hope in postmodern times', in D. Hicks and R. Slaughter (eds) *Futures Education: World Yearbook of Education 1998*, London: Kogan Page, 217–230.

—— (2001) 'Learning about global issues: why most educators only make things worse', *Environmental Education Research*, 7(4): 413–425.

—— (2002) *Lessons for the Future: The Missing Dimension in Education*, London: RoutledgeFalmer.

Hicks, D. and Holden, C. (1995) *Visions of the Future: Why We Need to Teach for Tomorrow*, Stoke-on-Trent, England: Trentham Books.

Hirst, P. (1997) 'Globalisation – ten frequently asked questions and some surprising answers', Brisbane: Griffith University www.gu.edu.au/gwis/akccmp/papers/Hirst.html (accessed 5 April 2001).

Hoffmann, F. and Stake, J. (1998) 'Feminist pedagogy in theory and practice: an empirical investigation', *NWSA Journal*, 10(1): 79–98.

Hoff Sommers, C., Simon and Schuster (2000) *The War Against Boys: How Misguided Feminism is Harming Our Young Men*, New York: Simon & Schuster.

Hollis, D. W. (1998) *The ABC–CLIO World History Companion to Utopian Movements*, Santa Barbara, CA: ABC–CLIO.

hooks, b. (1990) 'Marginality as site of resistance', in R. Ferguson *et al.* (eds) *Out There*, New York: New Museum of Contemporary Art, 341–343.

—— (1991) *Yearning: Race, Gender, and Cultural Politics*, London: Turnaround.

—— (1994) *Teaching to Transgress: Education as the Practice of Freedom*, New York: Routledge.

—— (2000) *Feminist Theory: From Margin to Center*, 2nd edn, London: Pluto Press.

—— (2001) 'Postmodern blackness', *Postmodern Culture*, 1(1) http://www.sas.upenn.edu/African_Studies/Articles_Gen/Postmodern_Blackness_18270html (accessed 29 January 2002).

Hopkins, A. G. (ed.) (2002) *Globalization in World History*, London: Pimlico.

Houston, M. (1994) 'Should public education be gender free', in L. Stone (ed.) *The Education Feminism Reader*, London: Routledge, 122–135.

Huggins, J. (1994) 'A contemporary view of aboriginal women's relationship to the white women's movement', in N. Grieve and A. Burns (eds) *Australian Women Contemporary Feminist Thought*, Melbourne: Oxford University Press, 70–80.

Hughes, K. P. (1994) *How Do You Know? An Overview of Writings on Feminist Pedagogy and Epistemology*, St Albans, Victoria: Victoria University of Technology.

Hughes, P. (1987) *Aboriginal Culture and Learning Styles – A Challenge for Academics in Higher Education Institutions*, Armidale: New South Wales: University of New England.

Hughes, R. (1991) *The Shock of the New: Art and the Century of Change*, 3rd edn, London: Thames & Hudson.

Humm, M. (1989) *The Dictionary of Feminist Theory*, London: Harvester Wheatsheaf.

Hutchinson, F. P. (1996) *Educating Beyond Violent Futures*, London: Routledge.

ILO (2004) *A Fair Globalization: Creating Opportunities for All*, International Labour Organization, Geneva: World Commission on the Social Dimension of Globalization, International Labour Office.

Ilyatjari, N. (1991) 'Traditional aboriginal learning: how I learned as a Pitjantjatjara child', *The Aboriginal Child at School*, 19(1): 6–13.

Inayatullah, S. (1990) 'Deconstructing and reconstructing the future: predictive, cultural and critical epistemologies', *Futures*, 22(2): 115–142.

—— (1996) 'Methods and epistemologies in futures studies', in R. Slaughter (ed.) *The Knowledge Base of Futures Studies*, Vol. I: *Foundations*, Hawthorn, Victoria: DDM Media Group and Futures Study Centre, 187–205.

—— (1997) 'Prabhat Rainjan Sarkar: agency, structure, and transcendence', in J. Galtung and S. Inayatullah (eds) *Macrohistory and Macrohistorians: Perspectives on Individual, Social, and Civilizational Change,* Westport, Connecticut: Praeger, 132–141.

—— (1998a) 'Causal layered analysis', *Futures*, 30(8): 815–829.

—— (1998b) 'Implications of *Sacred Pleasure* for cultural evolution', *World Futures*, 53: 41–51.

—— (2002) *Questioning the Future: Future Studies, Action Learning and Organizational Transformation,* Taipei, Taiwan: Center for Futures Studies, Tamkang University.

Inayatullah, S. and Gidley, J. (eds) (2000) *The University in Transformation: Global Perspectives on the Futures of the University,* Westport, Connecticut: Bergin and Garvey.

Iyer, P. (2000) *The Global Soul: Jet Lag, Shopping Malls, and the Search for Home,* New York: Knopf.

Jaggar, A. M. (1983) *Feminist Politics and Human Nature,* Sussex: The Harvester Press.

Jameson, F. (1982) 'Progress versus utopia; or, can we imagine the future?', *Science Fiction Studies*, 9(2): 147–167.

Jenks, C. (2001) 'The pacing and timing of children's bodies', in K. Hultqvist and G. Dahlberg (eds) *Governing the Child in the New Millennium,* New York: RoutledgeFalmer, 68–84.

Jennings, L. E. (1996) 'Dystopias', in G. Kurian and G. Molitor (eds) *Encyclopedia of the Future,* New York: Macmillan Library References, 211–212.

Johnson, J. (Summer 1996) 'The information highways from hell: a worst-case scenario', *The CPSR Newsletter*, 14(2), 16–18.

Jones, D. A. F. (1995) *Women of Spirit,* Sudbury, Massachusetts: Visions of a Better World Foundation.

Judge, A. (1993) 'Metaphors and the language of futures', *Futures*, 25(3): 275–289.

Judith, A. (1987) *Wheels of Life: A User's Guide to the Chakra System,* St Paul, Minnesota: Llewellyn Publications.

—— (1993) *Wheels of Life: A User's Guide to the Chakra System,* St Paul, Minnesota: Llewellyn Publications.

Kaigo, T. (1968) *Japanese Education: Its Past and Present,* 2nd edn, Tokyo: Kokusai Bunka Shinkokai.

Kapitzke, C. (December 1999) 'Global issues and local effects: the challenge for educational research', paper presented at the AARE–NZARE conference: Global Issues and Local Effects: The Challenge for Educational Research, Melbourne, Australia.

Kapitzke, C., Bogitini, S., Chen, M., MacNeill, G., Mayer, D., Muirhead, B. and Renshaw, P. (2001) 'Weaving words with the Dreamweaver: literacy, indigeneity, and technology', *Journal of Adolescent & Adult Literacy*, 44(4): 336–346.

Kearney, R. (1984) *Dialogues with Contemporary Continental Thinkers: The Phenomenological Heritage,* Manchester: Manchester University Press.

Keay, F. E. (1959) *A History of Education in India and Pakistan*, 3rd edn, London: Oxford University Press.

Keen, S. (1994) *Hymns to an Unknown God*, New York: Bantam.

Kellner, D. (1998) 'Theorizing new technologies', University of California www. gseis.ucla.edu/courses/ed253a/newdk/theor.htm (accessed 29 July 1998).

—— (2000a) 'Globalization and new social movements: lessons for critical theory and pedagogy', in N. Burbules and C. Torres (eds) *Globalization and Education*, New York: Routledge, 299–323.

—— (2000b) 'New technologies/new literacies: reconstructing education for the new millennium', *Teaching Education*, 11(3): 245–265.

Kelly, P. (1999) 'The geographies and politics of globalization', *Progress in Human Geography*, 23(3): 379–400.

Kenway, J. (1996) 'The information superhighway and post-modernity: the social promise and the social price', *Comparative Education*, 32(2): 217–231.

Kenway, J. and Modra, H. (1992) 'Feminist pedagogy and emancipatory possibilities', in C. Luke and J. Gore (eds) *Feminisms and Critical Pedagogy*, New York: Routledge, 138–167.

Kessler, R. (2000) *The Soul of Education: Helping Students Find Connection, Compassion, and Character at School*, Alexandria, VA: Association for Supervision and Curriculum Development.

Kesson, K. (2002) 'Tantra: the quest for the ecstatic mind', in J. Miller and Y. Nakagawa (eds) *Nurturing Our Wholeness: Perspectives on Spirituality in Education*, Branton, VT: Foundation for Educational Renewal, 30–48.

Koelsch, F. (1995) *The Infomedia Revolution: How it is Changing Our World and Your Life*, Toronto, Ontario: McGraw-Hill Ryerson.

Kofman, E. and Youngs, G. (eds) (1996) *Globalization: Theory and Practice*, London: Pinter.

Kramarae, C. (1996) 'Centers of change: an introduction to women's own communication programs', *Communication Education* ['The Women's University: A Symposium' feature], 45(4): 315–321.

Krishnamurti, J. (1974) *Krishnamurti on Education*, Pondicherry: Krishnamurti Foundation India.

—— (1985) *The Way of Intelligence*, Chennai: Krishnamurti Foundation India.

—— (1995) *Unconditionally Free* (also consists of *Concerning Education, Education and the Significance of Life* and *Letters to the Schools* reprints)', India: Krishnamurti Foundation.

Kristeva, J. (1981) 'Women's time', *Signs*, 7(1): 13–36.

Kuo, P. W. (1972) *The Chinese System of Public Education* (reprint of 1915 publication), Shanghai: Commercial Press.

Kurian, G. and Molitor, G. (eds) (1996) *Encyclopedia of the Future*, New York: Macmillan Library References.

Kushner, R. (1999) 'Is school the place for spirituality. Conversation with Marge Scherer', *Educational Leadership*, 56(4): 18–22.

Laenui, P. (2000) 'Process of decolonization', in M. Battiste (ed.) *Reclaiming Indigenous Voice and Vision*, Vancouver: University of British Columbia Press, 50–57.

Lankshear, C., Peters, M. and Knobel, M. (1996) 'Critical pedagogy and cyberspace', in H. A. Giroux, C. Lankshear, P. McLaren and M. Peters (eds) *Counternarratives: Cultural Studies and Critical Pedagogies in Postmodern Spaces*, London: Routledge, 149–188.

Lather, P. (1991a) *Getting Smart: Feminist Research and Pedagogy With/in the Postmodern*, New York: Routledge.

—— (1991b) *Feminist Research in Education: Within/against*, Geelong, Victoria: Deakin University Press.

Laukhuf, G. and Werner, G. (1998) 'Spirituality: the missing link', *Journal of Neuroscience Nursing*, 30(1): 60–68.

Laurie, S. S. (1970) *Historical Survey of Pre-Christian Education*, 2nd edn, New York: AMS Press.

Lawlor, R. (1991) *Voices of the First Day: Awakening in the Aboriginal Dreamtime*, Rochester, Vermont: Inner Traditions International.

Lechner, F. and Boli, J. (eds) (2000) *The Globalization Reader*, Malsden, Massachusetts: Blackwell Publishers.

Leck, G. (1987) 'Feminist pedagogy, liberation theory, and the traditional schooling paradigm', *Educational Theory*, 37(3): 343–354.

Lemonick, M. (2001) 'The end', *Time*, Time Australia Magazine Pty Ltd., 25 June 2001, 44–53.

Lesko, N. (2001) 'Time matters in adolescence', in K. Hultqvist and G. Dahlberg (eds) *Governing the Child in the New Millennium*, New York: RoutledgeFalmer, 35–67.

Levine, R. (1997) *A Geography of Time*, New York: Basic Books, HarperCollins Publishers.

Lewis, M. (1990) 'Interrupting patriarchy: politics, resistance, and transformation in the feminist classroom', *Harvard Educational Review*, 60(4): 467–488.

—— (1993) *Without a Word: Teaching Beyond Women's Silence*, New York: Routledge.

Lippincott, K. (ed.) (1999) *The Story of Time*, London: Merrell Holberton.

Little, A. (1996) 'Globalisation and educational research: whose context counts?', *International Journal of Educational Development*, 16(4): 427–438.

Looser, D. and Kaplan, E. A. (eds) (1997) *Generations: Academic Feminists in Dialogue*, Minneapolis: University of Minnesota Press.

Lucashenko, M. (1994) 'No other truth? aboriginal women and Australian feminism', *Social Alternatives*, 4: 21–24.

Luke, A. (2002) 'Curriculum, ethics, metanarrative: teaching and learning beyond the nation', *Curriculum Perspectives*, 22(1): 49–55.

Luke, A. and Luke, C. (2000) 'A situated perspective on cultural globalization', in N. Burbules and C. Torres (eds) *Globalization and Education*, New York: Routledge, 275–299.

Luke, C. (1996a) 'ekstasis@cyberia', *Discourse*, 17(2): 187–297.

Luke, C. (ed.) (1996b) *Feminisms and Pedagogies of Everyday Life*, New York: State University of New York.

Luke, C. (1997) *Technological Literacy*. Melbourne: Adult Literacy Research Network, Language Australia Limited.

—— (2000) 'New literacies in teacher education', *Journal of Adolescent and Adult Literacy*, 43(5): 424–435.

—— (2001a) *Globalization and Women in Academia: North/West–South/East*, Mahwah, New Jersey: Lawrence Erlbaum Associates.

—— (2001b) 'Dot.com culture: buzzing down the on-ramps of the super-highway', *Social Alternatives*, 20: 8–15.

Luke, C. and Gore, J. (eds) (1992) *Feminisms and Critical Pedagogy*, New York: Routledge.

Mackinnon, A., Elgquist-Saltzman, I. and Prentice, A. (eds) (1998) *Education into the 21st Century: Dangerous Terrain for Women?* London: Falmer Press.

Maharishi, M. Y. (1988) *Science of Being and Art of Living: Transcendental Meditation*, New York: SIGNET, Penguin Group.

Maher, F. A. (1987) 'Inquiry teaching and feminist pedagogy', *Social Education*, 51(3): 186–192.

Maher, F. A. and Tetreault, M. K. (1994) *The Feminist Classroom: An Inside Look at How Professors and Students are Transforming Higher Education for a More Diverse Society*, New York: Basic Books.

Manicom, A. (1992) 'Feminist pedagogy: transformations, standpoints and politics', *Canadian Journal of Education*, 17(3), 365–389.

Mannheim, K. (1936) *Ideology and Utopia*, London: Routledge & Kegan Paul.

Marien, M. (1996) *Future Survey*, 18(4).

—— (1997a) *Future Survey*, 19(9).

—— (1997b) *Future Survey*, 19(6).

—— (1999) *Future Survey*, 21(1).

—— (2003) *Futures Survey*, 25(8).

Marshall, A. (1999) 'Aboriginal culture, the framing of knowledge and ways of knowing: visual arts, performance and narrative in the mainstream curriculum', in R. Craven (ed.) *Aboriginal Studies: Educating for the Future*, Sydney: University of Western Sydney, 41–49.

Martin, P. (2000) 'The moral case for globalization', in F. Lechner and J. Boli (eds) *The Globalization Reader*, Malsden, Massachusetts: Blackwell Publishers, 12–14.

Martin, R. A. (2000) 'Paths of learning: an introduction to educational alternatives' http://www.PathsOfLearning.net (accessed 15 March 2002).

Marx Hubbard, B. (1998) *Conscious Evolution: Awakening the Power of Our Social Potential*, Novato, CA: New World Library.

Masini, E. B. (1993a) *Why Futures Studies?* London: Grey Seal Books.

—— (1993b) *Women as Builders of Alternative Futures*, Trier: Centre for European Studies, Trier University.

—— (1996) 'International futures perspectives and cultural concepts of the future', in R. Slaughter (ed.) *The Knowledge Base of Futures Studies*, Vol. I: *Foundations*, Hawthorn, Victoria: DDM Media Group and Futures Study Centre, 75–85.

—— (2002) 'A vision of futures studies', *Futures*, 34(3–4): 249–261.

Mason, R. (1998) *Globalising Education: Trends and Applications*, London: Routledge.

Massey, D. (1994) *Space, Place and Gender*, Cambridge: Polity Press.

Maurial, M. (1999) 'Indigenous knowledge and schooling: a continuum between conflict and dialogue', in L. M. Semali and J. L. Kincheloe (eds) *What is Indigenous Knowledge? Voices from the Academy*, New York: Falmer Press, 59–79.

Mayers, T. and Swafford, K. (1998) 'Reading the networks of power: rethinking "critical thinking" in computerized classrooms', in T. Taylor and I. Ward (eds) *Literary Theory in the Age of the Internet*, New York: Columbia University Press, 146–158.

McClintock, A. (1995) *Imperial Leather: Race, Gender and Sexuality in the Colonial Contest*, New York: Routledge.

McConaghy, C. (2000) *Rethinking Indigenous Education: Culturalism, Colonialism and the Politics of Knowing*, Flaxton, Queensland: Post Pressed.

McDonnell, K. (2002) 'The hurried child', *New Internationalist*, 343(March), 22–24.

McDonald, A. and Canchez-Cazal, S. (2002) *Twenty-First-Century Feminist Classrooms: Pedagogies of Identity and Difference*, New York: Palgrave Macmillan.

McGinn, N. (1997) 'The impact of globalization of national education systems', *Prospects*, 27(1): 41–55.

McGinn, B. and Meyendorff, J. (eds) (1989) *Christian Spirituality: Origins to the Twelfth Century*, London: SCM Press.

McHale, J. (1969) *The Future of the Future*, New York: Ballantine Books.

McLaren, P. (1998) 'Revolutionary pedagogy in post-revolutionary times: rethinking the political economy of critical education', *Educational Theory*, 48(4): 431–463.

McMurtry, J. (2002) 'Foreword', in W. Ellwood (ed.) *The No-Nonsense Guide to Globalization*, Oxford: New Internationalist Publications Ltd.

McPhail, K. (1997) 'The threat of ethical accountants: an application of Foucault's concept of ethics to accounting education and some thoughts on ethically educating for the Other' http://les.man.ac.uk/ipa97/papers/mcphai46 (accessed 12 October 1999).

Meeker, J. (1987) 'Reflections on a digital watch', Quoted in *Utne Reader*, September/October, 57.

Meredyth, D., Russell, N., Blackwood, L., Thomas, J. and Wise, P. (1999) *Real Time: Computers, Change and Schooling; National Sample Study of the Information Technology Skills of Australian School Students*, Australian Key Centre for Cultural and Media Policy, Boston: Houghton Mifflin.

Meyer, A. (1975) *Grandmasters of Educational Thought*, New York: McGraw-Hill.

Miles, R. (1993) *The Women's History of the World*, London: HarperCollins.

Miller, J. (2000) *Education and the Soul: Toward a Spiritual Curriculum*, New York: State University of New York Press.

Miller, J. and Nakagawa, Y. (eds) (2002) *Nurturing Our Wholeness: Perspectives on Spirituality in Education*, Branton, VT: Foundation for Educational Renewal.

Milojević, I. (1996) 'Towards a knowledge base for feminist futures research', in R. Slaughter (ed.) *The Knowledge Base of Futures Studies*, Vol. 3: *Directions and Outlooks*, Hawthorn, Victoria: DDM Media Group and Futures Study Centre, 20–39.

—— (1998) 'Learning from feminist futures', in D. Hicks and R. Slaughter (eds) *Futures Education, World Yearbook of Education 1998*, London: Kogan Page, 83–97.

—— (2000) 'The crisis of the university: feminist alternatives for the 21st century and beyond', in S. Inayatullah and J. Gidley (eds) *The University in Transformation: Global Perspectives on the Futures of the University*, Westport, Connecticut: Bergin and Garvey, 175–187.

—— (2002a) 'Creating communication spaces for not yet so virtual people', in S. Inayatullah and S. Leggett (eds) *Transforming Communication: Technology, Sustainability, and Future Generations*, Westport, CT: Praeger, 99–107.

—— (2002b) *Futures of Education: Feminist and Post-Western Critiques and Visions*, PhD thesis, Australia: The University of Queensland.

—— (2003) 'Hegemonic and marginalised educational utopias in the contemporary western world', *Policy Futures in Education*, 1(3): 440–466.

Minger, M., Mannisto, L. and Kelly, T. (1999) 'The future is bright, the future is mobile', *The Journal of Policy, Regulation and Strategy*, 1(December): 6.

Mok, K. and Welch, A. (eds) (2003) *Globalization and Educational Restructuring in the Asia Pacific Region*, New York: Palgrave MacMillan.

Moll, P. (1996) 'The thirst for certainty: futures studies in Europe and the United States', in R. Slaughter (ed.) *The Knowledge Base of Futures Studies*, Vol. I: *Foundations*, Hawthorn, Victoria: DDM Media Group and Futures Study Centre, 15–29.

Moody, R. (1993) *The Indigenous Voice, Visions and Realities*, Amsterdam, The Netherlands: International Books.

Mookerji, R. (1960) *Ancient Indian Education: Brahmanical and Buddhist*, 4th edn, Delhi: Motilal Banarsidass.

Moon, S. J. (2001) 'Introduction to feminism/postmodernism' http://www.geocities.com/Baja/9315/pe11.html (accessed 23 April 2002).

Moorcroft, H. (1997) 'Aboriginal construction of libraries and libraries' construction of aboriginal people', in S. Harris and M. Malin (eds) *Indigenous Education: Historical, Moral and Practical Tales*, Darwin: NTU Press, 71–80.

Moore, T. (2000) 'Foreword: the soul as educator', in J. Miller (ed.) *Education and the Soul: Toward a Spiritual Curriculum*, New York: State University of New York Press, vii–ix.

Moreton-Robinson, A. (2000) *Talkin'up to the White Women: Indigenous Women and Feminism*, Brisbane: University of Queensland Press.

Morphy, H. (1999) 'Australian aboriginal concepts of time', in K. Lippincott (ed.) *The Story of Time*, London: Merrell Holberton, 264–268.

Mosha, R. S. (1999) 'The inseparable link between intellectual and spiritual formation in indigenous knowledge and education: a case study in Tanzania', in L. M. Semali and J. L. Kincheloe (eds) *What is Indigenous Knowledge? Voices from the Academy*, New York: Falmer Press, 209–227.

Mulhern, J. (1959) *A History of Education: A Social Interpretation*, 2nd edn, New York: Ronald Press Co.

Mumford, L. (1922) *The Story of Utopias*, New York: Boni and Liveright.

Mwadime, R. K. N. (1999) 'Indigenous knowledge systems for an alternative culture in science: the role of nutritionists in Africa', in L. M. Semali and J. L. Kincheloe (eds) *What is Indigenous Knowledge? Voices from the Academy*, New York: Falmer Press, 243–269.

Myers, B. K. (1997) *Young Children and Spirituality*, New York: Routledge.

Myerson, G. (2001) *Ecology and the End of Postmodernity*, Cambridge: Icon Books.

Nakagawa, Y. (2000) *Education for Awakening: An Eastern Approach to Holistic Education*, Brandon, Vermont: Foundation for Educational Renewal.

Nakamura, L. (2000) 'Race in/for cyberspace: identity tourism and racial passing on the Internet', in D. Bell and B. M. Kennedy (eds) *The Cybercultures Reader*, London: Routledge, 712–720.

Nakosteen, M. (1965) *The History and Philosophy of Education*, New York: The Ronald Press Company.

Nandy, A. (1987) *Traditions, Tyranny, and Utopias: Essays in the Politics of Awareness*, Delhi: Oxford University Press.

Nasr, S. H. (ed.) (1989) *Islamic Spirituality: Foundations*, London: SCM Press.

Negroponte, N. (1995) *Being Digital*, New York: Alfred A. Knopf.

Nelson, R. F. W. (1996) 'Information society', in G. Kurian and G. Molitor (eds) *Encyclopedia of the Future*, Vol. 2, New York: Macmillan Library References, 479–481.

Nielsen, J. M. (1990) *Feminist Research Methods: Exemplary Readings in the Social Sciences*, Boulder: Westview Press.

Noddings, N. (1999) 'Longing for the sacred in schools', interview with Joan Montgomery Halford, *Educational Leadership*, 56(4): 28–32.

Norman, D. (1998) *The Invisible Computer: Why Good Products Can Fail, the Personal Computer is so Complex, and Information Appliances are the Solution*, Cambridge, MA: MIT Press.

Nowotny, H. (1994) *Time: The Modern and Postmodern Experience*, trans. Neville Plaice, Cambridge, UK: Polity Press.

O'Brien, M. (1989) 'Periods', in J. Forman and C. Sowton (eds) *Taking Our Time: Feminist Perspectives on Temporality*, Oxford: Pergamon, 11–20.

O'Sullivan, E. (1999) *Transformative Learning: Educational Vision for the 21st Century*, Toronto: OISE, University of Toronto Press.

Oakes, J. (1985) *Keeping Track: How Schools Structure Inequality*, New Haven: Yale University Press.

Orr, D. (1994) *Earth in Mind: On Education, Environment and the Human Condition*, Washington, DC: Island Press.

Orwell, G. (1949) http://allfreeessays.com/student/free/George_Orwell.shtml (accessed 23 June 2002).

Ostler, R. (1999) 'Disappearing languages', *The Futurist*, August–September, 16–22.

Ozmon, H. (1969) *Utopias and Education*, Minneapolis: Burgess Publishing Company.

Page, J. (2000) *Reframing the Early Childhood Curriculum: Educational Imperatives for the Future*, London: RoutledgeFalmer.

Painter, F. V. N. (1908) *A History of Education*, New York: D. Appleton and Company.

—— (1980) *The Recovery of Spirit in Higher Education*, New York: Seabury.

—— (1993) *To Know as We are Known: Education as a Spiritual Journey*, San Francisco: HarperSanFrancisco.

—— (1998) *The Courage to Teach: Exploring the Inner Landscape of a Teacher's Life*, San Francisco: Jossey-Bass Publishers.

Palmer, P. J. (1980) *The Recovery of Spirit in Higher Education*, New York: Seabury.

—— (1993) *To Know as We Are Known: Education as a Spiritual Journey*, San Francisco: Harper San Francisco.

—— (1998) *The Courage to Teach: Exploring the Inner Landscape of a Teacher's Life*, San Francisco: Jossey-Bass Publishers.

—— (1999a) 'The grace of great things: reclaimining the sacred in knowing, teaching, and learning', in S. Glazer (ed.) *The Heart of Learning: Spirituality in Education*, New York: Penguin Putnam, 15–32.

—— (1999b) 'Evoking the spirit in public education', *Educational Leadership*, 56(4): 6–11.

Papert, S. (1996) *The Connected Family: Bridging the Digital Generation Gap*, Atlanta, GA: Longstreet Press.

Parrish, A. M. (1991) 'Aboriginal world view in the aboriginal context', *The Aboriginal Child at School*, 19(4): 14–21.

Parry, S. (1996) 'Feminist pedagogy and techniques for the changing classroom', *Women's Studies Quarterly*, 24(3–4): 45–54.

—— (1997) 'A very recent past', in S. Harris and M. Malin (eds) *Indigenous Education: Historical, Moral and Practical Tales*, Darwin: NTU Press, 1–9.

Paul, P. (19 January 2004) 'The Porn Factor', *Time*, 73–75.

Petras, J. and Veltmeyer, H. (2001) *Globalization Unmasked: Imperialism in the 21st Century*, Nova Scotia: Fernwood Publishing Ltd.

Piercy, M. (2003) 'Love and sex in the Year 3000', in M. S. Barr (ed.) *Envisioning the Future: Science Fiction and the Next Millennium*, Middletown, CT: Wesleyan University Press.

Pieterse, J. N. (ed.) (2000) *Global Futures: Shaping Globalization*, London: Zed Books.

Pitsch, P. K. (1996) *The innovation Age: A New Perspective on the Telecom Revolution*, Indianapolis: Hudson Institute and Washington: Progress & Freedom Foundation.

Plaskow, J. and Christ, C. P. (1989) *Weaving the Visions: New Patterns in Feminist Spirituality*, San Francisco: HarperSanFrancisco.

Polak, F. (1973) *The Image of the Future*, Amsterdam: Elsevier Scientific Publishing Company.

Popkewitz, T. S. (1998) 'Introduction', in T. S. Pokewitz and M. Brennan (eds) *Foucault's Challenge: Discourse, Knowledge, and Power in Education*, New York: Teachers College Press, xiii–3.

Postman, N. (1993) *Technopoly: The Surrender of Culture to Technology*, New York: Vintage Books.

Pourrat, P. (1922–1927) *Christian Spirituality*, Vol. 1–3, London: Burns, Oates, and Washbourne.

Prakash, M. S. (1999) 'Indigenous knowledge systems: ecological literacy through initiation into people's science', in L. M. Semali and J. L. Kincheloe (eds) *What is Indigenous Knowledge? Voices from the Academy*, New York: Falmer Press, 157–179.

Prasad, H. S. (ed.) (1992) *Time in Indian Philosophy*, Delhi: Sri Satguru Publications.

Purpel, D. E. (1989) *The Moral and Spiritual Crisis in Education: A Curriculum for Justice and Compassion in Education*, New York: Bergin and Garvey.

Putnam Tong, R. (1998) *Feminist Thought*, 2nd edn, St Leonards, NSW: Allen & Unwin.

Rabinow, P. (ed.) (1984) *The Foucault Reader: An Introduction to Foucault's Thought*, New York: Penguin Books.

Rameka, N. with Law, M. (1998) 'Tiaki nga taonga o nga tupuna: valuing the treasures: towards a global adult education framework for indigenous people', in L. King (ed.) *Reflecting Visions: New Perspective on Adult Education for Indigenous Peoples*, Waikato: UNESCO Institute for Education, University of Waikato, 201–217.

Ravitch, D. (1 September 1993) 'When the school comes to you: the coming transformation of education, and its underside', in 'The Future Surveyed, 150 Economist Years', special supplement to *The Economist*, 39–45.

Reagan, T. (1996) *Non-Western Educational Traditions: Alternative Approaches to Educational Thought and Practice*, Mahwah, New Jersey: Lawrence Erlbaum Associates.

Regan, C. (ed.) (2002) *80:20 Development in an Unequal World*, Wicklow, Ireland: 80:20 Educating and Acting for a Better World and Teachers in Development Education.

Reignier, R. (1995) 'Warrior as pedagogue, pedagogue as warrior: reflections on aboriginal anti-racist pedagogy', in R. Ng, P. Staton and J. Scane (eds) *Anti-Racism, Feminism, and Critical Approaches to Education*, Westport, Connecticut: Bergin and Garvey, 67–86.

Reynar, R. (1999) 'Indigenous people's knowledge and education: a tool for development', in L. M. Semali and J. L. Kincheloe (eds) *What is Indigenous Knowledge? Voices from the Academy*, New York: Falmer Press, 285–305.

Rich, A. (1979) 'Toward a woman-centered university', in [collected essays] *On Lies, Secrets and Silences: Selected Prose 1966–1978*, New York: W. W. Norton, 125–157; originally published in E. Howe (ed.) (1975) *Women and the Power to Change*, New York: McGraw-Hill and Carnegie Commission on Higher Education, 15–47.

Riffel, J. A. and Levin, B. (1997) 'Schools coping with the impact of information technology', *Educational Management and Administration*, 25(1), 51–64.

Rifkin, J. (1987) *Time Wars: The Primary Conflict in Human History*, New York: Touchstone, Simon & Schuster Inc.

Robertson, L. (1993) 'Feminist teacher education: applying feminist pedagogies to the preparation of new teachers', *Feminist Teacher*, 8(1): 11–15.

Robertson, R. (1992) *Globalization: Social Theory and Global Culture*, London: Sage.

Robertson, R. (2003) *The Three Waves of Globalization: A History of a Developing Global Consciousness*, London: Zed Books.

Robertson, R. and Khondker, H. H. (1998) 'Discourses of globalization: preliminary considerations', *International Sociology*, 13(1): 25–40.

Rorty, A. O. (ed.) (1998) *Philosophers on Education: Historical Perspectives*, London, New York: Routledge.

Rosenau, P. M. (1992) *Post-Modernism and the Social Sciences*, Princeton, NJ: Princeton University Press.

Rossman, P. (1992) *The Emerging Worldwide Electronic University*, Westport, Connecticut: Greenwood Press.

Rousmaniere, K. (1998) 'Questioning the visual in the history of education: or, how to think about old pictures of schools' http://www.units.muohio. edu/eduleadership/kate/kate20.html (accessed 30 July 2000).

Roy, P. A. and Schen, M. (1993) 'Feminist pedagogy: transforming the high school classroom', *Women's Studies Quarterly*, 21(3–4): 142–147.

Ryan, M. J. (ed.) (1998) *The Fabric of the Future: Women Visionaries of Today Illuminate the Path to Tomorrow*, Berkeley, CA: Conari Press.

Sahtouris, E. (2000) 'The biology of globalization', in *New Futures*: *Transformations in Education, Culture and Technology*, proceedings from International Conference on New Futures, Taipei, Taiwan: Tamkang University.

Sai Baba, B. S. S. (1988) *Sathya Sai Education in Human Values I*, Bangkok, Thailand: Sathya Sai Foundation of Thailand.

Said, E. (1993) *Culture and Imperialism*, London: Chatto & Windus.

Sandell, R. (1991) 'The liberating relevance of feminist pedagogy', *Studies in Art Education*, 32(3): 178–187.

Sardar, Z. (1996) *Cyberfutures: Culture and Politics on the Information Superhighway*, New York: New York University Press.

—— (1998) *Postmodernism and the Other: The New Imperialism of Western Culture*, London: Pluto Press.

Sardar, Z. (ed.) (1999) *Rescuing All Our Futures: The Future of Futures Studies*, Twickenham: Adamantine.

Sardar, Z. (2000) 'Alt.civilizations.FAQ: cyberspace as the darker side of the west', in D. Bell and B. M. Kennedy (eds) *The Cybercultures Reader*, London: Routledge, 732–753.

Sardello, R. (1992) *Facing the World with Soul*, Hudson, New York: Lindisfarne Press.

Sargisson, L. (1996) *Contemporary Feminist Utopianism*, London: Routledge.

Sarkar, P. R. (1987) 'Tantra and Indo-Aryan civilization', in *A Few Problems Solved*, Part 1, Calcutta: A'nanda Ma'rga Praca'raka Sam'gha.

—— (1995) *Namah Shivaya Shantaya*, 3rd edn, Calcutta: Ananda Marga Publications.

—— (1998) *Discourses on Neohumanist Education*, Anandanagar, India: Ananda Marga Publications.

Scanlon, J. (1993) 'Keeping our activist selves alive in the classroom: feminist pedagogy and political activism', *Feminist Teacher*, 7(2): 8–13.

Schirato, T. and Webb, J. (2003) *Understanding Globalization*, London: Sage publications.

Schneider, B. (1999) 'New media and the global economy', *Journal of Futures Studies*, 4(1): 65–83.

Scholte, J. (2000) *Globalization: A Critical Introduction*, London: Macmillan Press.

Schwartz, H. N. (2001) 'Identity construction workers or how I stopped worrying and learned to love postmodernism' http://members.aol.com/ThryWoman/PFII.html (accessed 12 December 2001).

Scruton, R. (2002) *The West and The Rest: Globalization and the Terrorist Threat*, New York: Continuum.

Semali, L. M. (1999) 'Community as classroom: (Re)valuing indigenous literacy', in L. M. Semali and J. L. Kincheloe (eds) *What is Indigenous Knowledge? Voices from the Academy*, New York: Falmer Press, 95–119.

Semali, L. M. and Kincheloe, J. L. (eds) (1999) *What is Indigenous Knowledge? Voices from the Academy*, New York: Falmer Press.

Sen, G. and Grown, C. (1984) *Development, Crises and Alternative Visions: Third World Women's Perspectives*, New York: Monthly Review Press.

Shalaby, A. (1979) *History of Muslim Education*, 1st edn 1954, Karachi: Indus Publications.

Sharma, A. (1992) 'The notion of cyclical time in Hinduism', in H. S. Prasad (ed.) *Time in Indian Philosophy*, Delhi: Sri Satguru Publications, 203–213.

Shenk, D. (1997) *Data Smog: Surviving the Information Glut*, San Franscisco: HarperEdge.

Shiva, V. (1993) *Monocultures of the Mind: Perspectives on Biodiversity and Biotechnology*, London: Zed Books.

Shotton, J. (1992) 'Libertarian education and state schooling in England 1918–1990', *Educational Review*, 44(1): 81–91.

Shrewsbury, C. M. (1987) 'What is feminist pedagogy', *Women's Studies Quarterly*, 15(3–4): 6–14.

Sidhu, R. K. (2002) 'Selling futures: globalisation and international education', PhD thesis submitted to the University of Queensland, forthcoming 2004 as *Selling Education in the Global Market*, Mahwah, New Jersey: Lawrence Erlbaum.

—— (2004) *Selling Education in the Global Market*, Mahwah, New Jersey: Lawrence Erlbaum.

Siebers, T. (ed.) (1994) *Heterotopia: Postmodern Utopia and the Body Politics*, Michigan: University of Michigan Press.

Simon, B. (1994) *The State and Educational Change: Essays in the History of Education and Pedagogy*, London: Lawrence & Wishart.

Skolnik, M. (2000) 'The virtual university and the professoriate', in S. Inayatullah and J. Gidley (eds) *The University in Transformation: Global Perspectives on the Futures of the University*, Westport, Connecticut: Bergin and Garvey, 55–69.

Slaughter, R. A. (1993) 'Looking for the real "Megatrends"', *Futures*, 25(8): 827–850.

Slaughter, R. A. (ed.) (1996a) *The Knowledge Base of Futures Studies*, Hawthorn, Victoria: DDM Media Group and Futures Study Centre.

—— (1996b) *New Thinking for a New Millennium*, London: Routledge.

Slaughter, R. A. (1998) 'The knowledge base of futures studies', in D. Hicks and R. Slaughter (eds) *Futures Education: World Yearbook of Education 1998*, London: Kogan Page, 39–55.

—— (1999) *Futures for the Third Millennium: Enabling the Forward View*, St Leonards, NSW: Prospect.

—— (2002) 'Beyond the mundane: reconciling breadth and depth in futures inquiry', *Futures*, 34(6): 493–508.

—— (2004) *Futures Beyond Dystopia: Creating Social Foresight*, London: RoutledgeFalmer.

Smallwood, G. (1995) *Australia's Fourth World Nation*, Armidale: University of New England.

Smith, G. H. (2000) 'Protecting and respecting indigenous knowledge', in M. Battiste (ed.) *Reclaiming Indigenous Voice and Vision*, Vancouver: University of British Columbia Press, 209–225.

Snyder, I. (1997) 'Beyond the hype: reassessing hypertext', in I. Snyder (ed.) *Page to Screen: Taking Literacy into the Electronic Era*, Sydney: Allen & Unwin, 125–144.

Spar, P. (1994) *Mortgaging Women's Lives*, London: Zed Press.

Spender, D. (1982) *Invisible Women: The Schooling Scandal*, London: Writers and Readers Publishing Cooperative Society Ltd.

Spivak, G. C. (1985) 'Can the subaltern speak? speculations on widow sacrifice', *Wedge*, 7(8): 120–130.

Spring, J. (1998) *Education and the Rise of the Global Economy*, Mahwah, New Jersey: Lawrence Erlbaum.

—— (2001) *Globalization and Educational Rights: An Intercivilizational Analysis*, Mahwah, New Jersey: Lawrence Erlbaum Associates.

Sri Aurobindo (1962) *The Human Cycle*, Pondicherry, India: Sri Aurobindo Ashram.

—— (1965) 'Section I – Sri Aurobindo', in [compilation] *A True National Education*, Pondicherry, India: Sri Aurobindo International Centre of Education.

Stewart, F. (1996) 'Globalisation and education', *International Journal of Educational Development*, 16(4): 327–333.

Stone, L. (ed.) (1994) *The Education Feminism Reader*, New York: Routledge.

Stromquist, N. P. (2002) *Education in a Globalized World: The Connectivity of Economic Power, Technology, and Knowledge*, Lanham, Maryland: Rowman & Littlefield publishers.

Stromquist, N. and Monkman, K. (2000) *Education: Integration and Contestation Across Cultures*, Lanham, USA: Rowman & Littlefield Publishers, Inc.

Subramuniyaswami, S. S. (1993) *Dancing with Siva: Hinduism's Contemporary Catechism*, India: Himalayan Academy.

Sweet, L. I. (1991) *Quantum Spirituality: A Postmodern Apologetic*, Dayton, Ohio: Whaleprints, Spirit Venture Ministries.

Sweeting, A. (1996) 'The globalization of learning: paradigm or paradox?' *International Journal of Educational Development*, 16(4): 379–391.

Swift, R. (2002) 'Rush to nowhere', *New Internationalist*, 343: 9–13.

Tapine, V. and Waiti, D. (eds) (1997) *Visions for Maori Education*, Wellington: New Zealand Council for Educational Research.

Taylor, S. (2001) *Waking Up From Sleep*, unpublished manuscript.

Teilhard de Chardin, P. (1970) *Let Me Explain*, New York: Harper & Row.

Tenner, E. (1998) 'To glimpse tomorrow', in *Encyclopedia Britannica Yearbook of Science and the Future*, Chicago: Encyclopedia Britannica, 56–71.

Thacker, E. (2001) *Fakeshop: Science Fiction, Future Memory and The Technoscientific Imaginary*, http://www.ctheory.com/event/e087.html (accessed 31 March 2002).

The Mother (1965) 'The psychic and the spiritual education. Diverse educational insights', in [compilation] *A True National Education*, Pondicherry, India: Sri Aurobindo International Centre of Education.

Thiele, B. (1986) 'Vanishing acts in social and political thought: tricks of the trade', in C. Pateman and E. Gross (eds) *Feminist Challenges: Social and Political Theory*, Sydney: Allen & Unwin, 30–44.

Thomas, G. (1991) *The Australian Aborigines in Education: A Conflict of Cultures*, Brisbane: University of Queensland, Aboriginal and Torres Strait Islander Studies Unit.

Tierney, H. (ed.) (1989–) *Women's Studies Encyclopedia*, Vols I, II, III, London: Greenwood Press.

Toffler, A. (1974) *Learning for Tomorrow: The Role of the Future in Education*, New York: Vintage Books.

Tomlinson, J. (1999) *Globalization and Culture*, Oxford: Blackwell Publishers.

Torgovnick, M. (1997) *Primitive Passions: Men, Women, and the Quest for Ecstasy*, New York: Alfred A. Knopf.

Tracey, M. (1997) 'Twilight: illusion and decline in the communication revolution', in D. Cliché (ed.) *Cultural Ecology: The Changing Dynamics of Communications*, London: International Institute of Communications, 44–59.

Trend, D. (2001) *Welcome to Cyberschool: Education at the Crossroads in the Information Age*, Oxford: Rowman & Littlefield publishers, Inc.

Trenoweth, S. (1995) *The Future of God: Personal Adventures in Spirituality with Thirteen of Today's Eminent Thinkers*, Alexandria, NSW: Millennium Books.

Tuhiwai Smith, L. (1999) *Decolonizing Methodologies: Research and Indigenous*, London: Zed Books.

Twitchell, J. B. (1996) *Adcult USA: The triumph of Advertising in American Culture*, New York: Columbia University Press.

Tyrrell, B. (1995) 'Time in our lives: facts and analysis on the 90s', *Demos Quarterly*, 5: 23–25.

UN (1999) *1999 World Survey on the Role of Women in Development: Globalization, Gender and Work*, New York: United Nations.

UNIFEM (2000) *Progress of the World's Women 2000*, New York: United Nations Development Fund For Women.

Urry, J. (2000) 'Sociology of time and space', in B. Turner (ed.) *The Blackwell Companion to Social Theory*, 2nd edn, Malden, MA: Blackwell Publishers, 416–445.

USDE (1996) *Getting America's Students Ready for the 21st Century: Meeting the Technology Literacy Challenge*, Washington, DC: United States of America Department of Education.

Vaidyanatha Ayyar, R. V. (1996) 'Educational policy planning and globalisation', *International Journal of Educational Development*, 16(4): 347–353.

Valadian, M. (1991) *Aboriginal Education – Development or Destruction. The Issues and Challenges that have to be Recognised*, Armidale: University of New England.

Viergever, M. (1999) 'Indigenous knowledge: an interpretation of views from indigenous peoples', in L. M. Semali and J. L. Kincheloe (eds) *What is Indigenous Knowledge? Voices from the Academy*, New York: Falmer Press, 333–361.

Villemard (1910) 'A l'Ecole' (At School), *Visions de l'an 2000* (Visions of the year 2000). Chromolithograph, Bnf, Département des Estampes et de la Photographie.

Voigt, A. and Drury, N. (1997) *Wisdom from the Earth: The Living Legacy of the Aboriginal Dreamtime*, East Roseville, NSW: Simon & Schuster Australia.

Wagar, W. W. (1996) 'Futurism', in G. Kurian and G. Molitor (eds) *Encyclopedia of the Future*, Vol. 1, New York: Macmillan Library References, 366–367.

Wagner, C. G. (ed.) (1997) 'Women's preferred futures [collection of essays]', *The Futurist*, 31(3): 27–39.

Walker, B. (2000) *Restoring the Goddess: Equal Rites for Modern Women*, Amherst, New York: Prometheus Books.

Walker, P. 'Journeys around the medicine wheel: a story of indigenist paradigm research', paper presented to *Disrupting Preconceptions: Post Colonialism and Education*, University of Queensland, Brisbane, August 2001.

Weiler, K. (1988) *Women Teaching for Change*, New York: Bergen and Garvey.

Weiner, G. (1994) *Feminisms in Education: An Introduction*, Buckingham: Open University Press.

Weiss, L. (1998) *The Myth of the Powerless State*, Cambridge: Polity Press.

Wildman, P. (1997) 'Dreamtime myth: history as future', *New Renaissance*, 7(1): 16–20.

Willmot, E. P. (1986) *Future Pathways: Equity or Isolation*, Armidale: University of New England.

Wilson, A. (1999) *How the Future Began: Communications*, London: Kingfisher Publications.

Wolmark, J. (1999) The postmodern romances of feminist science fiction', in J. Wolmark (ed.) *Cybersexualities: A Reader on Feminist Theory, Cyborgs and Cyberspace*, Edinburgh: Edinburgh University Press, 230–246.

Wresch, W. (1996) *Disconnected: Haves and Have-Nots in the Information Age*, New Brunswick: Rutgers University Press.

Wright, E. O. (1999) 'The real utopias project: a general overview', Madison, WI: Department of Sociology, University of Wisconsin http://www. ssc.wisc.edu/~wright/OVERVIEW.html (accessed 24 November 2001).

Index